John Ruthven completed a PhD in Zoology before beginning his career as a BBC sound engineer. He soon found his way to the BBC Natural History Unit where with his interest in underwater photography he joined the first *Blue Planet* series as a producer, championing the behind-the-scenes shows, 'Making Waves'. Over the years he has written, produced and directed award-winning shows for the BBC, Discovery, National Geographic, PBS and others. In 2015, he received an Emmy for Best Environmental Film in the USA, producing and directing *Mysteries of the Coral Canyon* for PBS, which explored the inter-connected life on the extraordinary under-water corals of French Polynesia, known as the 'rainforests of the sea'. He also produced the widely acclaimed *Singapore Wild City*, commissioned for the fiftieth anniversary of Singapore and narrated by Sir David Attenborough, a series that won Best Asian TV Documentary, 2016. His most recent television work has been on *Blue Planet II*, for which he produced the episode on the open oceans, 'Big Blue'.

The Whale in the Living Room

A Wildlife Documentary Maker's Unique View of the Sea

John Ruthven

ROBINSON

ROBINSON

First published in Great Britain in 2021 by Robinson

1 3 5 7 9 10 8 6 4 2

A CIP catalogue record for this book
is available from the British Library.

ISBN: 978-1-47214-350-1

Typeset in Adobe Caslon Pro by SX Composing DTP, Rayleigh, Essex, SS6 7EF
Printed and bound in Great Britain by Clays Ltd, Elcograf S.p.A.

Papers used by Robinson are from well-managed forests
and other responsible sources.

MIX
Paper from
responsible sources
FSC
www.fsc.org
FSC® C104740

Robinson
An imprint of
Little, Brown Book Group
Carmelite House
50 Victoria Embankment
London EC4Y 0DZ

An Hachette UK Company
www.hachette.co.uk

www.littlebrown.co.uk

To India and Will – may all the oceans' creatures survive and thrive so that your generation can experience them beyond the history books

Contents

Introduction

This book is about whales and living rooms. In truth, more about whales than interior decoration and about making underwater 'films' to supply pictures of whales and other ocean creatures to your TV, which, although you may have one in the bedroom, kitchen or other parts of the house, is most likely in your living room. It is about more than that, too, because it's really a story of how we come to know our home better. I mean our whole home: the Earth, and especially the watery parts we don't often visit but are the very identity of this unusual and wonderful blue planet.

I love both whales and Wales, having grown up mainly on an old farm in North Wales where I walked all day with our sheepdog in tufty fields and along hedgerows, or explored in bluebell woods. I found newts in the mysterious waters of a tiny pond, hunted for fossils in the exposed shale of old lead mines, and cracked open suspiciously heavy stones to reveal their silver-grey cores of lead ore. It gave me a curiosity for nature and an understanding that life is far stranger than it seems if you only know cats and dogs. I was driven to seek that out, the other worldliness of creatures beyond the everyday, stranger things that in reality are just more pieces of life's jigsaw, promising us to be completed one day, but of course always with parts missing.

It's likely that a whale would fill your whole living room and spill over into the kitchen, with its tail bending uncomfortably up your stairs. If you're in a bedsit or small apartment it would certainly block your way to the door, and that's just your average whale and your average living room. In the more exclusive neighbourhoods of the world you might need a larger whale, but a blue is almost certainly too big.

Of course that is not what's meant but 'the whale in the room' is also a cousin of 'the elephant in the room', and just occasionally in our busy lives we should take note that she's right in front of us, waiting patiently to be noticed, hoping to be loved.

1

The Big Blue

The sheer volume of water

Have you ever been in deep water? It's so clear, so blue ... Why should it matter that there's two miles of water below you? What's the difference between swimming in a swimming pool and floating in the deep dark ocean – either way you're only immersed up to your shoulders? Yet when you're in the deep sea there's a gut-wrenching clarity, an immense feeling of volume, seemingly empty, but filled with the heartbeat of life on Earth.

My dive computer is going nuts, beeping an alarm in rapid descent: 43 ... 44 ... 45 metres – soon I'll be deeper than a scuba diver on air can safely dive. I'm tumbling head over heels like an ostracod – one of the many strange creatures of the deep that defy our imagination. It's hard to say what's up or down. I'm in freefall, an aquanaut lost in space. Then I see my diving buddy Mike above me, his silhouette against the surface giving me a point of reference. I put a burst of air into my stab jacket and slowly start to rise. I remember little model divers, Cartesian divers, I put in glass bottles when I was a boy. If you got the buoyancy just right, when you pressed on the cork the diver went down, and when you pulled, the model went upwards again. Something to do with the squashing and expansion of a little bubble of air inside it. Now I'm feeling as helpless as that miniature model might feel if only it could. But I am unbounded by glass, and floating in a trillion trillion tons of ultramarine fluid, with, I'd like to think, about the same concentration as the salts in my body. Sadly, that's not true, as seawater is three to four times more salty than your blood, but that doesn't mean we don't owe our life to the sea. I search for the submarine I know is coming our way.

The Johnson Sea Link submarine is one of the unsung technological miracles of the twentieth century: up there with Apollo and the fax machine, and hindered only by the fact that it doesn't have an on-board toilet – it's not big enough, and can only hold four people in cramped and relatively fixed sitting positions. It appears, quite literally out of the blue, coming up from below, huffing and puffing bubbles like some kind of steam engine. It has even got a train's name plate – *Harbor Branch* – mounted above the shining acrylic sphere of its main cockpit, and as a small, stubby submarine it is, of course, yellow. Mike signals to it in simple sign language to come past him for his first set of shots. I am filming Mike filming the submarine for the behind-the-scenes show. Slowly the sub chugs by underneath us, and I can see its top plate and the fans that are its vertical thrusters slowly turning. It purges its air tanks again and starts to sink away from us. We cannot follow to its depths, but it has been agreed that it will dive out of shot and then resurface. Sure enough, we start to see the silvery mirrors of bubbles in the water below and then the sub rises past us. It's June 1999, and we're about 300 miles out from

Port Fourchon, near New Orleans, in the Gulf of Mexico, filming what will become some of the first scenes of the deep programme of *The Blue Planet*.

These days I wonder whether the guardians of Health and Safety would let a film crew do that now: drifting miles from shore with two miles of water below and the chance of being run over by 12 tons of yellow steel, or chewed in its thrusters. Yet there is nothing to beat understanding the vastness of the sea than being fully immersed in it, free of walls, and vulnerable to its every whim.

The view from inside the sub is altogether different and a few days after our diving encounter I have the chance to experience the abyss from inside its chambers. It's very claustrophobic, of course, and I'm a deep sub rookie, which gives me mixed feelings as I anticipate returning to the most expansive place on Earth. I'm lying in the back; I have to, as I can't stand up – can barely even kneel on the mat lining the floor. I can squint through a port to my right, and on a screen above my head there is a live feed from the thick acrylic sphere, a separate chamber, up in front where Mike and the pilot are sitting, and from where Mike will control the main camera. Helpfully the crew dub the rear compartment 'the Coffin', and go on to tell me cheerfully about the only fatal incident to have happened in the craft, several years earlier. New safety systems have since been put in place, but in any case it's far too exciting to worry.

The 'flight check' before the dive involves the technician, in the rear with me, checking with the pilot by rapping out a litany of technical terms: 'Hatch secured. Meters on and checked, scrubbers on, O_2 flow is set. We have lights. All OK: we're ready to dive.'

Up on the surface, on the rear deck of the research vessel, *RV Edwin Link*, the Dive Ops Director (DiveOps) is standing by the winch listening intently to the pilot with the ear that isn't listening to the captain on the bridge.

Through the intercom of the sub comes a thin voice. 'We're ready to dive.'

'Roger. We're booming out.' DiveOps concentrates intently on making sure the sub lifts cleanly from the back deck.

We are suspended from an A-frame at the stern of the ship on just a single large cable. This giant movable gantry, whose roughly triangular shape and supporting crossbar form a giant 'A', allows heavy things like a sub to be safely swung out over the waves. *Mostly* safely, that is, because it still requires great care to judge sea conditions correctly during launch. On a later shoot in a smaller ship and a different submersible team, I witnessed what happens in a misjudged stormy swell, when the sub swings ever more violently, until the holding cable pings apart and, with decapitating velocity, flings its precious cargo seawards like a projectile from a Roman siege weapon.

The A-frame pivots the sub out about 5 metres from the aft rail. DiveOps has a last glance at the state of the sea, and his duet with the sub pilot continues. 'Release the locks.'

'OK. Here you go.'

Soon we are above the water, and there's that magic moment of immersion when you see the 'half-and-half': the above and below of air and water; two worlds clearly defined across the centre of the glass port. The sub starts to buck with the waves, but the ride is more comfortable than I expected.

'We have a seal.'

'We have a seal.'

The sub is lowered until its lift line slacks, and we feel the swell of the sea, so I'm glad we're not leaking.

'Blow it!'

'OK, release!'

The pilot releases the crane's line first and then, when he's happy the sub is riding correctly, a second tow line. We're free of mother ship.

We are on the surface, then just under it. I think of a whale, and I imagine this is what they might feel like before they dive, or at least as near as I'm ever going to get to understanding such an experience for a humpback, a blue or especially the deep diving sperm whales.

Some more half-heard communications from sub to ship – 'You're free and clear and have permission to dive'; 'Roger. We're diving' – a blast of bubbles, and we leave the surface in an aquatic elevator to the abyss.

Dan Boggess, in the acrylic cockpit ahead of me alongside Mike, became a sub pilot through the unlikely route of applying for the job in the local paper. 'After six years in the US Air Force,' he had explained to me, 'I was home and working in the long, skinny strip mall that is the Fort Lauderdale–Miami coastline, getting fed up with the grind of that semi-suburban life. One day in the *Vero Press Journal* an unusual ad caught my eye: "Wanted, exp'd Electronic Tech for Research Submersibles. Must be willing to spend 3–6 months a year working at sea & training for sub crew. Military exp. desired."'

That Sunday night PBS was airing a BBC David Attenborough special from 1986 about the Harbor Branch Oceanographic Institute. Dan watched avidly, which was just as well since neither he nor anyone he knew had ever heard of it, and it's best to be prepared at your interview. Not for the first time, Sir David had unknowingly changed the course of someone's life.

'I called their office on Monday,' continues Dan, and spoke with a guy called Jim Sullivan, known for his theory, "Success in life is based on the quality of your Plan B." He was the Sub Electronics lead, and ex-Air Force too, so knew exactly how my experience would meet his needs. Jim said they were heading out again soon for a forty-day Caribbean trip from St Thomas down to St Lucia. I did *not* faint. I managed to jot down some details, such as needing to get vaccines and a visa for our stops in Martinique and Guadeloupe. Two weeks later I was the newest sub crew member at Harbor Branch.'

So that, if you were wondering, is how you can become a research-sub pilot.

The Harbor Branch Oceanographic Institute (HBOI) is the marine research foundation on the coast of north-central Florida, with its quarters tucked away on an inlet off the Indian River. It was funded originally by the Johnson & Johnson fortune – the drug company probably most familiar from the baby powder in your bathroom. One of the institute's founders was Edwin Link, a famous aircraft engineer who also designed the Johnson Sea Link research submarine: hence the sub's double-barrel name and the name of the recovery ship.

As we go down, the light fades through various shades of ever darker blue. The depth gauge is in feet, a dramatic treat for a metric European, as feet are so much better value than metres. At 600 feet I can just see some light from the surface, but it's shrouded in a dim fog of blue, and we are about to pass what appears to be the dark horizon of the ocean into its eternal night.

Twelve hundred feet, and it's pretty black now. No – wait: there's a flash. What's that? My eyes tune in to the gloom through the window. A few white particles push past like snow. There it is again . . . and again: blue flashes! We are bumping into some of the inhabitants down here and they are reacting, perhaps even complaining, emitting their blue, biological light in a firework display of annoyed bioluminescence. Bumping into anything though must be strange for them in this void of water.

'Space is big. You just won't believe how vastly, hugely, mind-bogglingly big it is. I mean, you may think it's a long way down to the chemist's, but that's just peanuts to space.' I'm reminded of that observation from Douglas Adams in *The Hitchhiker's Guide to the Galaxy*, and chuckle to myself as we continue downwards. He might have written it about the sea. How could the sea compare in size to the universe, you ask? It does in one massive respect, if we consider the most unique property of our planet: *life*. The ocean is by far the largest liveable space on Earth, and hugely exceeds our conception of life's abundance. Its average depth is about 3.5 kilometres, or 2 miles, and, as is often mentioned, the ocean covers nearly three-quarters of the world.

It's the little things that count, though, even if often forgotten: the microbes. It's been estimated – how else? – that there are 44 *octillion* living cells in the ocean. That's according to the US short-scale definition of octillion, which has a mere 27 zeroes after it, and although nowhere near a googol (100 noughts – google it), it's still around 10,000 times the number of stars in the observable universe. And that's not even to start on the larger plankton, the teaming algae, the copepods like tiny shrimps and the gazillion eggs, larvae and young of pretty much everything from fish to crabs, barnacles and jellyfish that live in this huge 3D world.

Right now I'm falling through the Twilight Zone with the crew of the Johnson Sea Link. In proper scientific-speak this is known as the Mesopelagic layer. Musically speaking it would be confusing to call it the 'middle sea', because that's also a key on the piano, but that's what it is: neither the surface nor the seabed, just the bit in the middle. Except that it's not 'just', as it's the most important and massive – and ignored – habitat we have. Ninety-five per cent of all fish hide here. They include such horrors as angler, dragon and fangtooth fish, all with teeth so big they can hardly shut their mouths, and only slightly less scary when you realise they fit in your hand. Here too are nature's uglies, like the gulper eel, the spook fish, the sea pig and the vampire squid. But as solutions to living in dark, cold water under high pressure they're also really beautiful. Without our machines we'd be useless down here, and to them, I'm sure, we must also look very odd. Many were here first, of course, and are more representative of life on Earth than us.

At 1,800 feet the lights on the sub start to reflect off the seabed. There's a kind of mild fog – maybe the sub's engines stirring up the very light sediment at the bottom. Clumps of tubeworm bushes appear like the tumbleweed that bowls across a white sandy desert: it's like the set of a Western. Dan the sub pilot glides the vessel just a few feet above the seabed and, as we pass the bushes, I can see that they don't 'tumble' at all, but are firmly rooted. These are cold-seep tubeworms and life too, but not as we know it.

The worms need food but sadly are deficient in the gut, mouth and anus department: pretty much just a sac in a tube. Yet with the help of an intermediary, bacteria, they can break down the yummy rotten-egg-smelling hydrogen sulphide seeping from the seabed, and make a living out of it. Such places, where sulphides, oil and methane gas come up from below, are alien to us but common in the Gulf of Mexico. They're called cold seeps because no hot volcanic activity is involved. As if to prove the point, Dan stops the sub and deploys one of its crab-like metal claws to probe beneath the surface. Streams of bubbles trickle out of the damaged substrate along with, weirdly, what looks like a mass of yellow cheddar cheese. This, we're told, is something called methane hydrate, a frozen form of methane gas, that's also known as 'flammable ice', and which is already being extracted for fuel in China and Japan. Although it's one of the cleaner forms of carbon its burning will still become a new contribution to climate change.

The tubeworm bushes are massive – 3 metres; 10 feet high in places. They live on what to us would be a toxic cocktail, but thrive because of the assistance of their friendly bacteria, who in turn seek shelter in their twisted, tubular bodies. Clever experiments of staining the tubes with dye have shown that they are somewhat slow-growing, and many are over 200 years old. In this sunless world these animals are living like rooted plants, using chemical energy to build their bodies, and are some of the oldest living things on Earth. My looking-glass on life is starting to show the cracks, but the lust for stranger things is satisfied, even if I'm feeling curiouser and curiouser.

Mike deGruy is the cameraman in front. He is an extra-ordinary man: a polymath of the sea he loves, films and studies.

Beneath his white but youthful mop of hair is a brain that can master both the general and the specific: the significance of the oceans to life on Earth, as well as the detail of a beautifully framed and lit wildlife shot. Earlier on the surface he had fussed with the lights on the front of the sub, to the point where some of the scientific crew got grumpy about it, though grumpiness thresholds are variable, and sometimes, it must be said, lower than they ought to be.

Seawater is horrible stuff to film through. The main rule is to get rid of it as much as possible, by coming up close and wide to your subject. The other rule has to do with lighting: too much of it, and it just bounces back from particles suspended in the water, like driving in fog when turning to full beam paradoxically makes visibility worse. In underwater photography this is called backscatter, and it can be largely avoided by making sure the camera and the lights are off axis with each other, so you are not lighting the particles in the camera's path directly, but only subtly from the side. This was what Mike was trying to do by 'fiddling' with the lights on the sub and making sure the angles between lights and camera were right. It paid off.

Lying in the back of the sub, looking out on this alien landscape, feeling a bit cold and isolated from the sunlit world above, perhaps even disorientated, I was startled by what Mike lined up on the camera's monitor in front of me. It's a left-field moment that happens when you've been deeply immersed in something else – in this case, of course, quite literally. All we could see of the open end of this single giant tubeworm was just that, inside a dark tube. Then suddenly it blossomed. A beautiful crimson bloom that opened like a magician pulling a bunch of red feathers out of a sleeve. These animals that behave like plants have flowers.

The discovery of these cold-seep worms by deep-diving submarines has been called one of the most remarkable events in marine biology, but even as our knowledge of the sea slowly grows it just leads to more questions. How do the feather-flowers open so precisely, and every time, it seems, in exactly the same way? And should a crab threaten to nibble their heads they can withdraw again instantly – how do they do that with fewer nerve cells than you can rub together? Some of their shallow-water relatives have light-sensitive 'eyes' all along their feathery tentacles that close when they see threatening shadows overhead – so what about these that live in the dark?

Similar tubeworms grow in ocean gardens around the world, and one of the most spectacular displays of all is in Scottish lochs north of Oban, where their girdered bodies scaffold into reefs as big as proverbial soccer pitches scattered across the seabed. Dressed in feathers of red and white, football spectators in sloping stadiums, they support a city where crabs, starfish, snails and squat-lobsters find accommodation within their branches. Shallow water species like the Scottish ones feed on detritus but those we see from our submarine around the cold vents drink noxious sulphides that would kill most animals.

Absorbed through the worm's blood-red branching head and peculiar animal roots, sulphides are transported through the blood to the co-operative bacteria inside to be turned into something the worms can eat. Some think this union with bacteria evolved to protect the worms from the obnoxious forms of the sulphur in the first place – and then you might as well use it to advantage over those that can't do that and turn it into food. Forty years ago, we didn't even know these cold-vent worms existed and, having found them, it seems, as so often with marine creatures, their mysteries only multiply with exploration.

With exquisite control Dan gently nudges the sub over the seabed like a hovercraft or more precisely a magic carpet, gliding quietly above the tubeworm bushes in a mystical world without gravity. For what seems like minutes, but has in fact been two hours, we trundle along across this deep-water range, imagining the skeletons of whales and sunken vessels about us. This is the final resting place, it's thought, of the giant asteroid that ended the age of the dinosaurs. The meteorite landed in the bottom-right corner of the Gulf of Mexico, near Chicxulub on the Yucatán Peninsula, about 65 million years ago. Until I checked, I glibly thought it had been responsible for hollowing out the entire area bounded by Florida, Texas and Mexico, but the Gulf is much older even than that and, although in one part the space-bomb did indeed add miles to its depth, the Gulf was formed by the less dramatic slow creeping of plate tectonics pulling continents apart, a process that's been going on here for about 300 million years.

Up until the mid-Jurassic – say 180 million years ago – the Gulf was a vast but shallow water-collecting bowl, and in successive blinks of geological time saw many different sea levels. Many times it filled and evaporated, each time leaving more and more concentrated salt on the bottom. Thirty-six kilograms or about 81lb of salt is what you'll get when you evaporate a ton of seawater from the Atlantic, as well as a very big electricity bill! Yet countless trillions of tons of water evaporated here, to the extent that today the salt layer is in places no less than 5 miles (8 kilometres) thick. As the Gulf opened to the Atlantic the waters became deeper, and the salt layer was covered with sediment, but this super-concentrated salt is still here in vast pockets. Since salt is softer than the surrounding rock, it often gets squeezed upwards again, and appears in great lumps pushing through the sea floor. That's when things become very weird indeed.

Squinting sideways and ahead through the small port of my coffin, the rear submarine compartment, I can see a haze in the distance, lit up by the sub's lights. As we approach the fog clears to reveal what could be the strangest habitat on our planet: a brine pool. It's a landscape that seems carelessly misplaced: a lake at the bottom of the sea with its own pebble shore and shimmering water surface. As we slide over its banks, I can see that they're not pebbles at all but millions of very large mussels. They carpet the whole rim of the pool in quite a tightly defined band but, looking intensely at this mussel beach, I can see large anaemic-looking crabs here and there, thousands of pink worms, white and hairy worms, strange lobsters, a solitary giant woodlouse, and things I just don't have a name for. What seems like a heat haze over the briny lagoon is in fact dissolving salt. In places the pool has a dark blackness that beckons you deeper, and where the sediment is stirred up the water is milky white, but still clear enough to see a few feet, and there's an almost jelly-like texture, thicker and stickier than the surrounding water. In fact, this pool has at least five times the salt concentration of normal seawater. It's so dense, and this salt broth therefore so buoyant, that the sub couldn't dive far into the pool even if we wanted to. Even so, the thrusters whine as Dan tries to get a little more altitude. He told me later that sometimes he'd deliberately put the skids of the sub into the lake just so he could see the waves wash over its shore. I mean, you'd have to, right?

Such salt lakes on the bottom of the Gulf of Mexico, and there must be many, have been called 'hot tubs of despair' because they are much warmer and of course way saltier than the surrounding water, and so kill a lot of the animals unfortunate enough to swim into them. Mind you, like the sabre-toothed tigers and mammoths of the La Brea tar pits in Los Angeles, preserved in heavy oil, there must be lots of ancient marine creatures embalmed in the salt. I'd bet that one day someone might even find a whole megalodon, the massive whale-eating shark that roamed these waters only a mere 3.6 million or so years ago. That's just my daydream, of course; to others a nightmare.

Even so, there are some stalwart eels that can brave the brine pool, at least for a few seconds at a time, although it wasn't until *Blue Planet II* that this was properly caught on video. Presumably the very slender cut-throat eel doesn't do it for fun, but dives in to take advantage of the deadly lake's victims and an easy(ish) meal. The eel is playing hot-salt-tub roulette though, because if it stays too long it starts to go into what looks like a death spasm, and twist into painful-looking figures-of-eight, tying itself in knots. It reminds me of the face we make eating a lemon, although this is much more deadly, because if the eels don't escape the lake quickly enough they'll become one of the bodies they themselves are scavenging: a cut-throat existence indeed.

Coming up again is just as interesting as our descent. Dan turns off the sub's lights and the blue-green firework display seems if anything more intense as the vessel bumps into what appears to be a disgruntled glow of migrating plankton, escaping from the surface. Squinting upwards, I can see the water above getting lighter, as though we are sailing into the dawn. I find I've missed the sun; as fascinating as it is down here, I am a creature of the light.

Bladders bursting after about six hours squashed in the too-small-to-have-a-restroom sub, we bob on the water again. Dan has guided the yellow machine surprisingly close to the mother ship. It comes as a shock to see the face of a diver suddenly smiling at us through the glass, but of course someone has to hook up the lifting rope. Disgorged onto the deck, hissing and spluttering with dripping water and the effort of hydraulic arms, the sub is finally secured. Hatches open, everyone bolts to the loo, faster than a scallop swimming from a starfish, their fearsome predator.

The deep brine pools are one of the more recent finds in the sea, only known since navy surveys of the early 1980s, and the first detailed images came from those Johnson Sea Link subs run by the HBOI in Florida. Without government resources, such institutes are vulnerable to the whims of their benefactors, and in 2011, a decade after our dive with them, Harbor Branch lost a lot of its funding and redeployed the seven people (including Dan) who crewed and supported the two submersibles, marking an unceremonious end to a research programme that began in 1971. The subs were mothballed and their supporting research vessel sold.

When I called Dan up recently he sounded, retired now, a bit down, but his voice lit up as he talked about his time as a pilot. He sent me a copy of his dive logs, which showed 665 dives into the abyss, seeing as much of the strange places of our planet as any man alive. In their forty-two years exploring the deep, the Johnson Sea Link subs shone a light into our oceans, into the depths of our planet. I can't help thinking something is missing when we don't fund such things, because as expensive as they are, our world needs to be understood.

2

How Big?

Mapping the sea

It would have saved an awful lot of trouble for the European explorers if they could have just had some pictures of Apollo 8's 'Earthrise' shots or better, NASA's 2012 'Blue Marble' series of images, that showed the Pacific in all its glory cloaking much of our planet. We can get some measure of how far across the world these blue prairies stretch when we add up the deaths of the sixteenth-century sailors who first attempted to cross the Pacific from the west. Images of those ethereal underwater lakes we saw in the Gulf of Mexico bring gasps of disbelief and wonder to the living room, but to capture such things you have to know roughly where to look. That's why mapping the sea is the first stage: a process that began many centuries before the invention of television.

On September 20th, 1519, Ferdinand Magellan set sail from Spain towards Brazil in command of five ships and 270 men, in search of a fast western route to the Spice islands. Hugging the coast southwards towards Chile he made the remarkable discovery of a navigable channel into the Pacific, the first

European voyage of its kind. He and his crew imagined they would soon reach the Spice Islands, situated near what we know today as Sumatra. What they didn't know was that their voyage across the Pacific had only just started. Distance meant death for these early European sailors. Dwindling food and water was one thing, and even maggot-infested biscuits can be stomached, as long as there is one other vital component in the diet. It seems surprising now they didn't work it out sooner, though hindsight is a wonderful thing. Without vitamin C, which the human body can only extract from fruit and vegetables rather than make for itself, we soon get scurvy. Body tissue decays rapidly, and an agonising death follows. Even with favourable winds, and making good time, days turned into weeks for Magellan and his crew, and then into months, as they traversed the biggest patch of blue in the world. Before they reached Guam, nearly 8,000 miles, and about 120 days sailing from South America, they had lost eighty sailors, or one for every 100 miles of ocean: on average, a death every thirty-six hours. It must have given meaning like nothing else both to the excruciating length of their journey, and to the stupendous tracts of blue water on this planet. Only one ship with 18 men of the original crew would return home three years later, the majority dead for want of citrus juice. Magellan himself, often credited with being the first person to circumnavigate the globe, was in fact killed in a skirmish en route in Mactan, a coral island in the Philippines.

Viewing the Blue Marble from our space station is very different of course to riding those waves with the salt spray and sea wind in your hair, and even today, there's always going to be something new to find and understand. Thankfully there are still epic expeditions that set out to do just that. Recently, for example, the Khaled bin Sultan Living Oceans Foundation

(KSLOF or LOF), established by the prince and dedicated to the research and understanding of marine science, spent six years on a Global Reef Survey to explore coral reefs around the world. Why? Because we still don't know our planet in detail. Most marine scientists I've met are Extinction Rebels at heart, who are using their smarts to save the world from ourselves. Coral reefs weigh heavily on their mind, because they're really sensitive to changes in temperature. That's why the corals are sometimes called 'the canaries of the ocean', and their deterioration is one of the first signs of global warming, and that the sea as a whole, and our planet, is sick. It's therefore vital we monitor how coral reefs are changing – but from what? Until the KSLOF's Global Reef Survey no one had done a comprehensive and standardised global survey. Together with cameraman Doug Allan, I was asked to help film their work. When you're asked to film coral reefs all over the world, potentially for six years, you're probably going to say, 'Yes, please!'

It meant many months aboard the Living Oceans Foundation's *Golden Shadow*, a 66-metre yacht, originally built as a tuna-fishing vessel and consequently a superb platform for ocean research. Notice I don't call it a 'research ship', though, because even at that length, and with four decks, it's still considered a yacht, and only on loan to the foundation. For its day job *Golden Shadow* was the service ship to Prince Khaled's two other yachts in his *Golden* fleet. Prince Khaled bin Sultan Al Saud was the Saudi defence minister up until 2013, but he is also a keen scuba diver. The story goes that one day he was diving on the Great Barrier Reef in Australia, during, sadly, another epic year of 'bleaching', when corals go white in over-warm water. Everywhere he looked the reef was a blanched skeleton of its former self, and in places it seemed as if builder's rubble had been fly-tipped on the seabed; the builders in question being the little coral polyps, now deceased. So shocked was Prince Khaled that he vowed to do something about it, and started his marine research foundation.

Of course, for some there might be an irony about a Saudi prince whose family wealth comes in a large part from oil, promoting conservation when a large proportion, up to about 40 per cent, of all carbon dioxide emission comes from refined petroleum. We are, however, all connected to oil in one way or another. Whilst oil companies are the suppliers, we are the addicts and if anything it's the profligate consumption, not the supply, that is at fault. Even if we don't drive a car, or fly all over the world, we are all complicit in the use of the crude brown liquid every day, for food production, transport and a host of petrochemicals used in industrial processes that we hardly understand but certainly use about the house, most obviously in the form of plastic. It is this complicated relationship that I grapple with a lot, especially when making environmental films which often require journeying to far-away places.

So that's how I ended up sailing through French Polynesia's Society and Tuamotu Islands, living the adventures I had read of in Willard Price's *South Sea Adventure* when I was nine. Everywhere the *Golden Shadow* went it took on twenty or so local marine scientists, from the Bahamas and Jamaica to the Galapagos, Tonga and Tahiti, as it followed the coral barriers and bommies across the ocean. I don't keep regular diaries, but when something bubbles above the surface of daily routine I jot it down. Here's a page from my notes of over 100 days working with the Washington office of the KSLOF. We were coming to the end of a long trip and had just been diving off the island of Moorea, near Tahiti:

Just sitting in the *Heiva* catamaran, tied to the *Golden Shadow* ship in Papeete harbour, Tahiti. Early hours and can't sleep as a tropical downpour outside. The *Heiva* has been our home for the last two weeks, but we are leaving it today. Earlier I saw a few people cleaning the streets and a couple of market-stall owners setting up on the dock front, which is also a market. A few stray dogs and a couple of rats can be seen if you look closely. All along the high street there are trees with white and red flashing lights for Christmas – it's the shopping centre for the whole of French Polynesia.

Yesterday we had an exciting time underwater. We were looking for lemon sharks, and the day before scientist and dive guide, Nicolas Buray, assured us they would always come to bait. They didn't – for the first time since 24 September 2008, according to his records, and he's been diving here for over twelve years. The shyness of creatures is an occupational hazard for wildlife film-makers, but still that seemed hard. So yesterday we went to the same spot again (about 15 metres down, just outside the reef on the north side of Moorea, by the bay where Captain Cook first landed).

We waited for thirty minutes around one stinky tuna head buried in the seabed – nothing. The blacktip sharks circled around us – they are light brown with a distinctive black mark on the dorsal fin, about a metre long and remind me of scavenging seagulls. I was nearly falling asleep thinking, 'Typical – the lemons are camera-shy' and then the viewfinder of my camera went black! A 3-metre lemon shark swam closer than arm's length in front of me – the blacktips scattered like chickens from a dog, and suddenly we were surrounded by five adult lemon sharks nosing around for the food.

There were four males and a female, and the males carried scars from recent battles between each other in the mating season. Very different character to the other types of sharks we have seen – big bruisers that come in and own the place – no messing with these boys. But they were quite docile as it happened, coming very close, then turning away from you at the last moment, with a little toothy grin from their downwards facing mouth. The males have two 'claspers' that dangle below the tail. They are indeed a lemon colour, I suppose; yellowy green too if the light shines brightly enough on them, and they are also distinctive because they have two dorsal fins. There is a funny diver signal for a lemon shark that involves making a motion with your hands as if you are squeezing a lemon on a lemon squeezer!

They found the tuna, and in an explosion of flesh it was gobbled up by violent digging into the seabed with their heads. The conditions were not easy – there was a 2-metre swell in the sea that made us want to bob up and down, even at 15 metres, and the water was cloudy from the sand thrown up – but we had three cameras on them, and got 'two-shots' with the scientist who was photographing them and taking notes. Massive, beautiful animals!

Moorea's jagged mountains are an unforgettable sight: covered with jade and light-emerald-green vegetation on volcanic rock, they're like giant black shark's teeth piercing the world from the depths of the sea. That dive spot was just outside Cook's Bay, almost under the shadow of Mount Tohivea, the tallest and most beautiful of Moorea's dormant volcanos. In more romantic moments I imagined I was alongside the Royal Navy sloop *Resolution*, Captain James Cook's ship, after whom they renamed the bay, of course, where, unknown to him, the lemon sharks roam. In truth, I imagined it was his first ship, HMS *Endeavour*, but writing this I now realise that when he visited Moorea it would have been his second exploration ship, HMS *Resolution*, and his third global voyage.

Cook landed on Moorea in 1777, but his ghost is still here: for people like me our views of ocean exploration were formed around the celebrated adventures of Western European heroes like Cook and Magellan. The map of the world is drawn from our perspective. That's to be expected: over the last 500 years the fantastic endeavours of ocean superpowers from Portugal and Spain to Holland, France and Britain led them to rule the waves for much of that time. But don't you think the indigenous peoples would have been astonished to be told they were 'discovered'? They knew they were here all along, and probably explored much like the Europeans. Indeed, it has even been conjectured that a great fleet left from China to circumnavigate the whole globe one hundred years before Magellan. Although that plausible theory in Gavin Menzies' bestseller *1421* has been somewhat discredited, I don't care, as it's certain that some part of every society has a yearning to explore the sea. It's only a matter of degree, or more pre-cisely *how many* degrees they ventured from their shores.

25

And, all the time, unknown to them, they were pathfinders in the story of how the sea came into your living room.

It's about 11 p.m. and I'm on the phone in our bedroom talking to the one-time White House Chief of Staff and Secretary of Defence, Leon Panetta, about fish and chips.

I'm trying to make a point about the things in everyday life people know about and connect to the sea, and how that might be a route back from the TV to caring about the ocean (yes, it's a two-way journey). Apparently, there are fourteen other people in the 'back-in-time-zoned' room in Monterey, California, listening in on the conversation. It's a bit surreal, to say the least, and I've no idea really whether I'm getting my point across, and 'fish and chips' is probably a bit lost in translation, but there seem to be grunts of agreement coming from the background.

'This is how they do it in Hollywood,' I thought: fly a team of high-powered people in for a conference to big-up the film idea. The idea on the table was that of Barrie Osborne, producer of *The Lord of the Rings*, *The Matrix*, *The Water Horse*, and much else. Although what I'm most in awe of is that he was the production manager on *Apocalypse Now* and survived to tell the tale. His idea, to put it in Hollywood-pitch terms is: *Lord of the Rings* meets *Blue Planet*.

Just suppose you mixed the mythology of the sea with stories about the sea's animals and environment . . . What would you have? A host of wonderful characters from strange gods to sea monsters, and a rich way of inspiring us about the sea and conservation issues. So I was asked to write some test scripts.

I wrote about how Inuit people on hunting trips across Alaska are falling through the ice, sledges, dogs and all, much more than they used to. This is likely to be down to the accelerated melting of the Arctic in recent years, and so a sobering but human way to engage the audience with global warming. The opening scene is a hunter falling through the ice, and in his cold-bitten mind he dreams of Sedna, the Inuit goddess of the sea. There are various versions of the story, but most involve Sedna falling out of a boat, losing her fingers as she tries to cling to the side, and eventually plummeting into the dark depths – just like our poor Inuit hunter. In the myth, each of her fingers then turns into a seal, a walrus or a whale, and so in the film we go on to learn more about those Arctic sea mammals. I can't remember if we returned to save the hunter from an icy death. I hope so.

In another episode I wrote about how the wood for a *vaka*, or *waka*, canoe, used by the Māori close to the shore, was constructed from a single trunk of the very tall totara tree. One of the reasons its strong wood is so good for making boats is that it contains a chemical, totarol, that is resistant to rot. For it to be used as a boat, however, a Tohunga (spiritual leader or healer in Māori culture), must advise if the spirits will give permission to cut down the tree; if this is not done, the boat could grow back into a living tree. In the film, via the magic of *Lord of the Rings*-style CGI, we would see this happen. This in turn leads us to the natural history of the totara tree, a spiky-leaved giant that can grow over 40 metres tall and live for over 1,000 years. The 'spiritual permissions' required to cut it down show how much it is valued in Māori tradition, and perhaps how much we must take care of precious natural resources.

Like many projects in film and TV, in the end this one didn't get 'green-lit', meaning it hasn't been made (do step forward if you'd like to fund it!). But every idea that is developed generally leads to other things, reincarnated and reincorporated into other pitches, and eventually some of them do get financial backing and are filmed. Even if they don't, the research knowledge is still enriching, and often leads to a more rounded understanding in future projects. What it gave me was an interest in the amazing technology of the Polynesian (or more generally Oceanian) voyaging canoes and their conquest of the Pacific way before Europeans.

The Polynesians, or 'Lapita' people, were the first blue-water mariners. They make the Vikings look like beginners. We know only a little about the boats they used, because no complete examples of their awesome trans-Pacific canoes have survived, but we know at least that they were big enough for rats to have stowed away undetected for a free adventure, during which they also spread across the Pacific islands. We know too they must have been big enough to store food for long voyages, but not so large that their string bindings would break in the average sea swell or founder in the troughs between waves. It has been calculated that the ideal length would be 55 to 60 feet, although fragments of preserved voyaging canoes found in Huahine, west of Tahiti, gave a length of 72 feet. One of the few replicas today is *Hōkūleʻa*, made in fibreglass to a reconstructed Hawaiian design. It is 62 feet long, and nearly 18 feet at its widest point.

Clearly, for long-haul journeys they needed to use sails. These had a basic triangular form, with the apex pointing down, and were most often made from sheets of pandanus: palm-like fronds full of fibre and woven into mats. For the people of Oceania the major innovation in sea technology was to be able to sail against the wind, but they did it not with the heavy rudders Western sailors use; rather with perfectly balanced paddles raised and lowered into the water to make subtle movements turning the vessel into or against the wind, and also by using the trim of their sails. That way they saved the extra drag a permanently submerged rudder makes. Everything they did was designed to tune the double-hulled canoe to racing trim.

Their nimble craft were in many ways far superior to the heavy, leaking hulks, made from a forest's worth of trees, that enabled European expansion over the oceans. In fact, at the time many of the European captains who spied them commented as much. In 1686, William Dampier, the pirate and one-time British naval officer who spearheaded European ocean exploration, tried out one of the smaller sailing canoes to see for himself:

> I do believe they sail the best of any boats in the world. I did here for my own satisfaction try the swiftness of one of them . . . I do believe she would have run 24 mile an hour. It was very pleasant to see the little boat running along so swift by the other's side . . . The native Indians are no less dextrous in managing than in building these boats. By report they will go from hence to another of the islands about 30 leagues off, and there do their business and return again in less than 12 hours. I was told that one of these boats was sent express to Manila, which is above 400 leagues,[1] and performed the voyage in four days' time.[2]

A rough bit of maths gives 14 knots as the average speed for the vessel Dampier is talking about. From Papua New Guinea

---

1 400 leagues equals 1,381 miles or 2,222 kilometres.
2 William Dampier, *A New Voyage Round the World* (1697).

to Easter Island, pretty much the whole width of Oceania, is about 9,000 miles (14,500 km), so at that rate such a boat would cross it in just under a month. Of course, that's not how it works: it depends on the winds and currents, great navigation, and sufficient food and water for the journey, but it's still very impressive and makes us reconsider ocean journeys past. One thing I wondered was whether the Polynesians got scurvy too on long-haul voyages like the Europeans. Apparently not, as they carried vitamin-rich foods with long shelf lives, including pandanus palm paste and fermented breadfruit. If only the Europeans and Oceanians had exchanged notes!

Within a mere 300 years, starting nearly 3,500 years ago, humans conquered the Pacific. Their nimble craft were free to roam the 22 million square kilometres (nearly 9 million square miles) of its open waters and settle almost all its peppered islands well before precise navigation aids even existed. Before precise *European*-style navigation existed, that is. Patently you don't really need shiny brass instruments or accurate chronometers. Modern reconstructions, tracing ancient journeys in replicas like the *Hōkūle'a*, show that the citizens of Oceania did it with just an intimate knowledge of stars, currents, winds and wildlife. They even made maps from sticks and shells that recorded things like water currents and wind direction, but it's likely that these were used just for teaching and not taken to sea.

When the Polynesian voyaging canoe *Hōkūle'a* was built in 1975, as an archaeological experiment, it was by no means certain there'd be anyone to sail it in a traditional way. Luckily the team from the Polynesian Voyaging Society in charge of the project was able to find one of the few living people who could help them. Pius 'Mau' Piailug was a Micronesian navigator from the Carolinian island of Satawal (a dot 800 miles, 1,300 kilometres, north of Papua New Guinea), whose grandfather chose him in 1936 to study traditional sailing methods as an apprentice navigator from the age of four, and Mau became a master navigator able to steer by the stars, swells and methods such as following birds across the sea. With his help the *Hōkūle'a* sailed many long-haul routes, including a return journey between Hawaii and Tahiti – something that had not been done by traditional methods for 500 years – and demonstrating conclusively the potential for Pacific exploration by canoe several thousand years before the Europeans. But Papa Mau's achievement took great skill learnt from childhood, as modern-day sailors on Hawaii found out when they asked him if he would kindly teach them his methods: 'You? You are too old. Give me your children – I will teach them.'

Although there are no original voyaging canoes left, exciting discoveries of their remains do occur. In 2014 part of an ancient canoe was found in Anaweka, New Zealand, uncovered in a sand dune after a storm. It was clearly a large canoe, as it had drill holes and binding recesses for rope to 'sew' the planks of its decking and dual hulls together. And carved in raised relief on its shaped end: a beautiful, swimming turtle. Sea turtles were known to make long migrations in open ocean, just like human voyagers, and, coming from the deep sea onto land, they also crossed between the elements of water and earth just as sailors do. No wonder that in Polynesian culture turtles were associated with voyaging to the afterworld and assisting in a successful passage of the spirit after death. Faces on Lapita pottery seem to be representations of sea turtles, not of human beings, and connect with a popular legend about a person who rode on the back of a sea turtle. For us it's a unique and powerful symbol that brings to life the real people that sailed this vessel 600 years ago, and how keenly they must have observed the creatures of the sea.

It's humbling to reflect that mapping the ocean started thousands of years ago, and that it was really only about 200 years ago that the pieces of the Blue Marble were crudely put together into something resembling the globe we know today. Even now the largest part of the world, an area estimated to be equivalent to two Mars-sized planets, is uncharted to modern standards (100-metre resolution), although there's a new drive to correct that called Seabed 2030 aiming for a detailed and complete map of the ocean floor by 2030.

In the past maps were made with commerce and political power in mind, not so much to capture the wonder of the sea; but they define the jigsaw puzzle that helps us realise the scale of our precious, watery planet. As for knowing what it looks like below the surface, until relatively recently few people had ever seen *beneath* the waves, let alone observed the ocean in their living room. Remarkably, those crafty Victorians began to find a way to do so – and many years before the invention of TV.

3

Victorian *Blue Planet*

The first glass screen in the living room

S tanding in the corner of the living room is a glass screen. It's the focal point for all who pass through or sit down. The latest model, with great colour, has a resolution far better than 4K (Ultra High Definition). In fact, it's almost as if you were there. The screen is a portal to other worlds and other ways of living. On tonight's schedule: bright orange fish, like goldfish stand-ins shown in pioneering TV when technical problems frequently made programmes 'fall off air', but this technology existed way before television. As if you haven't guessed, aquariums, as we know them, were first seen in the 1850s.

For most of human history few people had ever seen beneath the waves, and the ocean was even more dark and mysterious than it is today. Part of the spin-off from the frantic activity of invention and exploration in the Victorian industrial age was the opportunity for people to observe marine life up close for the first time. They liked what they saw, and our awareness of the remarkable life forms with which we share our planet was changed forever.

During the 1800s the UK saw such a sudden enthusiasm for marine life, and so many dedicated natural historians, that I hardly know where to start. It feels like one of those pop quizzes on the radio when you get the chance to have a shout-out for your friends and you just know you're bound to forget someone. Still, here goes: more rock pool than rock 'n' roll, of course . . .

First, I'd like to have a shout-out for Philip Henry Gosse (1810–88), who almost single-handedly created the enthusiasm for aquariums not just in Britain but worldwide. Some say he was actually the inventor of the aquarium – he did indeed formulate the term out of the awkward 'aqua-vivarium' – but many others had had a similar idea ever since the Sumatrans kept fish in ponds 4,500 years ago, and probably before.

After helping London Zoo set up the first fish house, aka public 'aquarium', in the world, Gosse wrote the wildly popular *The Aquarium: An Unveiling of the Wonders of the Deep* (1854). The success made him realise there was an appetite for keeping aquariums at home, and so then he published *A Handbook to the Marine Aquarium* (1856), explaining in detail how you need to balance marine and plant life and be careful how you treat the water in a small glass tank. Part of what made those books hits were the illustrations, sketched by Gosse and beautifully embellished on woodblocks by the printers Hullmandel & Walton. There were only five illustrations in *The Aquarium*, but later there would be hundreds – 700 in *Actinologia Britannica*, which is still one of the foremost field guides to British sea anemones.

I'd also mention Jeanne Villepreux-Power, sometimes called Jeanette Power, a French dressmaker and naturalist who researched the free-swimming relative of the octopus, the paper argonaut. To solve the mystery of how they made their 'paper' shells, she knew she needed to observe them more closely. So she went to the Strait of Sicily where the animals were abundant, but that wasn't enough. The eureka moment came in 1832 when, to get a close-up look, she had the idea of putting them in a glass tank filled with seawater. Unfortunately, all her notes on the husbandry of argonauts came to naught. They were lost in a shipwreck by the removal company taking the Power family's belongings from Sicily back to London.

This may be why Philip Gosse is more frequently credited with the invention of the modern aquarium, but it's more likely because he was a great popular writer. One of his contemporaries wrote that he could 'impart to his readers something of the thrill of studying living animals at first hand'. Perhaps all we need to know is that he realised 'aquarium' would be a popular and easy name to remember.

A shout-out too for Amelia Warren Griffiths (1768–1858), who made seaweed-collecting and seaside holidays popular. With her great friend Mary Wyatt, who ran a tourist shop in Torquay, she produced two volumes on seaweeds. It started a popular pastime for Victorian middle-class women, partly because collecting and pressing seaweed was an unthreatening version of what was then the predominantly male preserve of marine biology and science. Pressing the red seaweeds in particular made beautiful pictures, and there's still a market today on eBay and the more craft-friendly Etsy. Or you can try it yourself: put some heavy paper in a tray of water, and place the seaweed on top. Remove the paper and seaweed from the water and lay several layers of newspaper on top, with some weight, like a brick, to press them down. Replace the newspaper every day until the seaweed is dry.

The first sea life I can remember encountering, when I was about eight, were the jellyfish of Prestatyn Beach in North Wales, where our mother took us on summer holidays. Half-terrified and completely fascinated, I'd try to work out exactly what this purple-flecked blob was. But those sandy beaches didn't have much sea life on their upper stretches, and the mud-coloured water wouldn't let you see anything below the tide. So my first real encounter with marine life was during my zoology course at Reading University, when in the summer of 1980 we were sent to the Scottish field station at Millport, on the Clyde's Isle of Cumbrae.

Half-remembered friends from forty years ago are difficult to put a name to. But perhaps it's better that this one stays anonymous, although he did show great initiative. Let's call him 'Phil'. From the pier outside the research station you could look down into quite deep water, but on the surface, milling around every evening and nibbling at detritus and even Scottish midges that got too close, were beautiful grey mullet. Perhaps *silver* mullet would be better, as the mosaic of their scales shines like many tiny mirrors across their blunt and slender 2-foot-long bodies. Phil was observing them keenly as they darted just under the surface looking for tiny morsels – perhaps surprising for such a large fish to eat such small food, but then again the giant whale sharks and the like are plankton feeders. A patch of troubled water would betray their presence each time they darted upwards, almost breaking the surface, flitting about in interweaving patterns for maybe thirty seconds and then diving back into the dark again, invisible until their next return.

Actually, Phil was watching them very keenly *indeed.* Then I noticed there was a brick in his right hand. A whole red brick.

He had it poised a few feet above the water, forearm bent, ready to fling hard at its target. It was a long, still, summer's evening, and Phil stayed motionless like that for what seemed like a couple of hours, all the time with the brick fully primed. His focus was exclusively on the patches of silver mullet as they raided the surface and almost came into our world. He stayed like that such a long time that eventually we got bored and turned our backs on him.

Suddenly: a huge splash, and a shout – and, turning around, we saw the flopping side of a large silver fish, clearly stunned and unable to return to the deep. I felt I was getting an insight into the long-lost skills of Stone Age man. Phil fished out the heavy fish and later that night cooked it with the help of the marine science teachers from Reading, who were very impressed. We all ate some of its soft white flesh, marvelling at how something could taste of the fresh, salty sea, exactly as the waters of the Clyde at Millport smelt. In truth, we probably said it was nice because of the way it had been fished, which made us all feel implicated in murder. But fish caught in nets have a far nastier and slower death, when they drown in air. It's more than that: anonymous death has no accusers, and we knew this fish now, because we had been watching the magic of its silver dance, rising and falling in the water like reflections on the sword of Avalon.

Why do I still remember this moment so many years later? Certainly because of the almost comical intensity and concentration with which Phil hunted his quarry, and the unusual murder weapon. But I think too it was a naked illustration of our relationship with the sea and nature's bounty. Our instincts to banish hunger are always with us, leaving us confused as to whether to play the role of protector or exploiter.

The mysterious beauty of the sea must die to give us food. 'Yet each man kills the thing he loves,' wrote Oscar Wilde in 'The Ballard of Reading Gaol'. Though he didn't intend it as such, I think it describes perfectly how we treat nature, then feel guilty for what we've done to the world we love.

When one day on the Firth of Clyde I saw three of my group diving into the sea beneath a pier I remember feeling very jealous. I vowed then that I would learn to dive, so that I too could enter the hidden world beneath the waves. Until then I would have to content myself with rock pools and chasing the tide until it went out far enough to uncover starfish and squat lobsters, and then only for a short time before it came back in.

In the rock pools I noticed the red[1] beadlet anemone, *Actinia equina*, probably the most widely seen in the UK as it lives high up on the seashore, surviving out of the water for hours at low tide. It has a bit-part in Gosse's famous book on anemones, *Actinologia Britannica: A History of the British Sea Anemones and Corals*, and although I would see many more exotic species, it's still my favourite. Alien to us yet beautiful, accessible to all who walk beside the sea, it signals that ocean life is life but not as we know it, stranger and less familiar. As with so many sea creatures, it's difficult to know if the sea anemone is plant or animal, and it doesn't help that it's named like a flower. It is in fact an animal pretty close to being a jellyfish, and jellyfish themselves have a sessile stage called a polyp that sits on the seabed and looks very like an anemone. When times are good, this polyp goes mad and starts budding off thousands of tiny medusas, the floating jellyfish we know. That's how jellyfish

---

1 Other colours are available.

swarms come about. Anemones, on the other hand, don't have the floating jellyfish medusa stage, but mainly just sit around. Or do they?

For a zoology project I decided to see if the beadlets moved between tides by painting a yellow line around them, near to, but not touching their base. Just six or so I circled, on a rock halfway down the shore, not expecting the Nobel Prize for Science, but intrigued nonetheless. Then I waited six hours for the tide to wash over them and drain back again. The tide waits for no man, but a man must wait for the tide.

Sure enough, these little red blobs had moved, some almost all the way across the rock they were on. Perhaps they were trying to get away from the yellow paint! But nowadays, when I read about their gift of feeble movement, I see it makes sense for creatures that shelter symbiotic algae, because the anemone will get more sugars by taking them to the light. However, the beadlet anemone is not one that has algae, and so you would think it makes no difference where they live – and yet it still moves around. Maybe it's always on the look-out for better currents to bring it food. Or maybe, more dramatically, it needs to move to make war on its fellows: around the top of the blood-coloured beadlet is a ring of 192 tentacles, but also a slightly smaller ring of beautiful, purple-blue stumps, or acrorhagi, and these are full of stinging cells that attack neighbouring anemones invading their pitch. Since compared to us anemones and their kind live life 'in the slow lane', the battles between rival anemones only become clear when speeded up by time-lapse photography. I once built some home-made underwater time lapse units to capture just this sort of thing, placing them next to large Dahlia anemones 20 metres (65 feet) deep off the coast of St Abbs in Scotland. Taking a shot every six seconds over a couple of hours and playing them all back in only a minute or so you can begin to get a fascinating insight into their world and see them eat.[1] It's fascinating to watch and a bit gruesome, and just because it's slow doesn't mean it's not a complex behaviour, even though anemones hardly have two nerve cells to rub together.

While there were helmet- and even scuba divers earlier than we might imagine, the art was not perfected until Jacques Cousteau's attempts in the 1940s, and in Victorian times diving often came with a good chance of drowning and a fatal dose of the bends. The history of diving apparatus is a book in itself, albeit curiously dry for such a wet subject. But I do have to mention an early French diving suit made by the Carmagnolle Brothers in 1878, that seems to tell the story of hard dive suit development all by itself. It looks like something from the art department of a Sci-Fi horror movie mixed with a medieval knight's armour. The helmet has 25 individual small glass viewing ports, spaced at the average distance of the human eyes, and it has no less than 22 sliding joints. It's the sort of thing you'd build if you had no experience of going underwater but were trying to cover all eventualities. I saw a picture of Cousteau making a proud pose beside it in the National Maritime Museum in Paris in the sixties. I could swear that his face expresses sadness for the quaint metal monster and the knowledge that he freed scuba divers from it forever, at least in the shallows.

---

1 You can see the results on my YouTube channel: https://www.youtube.com/c/IndoonaOceans

Without safe diving equipment, ever-resourceful nineteenth-century naturalists found other ways to bring ocean creatures above the surface to reveal their wonder to the public. Though they weren't able to bring their audience the ocean in glorious Ultra High Definition (UHD) video, I think it's likely that they were better observers than we are today, because making drawings and even small models often requires more detailed observation than simply pointing a camera.

The most beautiful example comes from a father-and-son team who belonged to a long line of glass workers, originally from Dresden. Leopold Blaschka, who died in 1895, and his son Rudolf, who lived until 1939, had an exquisite way of crafting glass models of plants and sea creatures that has never been bettered. What they did might have seemed bizarre if it were not for the quality and detail of their work, and many of their techniques, including the first uses of acrylic paint, remain a secret to this day.

Leopold's credentials as a glassmaker were well established, but it wasn't until the death of his father that his grief led him to take consolation in nature, and in particular in sketching the plants around his home. Then in 1853, when he sailed for America, the ship was becalmed, and for two weeks he had nothing to do except observe the sea, and in particular the strange light made by many creatures at night. 'It is a beautiful night in May,' he wrote, about what we today call 'bioluminescence':

> Hopefully, we look out over the darkness of the sea, which is as smooth as a mirror; there emerges all around in various places a flash like bundle of light beams, as if it is surrounded by thousands of sparks,

that form true bundles of fire and of other bright lighting spots, and the seemingly mirrored stars. There emerges close before us a small spot in a sharp greenish light, which becomes ever larger and larger and finally becomes a bright, shining, sun-like figure.

His sighting sparked an interest in marine life and, since many such creatures were transparent, he realised that glass would be an ideal substance to represent them. Like most of us, though, he needed to make a living, and had to concentrate on the family business, which was mainly making prosthetic glass eyes (as you do). Eventually, his skill at making accurate glass models caught the attention of patrons, of whom the first was Prince Camille de Rohan, who ordered a hundred glass models of orchids for his private collection. When the head of the Dresden Natural History Museum, Professor Reichenbach, also funded Leopold to make twelve glass models of sea anemones, Leopold knew he could turn his hobby into his main business.

Until the mid-1800s there had been no way to preserve soft-bodied marine creatures so that they kept their shape and colours. Pickled in alcohol, many specimens just turned a waxy-white and disintegrated, useless for teaching students or intriguing the public. What is interesting, though, is that by now there was such a huge appetite for seeing these strange and beautiful forms of marine creatures that, unlikely as it seems, the Blaschka marine glass-model business thrived. Museums and private collectors were all keen to buy, and at a good price, and in a business model worthy of Amazon the family produced a mail-order catalogue to ship their glass creations worldwide. The operation was a testament to their packaging and handling of the postal service as much as anything, as these models are beyond fragile. The ocean side of the business modelled marine invertebrates, including jellyfish, octopus and squid, in impossible detail, with clear tissue, eyes, spines and tentacles all perfectly rendered in glass. In a time before underwater photography they were the nearest thing to *The Blue Planet* in bringing the undersea world into the classroom, lab, public gallery or indeed living room.

Over 10,000 models that we know of were made of marine life by the Blaschkas (and about 4,500 flowers). Today it is Cornell University, one of the biggest original commissioners, that holds the largest collection, with many glass plants but also 570 marine-life models, and design sketches by Leopold and Rudolf made as a guide to crafting the glass models. The London Natural History Museum has 180, and I have filmed them twice, once for the BBC series *Wildlife on One*, with Sir David Attenborough, and once for the museum's own exhibition, *Treasures*, about the objects that changed our view of the natural world. The first time, I remember, they were at the back of the museum in wide mapmakers' drawers, wrapped in tissue. We were kindly allowed to spend a whole day filming them for an episode about the special adaptions of octopus, squid and cuttlefish, all represented in the Blaschka collection. The models were a bit dusty and occasionally broken, but still beautiful, and their colours unfaded. We rotated them gently on an electric turntable, which is a good way to make inanimate objects come to life. By the time I went back a few years later, their importance had become apparent and, thanks to the careful work of curator Miranda Lowe, they had been restored to their full glory, and each given their own specially-made padded box with a clear perspex panel on one side.

Today many of the Blaschka models are being scanned in 3D and digitised on computer. It occurs to me that that is one of the stages used in digital animation – making a digital 'wireframe' model – and from here it isn't too much of a leap to making that model move, animating it in different seascapes. It would be fun to bring this glass menagerie to life like that and capture the enthusiasm and wonder of the Victorians and their excitement at new discoveries in a *Victorian Blue Planet*. Tiny, delicate and beautiful, the Blaschkas' glass models captured the ethereal mystery of the deep sea forever.

I'd like to move on to the work of the flamboyant doctor Ernst Haeckel, born in 1834, an extraordinarily prolific marine and anatomical illustrator the Blaschkas themselves used for inspiration, especially for depictions of microscopic marine life. But after a disastrous talk recently to a group of eager young film-makers about the technology of wildlife film-making, in which I went into far too much detail about esoteric gadgets and nerded them to death, I feel I must pause and come up for air. Don't worry, Ernst; I'll fit you in if we ever get around to discussing plankton and how tricky it is to film.

I had, come to think of it, been hooked on the very thing about the sea that hooked Gosse and the Victorians – a rock pool full of mysteries, a miniature of the sea as a whole. But my journey to the ocean took a few detours as it flowed downstream into the deltas and estuaries of time, always tied up as it was with seeking out the stranger forms of life.

After doing a zoology degree I decided that the next thing was to do another zoology degree, and in 1982 I found myself starting a PhD on tarantula spiders. I'd like to say as a joke it has always stood me in good stead, but it truly has, in ways I didn't realise at the time. In other ways it just made me peculiar, and certainly not as glamorous as that other more well-known Spider-Man. My son's affectionate (I hope) name for me today is 'WOM' – Weird Old Man – and I suppose that's fair: some of that strangeness I seek has rubbed off on me.

Certainly, spiders are strange to us: they do almost everything differently from animals like ourselves. Their legs, made from seven segments, use hydraulic fluid to move; they have six to eight eyes depending on the species, and their bodies bristle with sense organs (the subject of my research), including some 3,000 slits in the skin that pick up all sorts of stresses and vibrations, which they are very good at analysing. That's why spiders don't run after the vibrations caused by rain: they can tell raindrops on a web or leaf make much lower notes than the frequencies produced by the beating wings of a juicy fly.

Yet such animals are not 'peculiar' at all: the arthropods to which spiders belong are among the most common and successful animals on Earth, far more so than us, many would say. And arthropods too came from the sea, and still dominate the ocean and our planet: hermit crabs and horseshoe crabs, barnacles and copepods, amphipods (like shrimps) and isopods (like woodlice), and even sea spiders that don't have a body as such but pack in all their organs into their legs. Although it must be admitted that the most diverse group of arthropods, the insects, are strangely lacking in the sea, and only the sea skaters (or 'striders' in the USA), *Halobates*, are found far out in the ocean. No one knows exactly why; perhaps the crustaceans (crabs, lobsters, shrimps and barnacles and the like) got there first or perhaps crustaceans and insects are actually more closely related to each other than we realise.

How does a degree in tarantulas get you into the BBC? Is it necessary? Well, in 1984 it was decided to send me to a research group in Frankfurt for a year. There was no internet then, and so I listened to the BBC World Service every day to keep in touch with home. Back in the UK a year later, I saw an ad for a post called Studio Manager, that asked for an interest in both science *and* art; for technical knowledge as well as an appreciation of music and sound, which would help in running a radio studio. It had long irritated me that people divide life into science and art, as though you have to be either logical or emotional. I knew a lot about recording sound because of the spider work, and the job was with the World Service, which I had just been listening to all year. Add in a little hospital radio experience and the job was mine.

A few years of writing radio scripts for science, moving from London to Bristol, home of the Natural History Unit of the BBC, to make wildlife radio programmes, and then moving to wildlife television while developing an interest in underwater photography as a hobby, left me perfectly placed in 1998 when the opportunity arose to join the *Blue Planet* team.

4

Lucky Dips

The surprise of discovery

I still remember Lucky Dips: barrels of sawdust with sweets and toys in them and the excitement mixed with caution as I trusted my hand to find something in the wood shavings. Exploring the oceans is exactly like that: the surprise of discovery, and sometimes too the fear that, groping to find its treasures, you might get your hand bitten.

As I write it's fifty years since Apollo 11 took off to go to the Moon. I listened to the soundtrack of the lift-off again today – maybe it's fifty years too since I last heard that, although it will have been mixed unobtrusively into countless history, science and news shows I'll have watched over the years. So, the first time I'm *consciously* hearing it, then, and it takes me back to the little plastic black-and-white telly perched on a sideboard in a farmhouse-snug living room in North Wales, July 1969. I can't remember the colour of the walls, the curtains, the exact detail of the sofa, or the sideboard, but I do remember seeing the images of the Apollo launch on that 16-inch screen (it was inches: in the UK they didn't have centimetres back then).

The crackle of the Apollo soundtrack still gives me the thrill of a great adventure about to start, like a family holiday in August, car loaded, and shrimp nets packed. The crackle isn't the static of a bad recording – it's quite high-quality, in fact – but comes, I think, from the strains of take-off: the massive fuel burn, the ice falling away from the sides of the giant launch vehicle, the slow rise of mass on an improbably pencil-shaped object, so tall yet managing not to fall over. And mixed in with that audio the confident commands of men (there was only one woman, JoAnn Morgan, in the launch firing room) who knew what they were doing, although knowing even as it was happening they only had a 50:50 chance of success. The fifty years in between disappear, and now I also see Apollo 8's close-ups of the far side of the Moon. Sent about six months earlier than Apollo 11, as a dress rehearsal for the landing, its astronauts were the first people to ever see the Moon's dark side; I see the somewhat jumpy motion of craters and white dusty seas passing by, and I sense the awe, of both the adults in the living room and the astronauts themselves who are touching the face of God. Probably the TV room smelt of my Dad's rollies – Player's Medium Navy Cut, tobacco strong enough to make a thieving goat regretful – which he chain-smoked without regard to the secondary inhalation by his family. Although like climate change, mental health, talking about cancer, and gay marriage, that wasn't a thing then. But maybe Apollo was part of the change that brought those issues out into society, accelerated by a picture of Earthrise over the moon? Looking back on ourselves is a powerful thing.

Just before the Moon age, in 1960, we had decided that it was worth exploring the deepest parts of our ocean. Jacques Piccard and Don Walsh bravely piloted a curiously shaped submersible, the Trieste, right into the Challenger Deep, going down to 10,911 metres (35,797 feet). More correctly their craft was called a 'bathyscaphe' and had a very cramped spherical crew compartment sitting under 32,000 US gallons of gasoline that acted as a pressure resistant float. About 100 years earlier the British survey vessel HMS *Challenger* first identified this spot, now named after the ship, as the deepest in the world. What they had found was a valley in the so called Mariana or Marianas Trench about halfway between Papua New Guinea and Japan. Funnily enough, if you search for 'Challenger Deep' on Google Earth (as I just have), you just get a sky-blue box with a red lollipop in the middle marking the spot, and it's not until you pull out to the coast of the Philippines and a bit of Papua New Guinea and North Australia that you can see where you are, which is yet another demonstration of the fantastic amount of water there is on this planet. It's also a reminder of how unfathomable the sea remains; I mean, 4,000 square miles or so of the planet can't possibly be *featureless*, can it? At any rate, there must be a gigantic scar in the Earth around the famous trench filled in with water. There are several in the same region actually, and at least five narrow trenches over 10,000m, 6.2 miles deep in the Pacific. The sea can get to such astonishing depths because of course the oceans are not uniformly distributed across the world, and there are gigantic mountains as well as gaping chasms, but if the Earth were a perfect sphere with a porcelain-smooth surface, then it's been estimated the average depth of the ocean on such a silky globe would still be 2.6 km, or 1.6 miles.

As with the Moon landings it's been a while since we have made any substantial effort to continue the exploration of the oceans. In 2012 James Cameron's *Deepsea Challenger* returned to the Challenger Deep, and that seems to have rekindled a new era of deep exploration. Several companies, including Virgin Oceanic and Triton Submarines have taken on the challenge of the Challenger Deep in recent years. The most successful was led by Dallas businessman and explorer, Victor Vescovo, of the Five Deeps Expedition, going to the deepest point in five oceans. Vescovo set another record for going to the deepest part of the Challenger Deep in 2019, albeit breaking the Piccard and Walsh record by only about 40 feet, 11 metres or so, which doesn't seem much when you are so deep. However, using a Triton submersible called the *DSV Limiting Factor*, Vescovo and his team cracked making five dives to the bottom of the Challenger Deep in just ten days, while there had only been two successful manned dives there in the previous 59 years. In 2020 and 2021 the 'Ring of Fire' Expeditions, with Vescovo, returned making at least nine further crewed dives into the Challenger Deep to date. Although, as any deep-sea researcher will tell you, and probably lunar explorers too, there are less-spectacular expeditions all the time. Using deep-ocean trawls, remotely operated vehicles (ROVs), landers (awkward-looking metal frames with cameras, but getting smarter all the time) and sometimes various piloted but relatively shallow working submarines, ocean science moves on at a pace that cannot be hurried, it seems. A pace of course that depends on the vogue for funding as well as advances in engineering and material technology.

Mapping and sounding the oceans was essential in understanding marine creatures, as we realised, for example, that polar bears lived right across the Arctic seas, that sperm whales were frequently encountered in the deep waters off the Azores, or that leatherback turtles nested on the beaches of Trinidad. Knowing where to look is the biggest part of discovery, yet so strange are some of the creatures in the sea that knowing what you're looking at is often something of a puzzle too.

Have a look at the wonky drawings of rhinos that European artists from medieval to Victorian times drew from hearsay. They reveal our curiosity, but also how little we understood until recently about our planet. And if that was the case on land, then all the more so in the sea, where even today the ocean's rhinos are only partially drawn. Hardly more than a century ago the deep was a place of at best horrific thrills, at worst ill omen, where terrifying monsters devoured everything in sight. Judging by the continuing hysteria about sharks, many would still agree.

So what creatures remain to be discovered in the 95 per cent of the seas we haven't thoroughly checked? Ward Appeltans, a marine biodiversity specialist, and colleagues suggest maybe between one and two thirds of all marine life has not been discovered. Even more sensational, though also controversial, are the estimates from ecologist Charles Paxton, based on the rate of previous discoveries, that there may be as many as 18 marine creatures greater than 6 feet or 2 metres still waiting to be found. For me these unknown unknowns are surely the greatest pleasures and excitement. In the oceans the great age of discovery is not over, and equipped with a camera we still have an awesome journey ahead of us, one which, of course, we'll never finish.

During the long reign of Queen Victoria in Britain, we see a developing understanding of our deep oceans and the creatures that live there. At the outset it was thought the phenomenal pressure of the water crushed all life down there to extinction, although the exact depth at which this occurred was a matter of dispute. And even if it were possible to withstand the water's weight, scientists conjectured that there were no deep currents to stir up the nutrients and gases necessary for life, and so the ocean floor was stagnant and barren. As with our present quest to find life on Mars, it seemed literally unfathomable to try and sound out the existence of life on the seabed with the plumb-line technology of the day.

A self-taught young professor called Edward Forbes, who wrote carefully observed field books on subjects as varied as Austrian botany and British starfish, came up with the idea that life ceased to exist below 300 fathoms (1800 feet, 550 metres). He came to this conclusion because in 1841, on a survey ship in the Aegean Sea, he noticed that water samples from ever greater depths had fewer and fewer and smaller and smaller creatures. The logical extrapolation from his own measurements suggested that at the boundary of 300 fathoms life would stop altogether.

Over the next twenty years Forbes's azoic or 'lifeless' theory took on a life of its own. It just shows how folk follow the pack and believe what is easier to believe. Turns out that the Aegean seas are relatively barren, and that Forbes's gear wasn't up to catching much. Besides, there was already much evidence for deeper life by then, with deep-water fisheries established in the early 1800s catching fish from far greater depths. For example, from the early 1800s the black scabbard fish was fished from over four times the depth of Forbes's azoic zone, on 4,000-foot-long lines (about 1,200 metres); in Madeira it's a famous and fearsome national dish.

What really opened up the secrets of the deep sea, however, was the need to lay copper wires for international telegraph lines – vital by the 1840s, as the electronic age beckoned. Copper by itself, of course, is no use carrying signals underwater, as it would just short out: you need to insulate the wire. At the time all that was available in sufficient quantity came from the sap of a Malaysian tree called the percha. The sap or latex it produced, called *getah* in Malay, became known in English as gutta-percha and, ironically for the recent history of the oceans, was a somewhat pliable, and natural, precursor of modern plastic. In 1840, 150,000 tons of the stuff was imported into the UK, mostly for cable insulation. Even so gutta-percha ocean-telegraph cables didn't last too long, and were frequently brought up to repair. In the 1860s a damaged cable between Sardinia and the Algerian coast was fished up from over 1,000 fathoms (6,000 feet; approximately 1,830 metres), and found to be encrusted with abundant marine life, finally killing the notion there was no life in the deep.

For many there was now a great fear of what might be found down in these ocean depths. 'It is still possible that in the end the prophecies of the myths will come true and gigantic animals will appear from the depths,' wrote Gustav Jäger, a prominent German naturalist, in 1868. And he hadn't even watched Shark Week.

As more creatures were dredged from the deep sea, people were confronted with a strange new world and exciting new life forms. The British Empire was at its height, the Victorians were on fire, exploring science and the world as never before, and with public interest now on their side they could set out to reveal what really lay beneath the waves that Britain ruled. From 1872 to 1876 a now-legendary global expedition was made in a converted British warship, HMS *Challenger*, that ship that found the deepest part of the ocean. The expedition was led by Sir Charles Wyville Thomson, a professor at Edinburgh University who had already made his reputation with new finds in the North Atlantic.

Originally a Royal Navy Corvette, the guns and ammunition were thrown off, to make a state-of-the-art research vessel. I would say 'oceanographic vessel', but HMS *Challenger* was the ship that invented *Oceanography*. With its own laboratories and microscopes, it also had the latest scientific equipment of all kinds. There were many types of samplers to grab rocks and sediment from the seabed, and nets that could target creatures from specific depths. It also had several types of powered winches – essential kit on scientific vessels today – although then driven by steam they were still capable of lowering miles of cable into the abyss: a slow job without such power-assistance, as I can attest, having manually dropped and recovered 500 metres of fibre optic cable, with film-maker, Martin Dohrn and his team in the Azores in 2011 (see Chapter 12). To do it on a regular basis, and to depths that demand turning drums of cable weighing tens of tons, Victorian steam technology gave what was needed for the first time.

Wyville Thomson and his team of scientists were the first to methodically gather data on a whole range of ocean features, such as seawater temperature, chemistry, currents, marine life and the geology of the sea floor. They had planned and regular sampling stations, and at each one lowered nets and samplers to various depths from the top to the bottom of the sea, pulling their bounty back on board and storing it in the spacious holds of the onetime warship.

Over three years the *Challenger* explored 363 locations and discovered nearly 5,000 species new to science. Some of its findings are well known today and, as we've seen, it uncovered one of the deepest parts of the whole ocean – the Marianas Trench in the western Pacific, where the seafloor is between 5 and 7 miles down (approximately 8–11,000 metres), today honoured with the name Challenger Deep. In its ocean odyssey the ship sailed nearly three times around the planet and made the first maps of ocean basins, including the discovery of an underwater mountain range rising from the middle of the Atlantic Ocean that we now call the Mid-Atlantic Ridge.

In all, the HMS *Challenger* expedition produced fifty biblical-sized volumes of new information on the sea that took nineteen years to compile, collecting so much data and so many samples that scientists are still looking at them, sometimes with an intent never imagined at the time – such as to understand how the temperatures of the sea have changed with global warming over the intervening 150 years. I'd like to say it was the beginning of our understanding of 'marine life as we know it', but it really wasn't even the start of the beginning, as some of the things HMS *Challenger* dredged up are still pretty mysterious to us today.

5

Eel with Mouth Like a Pelican

Strange marine creatures revisited

This strange monster combines the shape of a spoon and a funnel and can do little more than to wiggle along the ocean bed; it hides in the mud with only its open, nearly toothless mouth protruding, patiently waiting.

William Marshall

Exactly 117 years later than the German writer of biological science William Marshall wrote these words, I was staring at the same animal, brought up from the deep sea, in a trawl, just as they did in Victorian times. Although it's now clear it is a mid-water, not a bottom-dwelling creature.

'It may be worth getting his eyes before they cloud over,' suggested Ron Douglas, a deep-sea biologist who specialised in fish vision. The sad fact is that we were filming a dying animal, a fate that happens to all creatures drawn from the deep into our world. The best we could do was to get as fresh a record of this animal as we could.

Our little filming team included Julian Partridge, another deep-sea expert and a scientific adviser on *The Blue Planet*, which is how I had got to know him. Julian had invited me aboard the Scripps research vessel *New Horizon* when a scientist dropped out. Scripps is a famous marine research institute in San Diego, California that also hires out its survey ships to whoever can fork out $40,000 a day. On this occasion the mission was organised by Tammy Frank, then of Harbor Branch in Florida. I was on my own dollar, so had brought some low-end jerry-rigged filming kit that was all I could afford, because I knew it was a chance not to be missed. It was 2005, and I had recently left the BBC to become freelance.

I had met Ron when I had asked him if it was possible to bring a chameleon and an owl to an optician for an eye test – we were doing a science show called *The Human Senses* and wanted to compare the infamous acuity of owl vision, and the 360° swivelling eyes of chameleons, with human vision, as you do, in those sorts of show at least. Julian had tipped me off that his friend Ron, who was teaching on the ophthalmology course at London's City University, probably wouldn't be too fazed by the request and might be able to bend the arm of an optician with a shop.

'We need a little bit more light,' I said, tilting the large lens of my camera for close-up filming – 'it's so dark.' We tilted the light, a $30 arc lamp bought the previous week from Home Depot, a bit more so it bounced off the ceiling to make the filming tank slightly brighter. 'Funny little pectoral fins he's got.'

That's not the most obvious thing to remark on when you see a pelican eel for the first time. The most amazing thing is its balloon-like face, which splits open with a massive, gaping grin. Two lentil-sized eyes peer over the top rim of its upper lip. If you can imagine the bill of a pelican without a pelican on it you're getting quite close to what a pelican or gulper eel looks like. Given that it comes from such a difficult place to reach, perhaps it's not surprising that, well over a century after its discovery, we still know very little about it.

Even in the present day the method of finding these creatures is still crude. The *New Horizon* was mixture between a spacious research ship and a trawler; it had a special large trawling net, with a wide mouth stretched across a boom. It took several people to untangle it and put it in the sea, and of course there was a massive steel-cable drum with miles of wire on it to lower it to the abyss. The net could be opened and closed at specific depths, so you knew roughly where the creatures caught had been taken from. At the end of the net, called the 'cod end', there was a large plastic cylinder, about the size of a small person, that collected the samples. Even though the creatures of the 'middle sea' live in the biggest habitat on the planet, and are therefore possibly some of the most numerous, their population density is very low. This means that to catch anything a six-hour trawl was not uncommon. There was great excitement when the net came up and the cod-end's contents were carefully spilled into a large plastic trough – that lucky dip feeling again. Each scientist took their specialist creatures – shrimps, squid or deep-sea fish – and our makeshift filming team was often allowed to film the pick of the crop before the research began. The animals were stored in the dark in a cold room to keep them fresh, but sadly they would not survive the pounding in the trawl, or the temperature and pressure changes on being brought to the surface. Although they were just a handful in the scheme of things, there was an onus on us all to be respectful and get the maximum knowledge from them, and by filming make a permanent record of all their amazing forms. Perhaps we were not so unlike the awestruck Victorian artists who a century ago recorded details of these deep-sea animals.

For filming we had a shipping container on the back deck, and inside it the space for a round acrylic tank about 4 feet (1.5

metres) in diameter, fed with fresh seawater by a filter pump. Such a tank is more properly known as a Kreisel, from the German for 'merry-go-round' and the same design as used in public aquaria for displaying jellyfish, with a circular water flow to keep the animals inside from touching the front. For the price of a curry and some beer, a friend and colleague, Jonathan Watts, of British Technical Films, had kindly machined some attachments for a special macro lens to put on the front of my video camera, which worked really well, as we could get right up to the side of the tank and film through the plastic front.

Trawling is used when tissue samples are needed for chemical analysis, but is also considerably cheaper than sending down submarines, and of course covers more sea area. Nowadays low-cost 'drop cameras', and new ways to retrieve them or even get live video from the seabed – sending a 'forest of camera eyes' into the ocean, something many people, including myself, are working on – promise a way of seeing more of the deep sea's amazing creatures. Great camera technology has got amazingly cheap, but the deployment and retrieval of the cameras in the deep remains expensive. Reducing cost is the key to exploring more of our deep ocean.

When I was filming the pelican eel and other amazing and curious deep-sea creatures in 2005, I didn't really know what I would do with the footage. It was interesting, and you could see the animals clearly in the filming tank, but high-quality wildlife films require very steady and artfully shot material on high-quality video formats. My footage was more 'opportunistic', to put it politely, and the video equipment at best semi-professional. At times the images bounced with the vibration of the ship, even in our isolated container. Worse still, I couldn't follow the animals on my clumsy tripod without making jerky movements that were difficult to watch. For broadcast wildlife films these images just wouldn't cut the mustard.

For several years these amateur marine videos, although full of extraordinary creatures, sat on the shelf. Apart from our egos, manifested in an unusual need for attention, film-makers are usually people who are so amazed or intrigued by something that they want to share their discoveries with the world. But I was also troubled by that ethical issue: to make sure these creatures had not been caught in vain. So I was delighted when I realised that YouTube – founded the same year as I'd seen the pelican eel – could give me the opportunity to share this shaky fascinating footage with everyone. Well, everyone that wants to see it, that is. On 29 October 2011, I started a YouTube channel on sea creatures called Indoona, and to date it has had nearly 2 million viewers: modest by many standards, but still a football stadium-full of audience every month.

I'm still learning whether it matters what you call your YouTube channel, but *Indoona* comes from the name of the boat my father's family had when he was a boy growing up in Essex. He said it was the happiest time of his life, as a young teenager sailing on the sea, and it's that innocent feeling of joy and fascination with the ocean I wanted to capture, at least in my mind anyway. In the end the emotional connections are more powerful than all the wonderful facts. Not surprisingly, the ocean master himself, Jacques Cousteau, puts it best: 'The sea, once it casts its spell, holds one in its net of wonder forever.'

YouTube's production values are often a long way from *The Blue Planet*, and most individuals on the platform are making a relatively tiny inroad into new media, but I embrace the new access to what is essentially a democratic way of making video content. Once making TV was a privileged reserve of the few who were lucky enough to get into it: intelligent, witty, humane, competitive, no doubt – but also people whose 'face fitted'. Maybe it's still a bit like that now, but on YouTube anyone who has an internet connection can be a kind of broadcaster, film-maker and presenter – which limits the pool of producers to potentially almost 5 billion and counting.

I always envied theatre for the immediate response of its audience. Every line written, every musical score, every fine piece of acting, all the nuances of the production, could be tested on an audience every night, and you would see their immediate delight or disappointment. As a producer in conventional, 'terrestrial' broadcasting it's pretty difficult to tell what's going on. Today in the UK, research is conducted by BARB, the Broadcasters' Audience Research Board, which uses 12,000 people across 5,300 households representative of the overall viewing public (I've never met one – have you?). There are also automatic loggers that give a percentage share of the audiences across about 231 mainstream channels at the time of writing, and in the BBC there are 'Audience Logs', an internal report of audience feedback (people who ring, email or write in). With YouTube, however, I can see the audience reaction to a video clip as though I was watching the audience live in a theatre: by the second, hour, day, week, month and year from all over the world – and the database I have comes from 2 million people.

One of the things that most interests me is what it reveals about how people think about the sea and the animals that live there. The pelican eel video is one of the most viewed clips, with half a million hits and about 300 comments, and one of the most common reactions to it is fear. Here are some of them:

'This is why I hate the Ocean' *Grant Hashimoto*

'Well no sleep for me today' *Zealotscout*

'Noooooooooooo!!! KILL IT WITH FIRE!!!!'
 The BeastWithin

'This is why I don't want to swim in un-seethrough
 water' *Archaeic*

'Cool. Who needs to sleep again, ever, anyway?'
 PJE Davey

'Your worst nightmares couldn't create something
 that terrifying' *Saturdays Child*

'Why are sea creatures so scary?' *The flying chicken*

'AAAAAAAAAA' *Rex* Lana

To be fair, there are quite a few amazed and somewhat com-
plimentary comments too:

'Just another one of God's beautiful creatures' *Erich*

'Pretty Cute to me' *kennyVargaz 1941*

'Shame that most of us can never see these deep sea
creatures when they are alive. Only from TV
documentaries' *Met3Angel*

'I think the eel itself is cool, but the gills creep me out,
with all those little spiky things inside of it.
Nevertheless, it is a fascinating animal' *Maxwell Dacre*

'It looks like a broken shoe' *RazgrizOne*

My favourite of all the comments on this clip titled 'Eel with
mouth like a pelican' is this one:

'Eel with mouth like a *politician!*' *Amadaeus*

You may find it surprising that I talk about YouTube channels that make a few cents when I also worked on *The Blue Planet*, some of the most expensive wildlife television ever undertaken. Wildlife films can be made in many different ways, and today you could decide to go and film some flowers or snails using a camera on your phone at a quality unknown only thirty years ago. They would probably not be polished, high-end documentaries (forgive me), but they would be a 'wildlife film' of sorts, and now the Internet provides a democratic way for people to judge if they are of interest.

Making low-cost films or just a short clip is very liberating. You can decide to do it one day and film right away, without spending months on research, logistics planning, meetings or getting executive permission to spend money. Although in the pioneering days, it seems, money wasn't such an obstacle for those making natural history documentaries, at least for those in the system. Sir David Attenborough, one of the first producers ever in documentary TV, mentions that in the old days he would be asked to 'go and film monkeys in Borneo and come back in six months.' What freedom, what joy!

Since then it has got a bit more controlling and measured. The modern-day protocol in broadcast production companies is to develop ideas within a development team and then have an executive present them to channel commissioners, like Discovery's Vice President, the gatekeepers of the budgets, in a semi-formal way, at set times during the year. Within the BBC that's called 'offers'. It's a somewhat random process that depends on how the commissioner controlling a channel sees the ideas fitting into the daily schedule, but also on whether the idea is within the remit of the channel's brand. It's still relatively well funded, though, and the expense of spending a lot of time making wildlife films is well recognised. We are talking hundreds of thousands of pounds an hour versus the almost nothing that most YouTube channels, especially the factual ones, have to play with.

Yet it's obvious that the whole TV landscape has been changing rapidly, and that the streamers and YouTubers or something similar not yet named are going to take over. Big players have already altered the film world beyond recognition in just a few years, and Netflix, Disney, Amazon and Apple are currently in a streaming war whose main weapon is cash, and with loads of new ideas, and scheduling documentaries to be watched in any order or in one glorious binge. Add to that the vast new data from online analytics that tracks if you've had Kellogg's Cornflakes or Weetabix for breakfast and what that says about what you want to watch, and you'd be silly not to try and understand this new world if you have even a pixel of interest in digital media and film-making. Such things are the hinterland of making films about anything, but especially about the sea where just having enough money to be there is a struggle. I like to understand them, even if I have very little control over how TV and the opportunities to make ocean films will evolve, so that I won't miss a chance to help explain such creatures as eels that look like pelicans.

Pelican eel, *Eurypharynx pelecanoides*. From *Oceanic Ichthyology* by G. Brown Goode and Tarleton H. Bean., published 1896.

6

The Saltwater Country

A feature-filled sea full of colours

The aboriginal Australians call the sea the saltwater country, which is a beautiful understanding of the ocean, and say it's not plain blue at all but all the colours of the rainbow. When you get to know it, they think, each part is distinct, with features that can and should be mapped, just like the land.

Marcus Barber did his PhD research by living for two years with the Yolngu people of Yilpara, right by the coast at Blue Mud Bay in north-east Arnhem Land in Australia's Northern Territory. I came across his work over a decade ago in researching programme ideas, and it has stuck with me, because it was remarkable and clever to learn directly from people who live with the sea, by directly 'living' their experience. His thesis has the magical title 'Where the Clouds Stand', which refers to the way the clouds sit above the sea on the horizon, and it's far from a dry, academic work. Rather, it's about the relationships between people, water and places in the everyday life of the Yolngu, and makes us reflect on how everyone might perceive the ocean and the rivers that flow into it. As conservation issues become ever more pressing, it's clear we could do with some new perspectives.

The Yolngu, Barber shows, give a greater priority to the ways in which fresh and salt water mix, to the path water takes to the sea, and to the currents stirred up in its depths, than they do to the division between land and sea itself. They are keenly tuned to the way water is continually moving and mixing. Their approach demonstrates, lest we missed it, that the river, the sea, the tides, currents, clouds, rain and seasonal weather are all part of the same system. To understand it as part of a spiritual world where water and the sea constitute rich metaphors for life itself. For example, to the Yolngu we are all connected to our first ancestors in the same way that one thrown pebble can cause ripples to spread out across a pond. The pebble is the beginning, and our lives are only a ripple. In water, a wave is only passing energy, the transference of vibrations from one water particle to the next. So, in the same way, we are all seamlessly connected to the past, present and future, as the generations travel through an ocean of time.

To be honest, I find some of these concepts hard to grasp, and part of me feels uncomfortable mixing science and the meaning of life in one sentence. Yet I know there's something immensely valuable here that I've been missing, and that the Yolngu conception of the ocean enables dots to be joined, if nothing else making me better at filming at sea, where the task is to find any animals to film in the first place, a better hunter of images. More importantly, of course, we need a wider and wiser net of ideas to grasp how our planet ticks, and how to live on it in more sustainable ways. It is ironic that this ancient wisdom comes as news to us, an inquiring but sometimes blind science-based culture, but we need to incorporate these ideas and realise they reinforce the picture we already have of the ocean.

Part of my blinkers are that I've been brought up with an old-fashioned atlas, where the sea is mostly depicted as a featureless blue. As Marcus Barber points out, that's a big omission in the commonly used maps of the world:

> The detail of the land is contrasted with the flat blue of the ocean; no depth, no variation in colour showing different water bodies or movements. No sign of distinctions in the seabed, such as are made on land. Rocky reef is not differentiated from mud, nor seagrass from sand. This is partly a reflection of the capacities and deficiencies of remote mapping systems, yet it is also the result of a difference in perspective, an assessment of what is important to know.[1]

To the Yolngu such differences are vital, because they're a subsistence-hunting people, and their lives depend on it. Every nuance in the structure of the ocean is an important clue as to where their food might be.

And this reveals another error in our maps. Water is dynamic: it never stays still, and huge changes can occur within only a few hours, never mind seasons. Maps are tools of precision, with clearly defined borders and definitive lines, but the churning sea is so hard to show on a static map, though its flux of currents is key to where creatures swim and feed.

Most sea maps are further limited, Barber goes on to explain, because they don't show the sky, and 'to remove the sky is to

---

1 M. Barber, 'Where the Clouds Stand: Australian Aboriginal Relationships to Water, Place, and the Marine Environment in Blue Mud Bay, Northern Territory', *Australian National University, Open Access Theses* (2005).

destroy the system'. In writing the *Blue Planet II*, 'Big Blue' script, we wanted to say how much the power of the sea and the clouds are connected, and how the way they work together drives the weather. The simple fact of the sun evaporating water from the vast surface of the open ocean is vital to the whole world's climate, an idea not so far from the Yolngu's understanding that sea and clouds meet on the same 'map'. At one point in the many drafts of the script we tried to find a figure for exactly how much water is evaporated from the world's seas each day, although we subsequently chickened out of this mathematical rigour to say something vaguer, and let the images of the clouds building over the sea do the talking, to a voiceover that went: 'As the vapour rises, it condenses into clouds; they rapidly build into gigantic burgeoning towers, which eventually generate violent storms, some a thousand miles across.' That's a more imaginative way of doing it, and in any case numbers are so hard to grasp in the short time you have to take in everything along with fast-moving pictures. Still, here is the unused 'back-of-an-envelope' calculation I made, based on United States Geological Survey data: 280 cubic miles (1,170 cubic km) of seawater evaporates from the surface of the sea a day. Which means precisely not very much to anyone. So then I looked for a better way to understand its significance. You might know that there are minute amounts of gold in seawater, and if you did evaporate that amount of seawater, the gold you'd be left with by midnight each day would be worth about $3 billion. That's how powerful the sea-sky system is and, as the Yolngu tell us from their 40,000 years of experience, it's not to be ignored.

I'd have to admit however, that it's not practical to put an ever-changing sky on a paper map, or even to show the currents in anything but a vague, generalised pattern. Although it would be possible, of course, to capture its movement on video, and we need to work on that. But the bottom line is that our description of the ocean is inadequate. Perhaps that's why the Yolngu have over thirty-eight names for seawater, such as *morri*, which means 'calm saltwater', or *dhangayal*, which denotes the 'white chop on the sea', and they have about three times as many names for clouds as we do, who hardly know our altostratus from our pannus despite the UK having some of the best clouds in the world!

It would be hard to find someone more different from the Yolngu people than Peter Scoones, probably the greatest underwater wildlife cameraman that ever lived. I met him first when we did a filming trip together in Africa to Lake Malawi and he was sixty but still a better diver than myself. He had quite thick glasses and a purposeful stare, and a wild explorer's beard that seemed to contradict his English reserve. And yet in its extent and passion, Peter's detailed knowledge of the sea and water was surprisingly similar to the Yolngu's.

I suggested earlier that the aboriginal Australians of Blue Mud Bay were more in touch with the sea than we are, and if you get your food directly from the ocean instead of a supermarket that's not surprising. Yet different cultures often couch the same basic concepts in different terms. Even our somewhat mechanical, scientific culture comes up with the idea of 'habitats', labels the whole idea of nature as 'green' and calls our planet 'blue'.

Peter once told me how he came to be an underwater cameraman. His skills in photography were forged in the RAF in the late 1950s, when he flew sorties down the Gulf of Arabia as a technician photographing embargoed oil tankers. It was a filming job right up his street, and a life he obviously loved. Based in Singapore, he went sailing and, while cleaning the hull of his boat one day, he found himself fascinated by the fish. Never worried about tricky engineering, he started to make his own waterproof camera housings with spare acrylic from aircraft cockpit canopies. (This when Jacques Cousteau himself had only been making underwater films for less than a decade.) Clearly, Peter had a technical genius for all things camera and underwater, and the RAF helped him form a new dive club in Singapore, in those days all with home-made kit. Back in civilian life after National Service, he soon made a living providing inspection equipment for oil rigs. One thing led to another and, after a lucky break filming the first ever shots of a live coelacanth, the long-lost prehistoric fish, from the Comoro Islands north west of Madagascar, his next career was set.

Although he didn't describe the sea in mythical or spiritual terms but had his own scientific explanations, Peter would have agreed with the Yolngu that maps of the sea could have all the detail and more of a map of the land, and that every part of the ocean was unique. Even before I'd read about the Yolngu, in his own straight, British way he'd already told me something similar. Every patch of sea, he emphasised to me, is unique in its colour and its currents. He was himself the master of colour, and how light travels through water. Peter even carried with him a book of small 'coloured gels' from the catalogue of a theatre-lighting company. Gels are just pieces of coloured plastic you can put in front of lights or lenses to change the colour, and Peter's free sample book contained maybe fifty or so in the blue to magenta range, all within a very similar colour palette, yet all subtly different. He put them in the underwater camera housings wedged in front of the lens to adjust the water colour exactly, making the picture balance more what the human eye is used to above the surface, and working to the best efficiency of the camera's digital chip, which again had been designed only for surface use. I once saw him open and close a complex pole-camera housing four times, a faff on land but on a moving boat nauseating, as he tried slightly different shades of purple to filter its colour opposite, complementary green, and make the image sparkle. That is how unique one specific body of seawater can be. In fact in 1951, Swedish oceanographer, Nils Jerlov, created a very precise classification for clarity and colour of different waters that is still in use by scientists today.

I talk of Peter in the past tense because he died in 2014, but I was lucky enough to work with him on several occasions, as he was filming and scuba-diving well into his seventies. We had one of the most amazing experiences together, which for reasons that will become clear I've hardly mentioned to anyone: almost a spiritual moment in our quest to bring the waves to your door.

7

The Accidental Whale Riders

Close encounters of the whale kind

Peter is just smiling, standing like a figurehead at the bow of the rubber inflatable. He's standing at about 45 degrees, actually, the same as the rest of the rib. He's laughing as about £150,000 of his camera gear slides down the boat's floor and clatters to the stern. We're right in the middle of the Bay of Fundy, Nova Scotia, perhaps 40 miles out to sea, but as I look over the side my mind rebels in disbelief. All I can see is what seems to be an inordinately fat man in a very thick wetsuit. It is in fact the glistening, warty, black skin of a whale that's surfaced under the little boat and taken us right out of the water on its back. I can't see any seawater at all, in fact: just whale. The quick-thinking scientist on the tiller has already stopped and raised the outboard so that it doesn't hurt the whale or make us unbalanced and tip over. Then there's a massive blow of warm air that envelops us, and a deep and resonant rumbling sound like someone blowing madly over the largest of pipes in a massive church organ.

Phwoaaaaaaaaaah.

Perhaps it also sounds like a very slow, prolonged version of 'Phwoarh!', a sign of sexual attraction, because, as I'll explain, that's what got us into this unusual situation. The fetid air now smells like concentrated garlic, and I realise I'm breathing what has been inside the whale for the last twenty minutes as it held its breath in a dive.

Now we are completely connected to this whale, and I am just waiting for the boat to tip over and for us all to be thrown into the sea. Perhaps the connection is a direct line to the whale's brain, because I can almost hear it thinking, 'Ah, that doesn't happen very often – I mean, what *have* I got on my back?' The boat is now at its steepest angle, with the whale as far out of the water as it could be, and still we don't fall off, gently balanced on its back as though the whale, despite its massiveness, is trying to be as careful as possible with us. 'Oh, I'd better let them go now. Let's see . . . if I dive slowly, they'll just float off.'

And that's what it did.

At the time I felt this was a disaster. The whale in question was a highly endangered North Atlantic right whale, and there are strict rules about coming close to them, and many other marine mammals, especially in US waters. To film them at all you have to be with a research scientist who has a licence to be near. Riding whales with rubber boats is absolutely forbidden, a complete and utter no-no. Yet we had been very careful to be as low-key as possible and observe all the non-harassment protocols, because, first, we don't want to distress any animal we film, and secondly, it would be a stupid thing to do because if someone saw you you'd be fined heavily and never allowed near another whale again.

In our defence, it was the whale who surfaced under *us*, and we hadn't even seen it until it replaced the sea with its skin. In the distance we had seen the raised pectoral fin of another right whale, and in hindsight she was probably a female, and likely to have been on her side with her pectoral in the air as part of her mating ritual. Probably she was calling to other males to come to her, as elephant females do when they want a bit of sexual competition to be sure of getting the best mate. *Love Island* wasn't thought of first by humans. So we had inadvertently got in the way of a male charging in towards the female, and by some extraordinary coincidence it needed air at exactly the same spot where we found ourselves, and that's how we all met. Luckily it hadn't yet decided to deploy its 12-foot (4-metre) penis – though that would have been a story to tell.

As it was, I was immensely impressed by the gentleness of the massive beast, and how carefully it let us back onto the water. 'Neither whale nor human was harmed in the making of this film,' as they say, and I hope our friendly giant carried on his courtship and was at least considered by the choosy female of his endangered species. The whole thing was filmed from our support ship, but I've never mentioned it until now because of concerns that it would be held against us and misinterpreted as harassment by film-makers. Typically, it was probably the most exciting never-seen footage from 'behind the scenes' of the original *Blue Planet* series. One of the unwritten rules of documentary TV is that what is censored is almost always the most compelling.

Peter, of course, was unfazed. He'd enjoyed the whole experience immensely, completely unconcerned about the potential loss of all his kit. Or the peril of being thrown into icy water so far offshore. Perhaps it was his 1950s Brit cool, but I suspect he realised that he had unintentionally become a 'whale rider', maybe even felt the call of the Māori ancestor named *Paikea*, the original whale rider who survived a marine disaster by invoking the denizens of the sea to take him home on the back of a whale.

Those five weeks in the Bay of Fundy turned out to be an epic shoot for *Blue Planet*'s first series. We went on to film fin whales, which are much faster than the 'rights', and a relative of blue whales, with which they can sometimes cross-breed. They have a small dorsal fin like the head of an axe in the middle of their back from which they get their name, and they are a little smaller than blues, which demotes them to only the second-biggest species that ever lived. And they're black, not blue. Actually, that's not quite true, because fin whales are the only asymmetrically coloured marine mammal. Many ocean animals have lighter bellies to match the brightness of the surface, and a darker back to appear invisible when looked down on in the depths. Such countershading occurs throughout nature, and we even use it on military aircraft, as I remember from making model Spitfires from Airfix kits as a boy, painting their tops mottled green and brown and the undersides of their wings a light duck-egg blue (Humbrol model paint number 23); so countershading must be helpful as camouflage for things that fly and swim with different backgrounds above and below.

Fin whales are odd, though, because they have what is called 'asymmetric body pigmentation': the left front side is dark while the right front side is lighter and the right lower jaw is white. It's one of the very few animals to have this kind of side-to-side rather than up-and-down shading, and no one knows why. One theory is that they use it to co-ordinate the whole pod and all keep going in the same direction; another is that it's to do with feeding and that they herd fish by swimming in clockwise circles, to present their startling white flanks. Without further evidence of this fish-chasing theory, which in any case would be almost impossible to see, I'd have to go with the first idea, and a spectacular encounter with the Fundy fin whales seemed to prove it.

Standing on the deck of our small filming boat, we watched seven massive fin whales come towards us with the precision of an aircraft display team – '*Calling pod leader, I can see your white side at three o'clock and I am two whale lengths starboard; we are all going in the same direction,*' is the sort of thing the me who built model Spitfires would imagine them saying to each other.

It was truly awesome to see these seven fin whales at top speed (20 knots or more) coming straight towards us in formation, which is why I remember it so clearly. Filming whales involves hundreds of hours of nothing, and then for just a few moments you are in the right position for a shot. Five minutes before there had been nothing to see, although another ship had radioed a sighting of the whales. Then this moment, literally out of the blue: a salvo of seven whale-torpedoes running true and about to hole us side-on at any moment.

But just before impact they dived beneath the vessel without collision. One by one they slipped from the surface, leaving only a footprint of smooth water in their wake, as the displacement of a diving whale pulls water into its void. Beneath us you could clearly see their dark shapes cutting the ocean as they went under our hull. The formation had a lead whale and a tail whale, each with perhaps five seconds of swimming distance between them. Peter got the surface shots clearly from the deck, but next time, if there was a next time, we would need the pole camera ready.

Many of the days we spent on the Bay of Fundy were frustrating because it was almost always foggy, especially in the morning. For nearly fifty days we were in the bay, and for perhaps a third of that time it was foggy. Days when we could hardly see further than the hotel room window. Fog is what I remember most about the Bay of Fundy. Not relaxing, and quite stressful, because you know that, despite all your efforts and the cost, there's nothing to show for it.

So frustrating was it that eventually we would try to go out to sea even though we could hardly see beyond the ship's bows. It was eerie, like a scene from a pirate horror movie, but I was so impressed one day when we heard the rumbling blows of whales all around us as they came to the surface to breathe, even though we couldn't see them. Those days in the fog were not wasted anyway, because I spent them listening to Peter discussing the colour of water in *great* detail.

A few days after 'the magnificent seven' we did get a chance with a pole camera to film fin whales underwater. Peter Scoones is one of the people credited with the invention of 'pole-cam' in the first place. In some ways no more than a camera on a stick, the camera itself has to be in a waterproof housing, of course, and the stick has to be both light and strong, with a clamp to attach the camera at a slightly downward angle when the stick is held vertically. Pole-cams come in all sorts of varieties, and the more luxurious ones have video monitors and remote controls on the dry end for iris and focus. It allows you to get quick underwater shots when it might otherwise be difficult or dangerous for an underwater camera person.

That first encounter with the fins had indeed showed us that being quick was essential.

The best way to use a pole camera is from a boat very low to the water, like a RIB (Rigid Inflatable Boat) or rubber dinghy. So we separated from the mother boat to a small inflatable, launching in a similar area to where we had seen the fin whales a few days earlier. The fog had lifted a little, but you could still see it on the horizon. For long enough to get hungry we drifted in the hope of a fin whale encounter. Peter was controlling the pole-cam, and had it in the water to one side of the bow of the dinghy. He'd asked me to look at the monitor, which sat in a waterproof Pelicase connected to the camera with a 12-foot (4-metre) cable. I had to put my head under a black blanket to see the screen properly, a nauseous experience when you're floating on the surface but have underwater as your only viewpoint.

As usual we were being guided by a local research scientist, Dan Dendanto, who was keenly tuned in to both weather and whales, with many years of research experience. As we were about to give up, he suddenly shouted that there were fin whales right ahead of us. Unless they came close-up, though, say within 20 feet, within the visibility of this churned-up Fundy water, we didn't have a chance at an underwater shot. Then suddenly I saw a huge animal on my screen – a bit too fast for me to hit record, I'm afraid – and I only got its tail just before it went out of shot. However, from the previous encounter I now knew that another one would come by in five seconds or so, and I left the pole camera recording. Sure enough, out of the hazy blue another fin whale comes straight up to the camera, and for a whole nine seconds fills the screen as it slides past us like a train on another track and disappears into the blue tunnel. I got the shot, and felt the sudden stab of joy, the shot of endorphin that is the film hunter's reward. It wasn't much, really, but underwater shots like that are unusual, and every little piece we get over the weeks becomes part of a bigger sequence of images through which we can tell the story of how creatures live out here.

The third encounter with Fundy's fin whales was both our most memorable and the saddest. We had been on our daily routine, going out of Westport, Brier Island, Nova Scotia. It was a clear day and we could see for miles, but had been travelling all morning without seeing anything (situation normal) when suddenly in the distance we saw what looked like a big, black, floating log. As we got nearer, we could see it was a barely alive fin whale. As it arched its back above the surface its rib cage was clearly visible; hardly capable of moving, it was floating listlessly. As we got closer still we could see the problem: it had maybe a 200-foot-long thick rope net wrapped inside its mouth. Encounters with humans continue to be dangerous for whales even after the days of whaling have largely passed. We leave debris everywhere, and fishing gear does its damage even when lost: so-called 'ghost fishing'. So we were really motivated to get the shots of this starving leviathan, to show how serious a problem entanglement is for such animals.

The net trailed right through its mouth, with loose ends maybe 30 or 40 feet on either side. It seemed to consist of both nylon and hemp rope, and so perhaps several nets had clumped together and somehow been caught in the whale's mouth. To the credit of the Canadians, in the Bay of Fundy all interested parties, from conservationists to the tourist industry and the fishermen themselves, participate in attempting to safeguard the whales. Particularly of concern here are those North Atlantic right whales, of which there might only be 450 or so left, that are on the brink of extinction. The resources needed to tackle this are huge and expensive, and there needs to be constant vigilance, as whale entanglement occurs on a weekly basis. Several organisations, the Marine Animal Response Society, Fisheries and Oceans Canada, and the Campobello Whale Rescue Team (CWRT), founded in 2002, now work together to respond to marine animal emergencies.

This particular whale's condition seemed much more urgent, and the only fully equipped and trained rescue ship, with which we were in touch, was otherwise preoccupied with more pressing right whale protection, and in any case many hours away. Nowadays organisations like the CWRT have to be licensed and permitted by the government authorities to conduct whale disentanglement and release operations. However, our captain (let's call him Eric) had had entanglement training, and I could see he was struggling with the idea of leaving the poor animal to die. I had already strongly expressed my wish to capture a really powerful, emotional shot of the whale with a net in its mouth, from underwater, that would do whalekind a favour in the living room of public opinion.

I hadn't really noticed until now the several large buoys on the back of our ship. The captain told me that we had to make sure, if we got into the water near the whale, it couldn't dive halfway through disentanglement. That would be dangerous for both the people and the whale. The way to remove the netting was to stop the whale swimming by gradually attaching the big buoys to the entangled net ends, until there was too much buoyancy for it to escape and dive away. It would take about six buoys in total, Eric reckoned, to resist the strength of even this severely weakened whale. When it was temporarily immobilised by the resistance of the buoys we could then cut the ropes from its mouth.

Coming up alongside the whale, Eric fished the water for the trailing ends of the net and tied the first buoy onto it, and via another short rope tied the buoy to the stern of the boat. He then came towards the whale again and repeated this with a second buoy. I was hopeful that we would now be able to release the whale and to get the important but heartbreaking shots of the whale's mouth and its skinny body.

There's a lot for a TV producer to consider here – safety being foremost. Probably the correct procedure is to write a twelve-page 'risk assessment' and get it approved by several line managers, not to mention applying for the correct permissions, before you'd even attempt such a complex operation. Did that occur to me over twenty years ago? I can't remember, to be honest, but I do remember the conviction that it was important to rescue this whale and get shots of it to show the damage of fishing nets, and Eric, Peter and the crew agreed with me.

Filming is an 'all-or-nothing' situation: you need pictures to show the story, and if you haven't got any it's a bit second-hand at best. But this is a book, and I can tell you what I saw as it was all recorded in my head, if not the camera. In my mind the images as I play them back are there still and real. I can see the bony skeleton of the fin whale; I can feel its despair, whether real or imagined, that still sits like a scar in the heart when I recall this scene. In the camera of my head I see the captain threading the third buoy onto the net lines, and I can see the whale stirring, perhaps hurt by the rope now tugging in its mouth. It started to dive, and I hadn't realised this was a danger for us all. The two buoys on the surface started to skid across the water and be pulled under, and in turn the rope tying them to a post on the stern started to pull the entire rear of the vessel underwater.

Even a starving whale weighs many tons, and I was beginning to understand that it really could take us all with it. Eric knew, though, and that's why he had a hatchet out on deck near the rope lines. Without hesitation he drew it back and flicked it down on the rope as though it was a carrot on a cutting board, and the lines pinged off into the sea to become another small part of that tangled mess in the whale's mouth. Then he reached out to cut the buoys away from the whale. With a feeble gurgle the stricken animal disappeared into the black depths. In theory it should have surfaced again within its diving cycle, perhaps forty minutes at most, but though we waited for a couple of hours it never reappeared. It was perhaps its final blow.

So here's the challenge. You've been given millions to make a series about the sea, and it has to be made in, say, seven to ten parts: how do you define those episodes? You could do it by geography: going to each of the continents in turn. You could do it by animals: sea mammals, fish, jellyfish, molluscs, corals and plankton. Perhaps you could do it more conceptually, for example by following the major currents of the sea, and telling the story of the migration of humpback whales, sea turtles, and the 10,000-mile wanderings of an albatross? Or through the fishing cultures of the world. I'd like to do that last one, in fact – human and marine creatures both facing the hardships of the sea – but pure blue-chip wildlife documentaries like *Blue Planet* seldom have people as the main focus.

It's interesting, then, that both series of *Blue Planet* are split by habitat, defining the sea, albeit in less precise detail, as the Australian Yolngu do, by a sense of distinctive places in the Saltwater Country. In my mind each of these places has a colour too: the sandy and silty coasts where the estuaries flow are brown. The seaweed-filled shallows where tall kelp forests grow are green. Corals with the brightest colours I think of as red and orange and, as we get out into the open water – near the surface, at least – it's a wonderful ultramarine. Then, as you go deep, all the light disappears and it becomes an inky black, or we may also venture to the poles, to the ice-filled landscapes of a white sea.

8

Brown Planet

Life on the coast

Alan signals to the cuttlefish with what is apparently the universal stop sign: hand straight, palm out, facing upward, like a policeman directing traffic. The cuttlefish obediently comes to a halt no more than an arm's length in front of him: a perfect position for a photograph. The zebra-striped cuttle hovers in mid-water a couple of metres (6 feet) off the seabed; it has exquisite control, and can inch forwards or, more surprisingly, backwards, as an undulating wave wafts along the hovercraft skirt around its lower body.

This is the fleshed-out version of the cuttlefish bone you see washed up on the strandline of beaches all over the UK. It's not a bone at all, of course, but a honeycombed structure made of aragonite, a crystal form of calcium carbonate pretty similar to chalk. There's a lot of it in the sea, and nature has a way of making use of what it has got to hand. Molluscs like the cuttlefish are particularly good at extracting it and building their body framework with aragonite, and as well as strength it gives the cuttlefish an internal life-jacket of buoyancy.

I remember being fascinated by these oval white shapes as a boy when I saw them in budgerigar cages. They obviously had some interesting properties, because I could see they were both ridged and soft at the same time – beak marks easily indenting them, yet snapping when they were bent. I never imagined I would meet the alien creature that owned them face to face one day, and spend hours filming and studying them.

I started looking at cuttlefish when I had recently learned to dive in open water, and they are wonderful introductions to the behaviour and sophistication of sea creatures. Successful and rewarding first encounters fuels enthusiasm for bigger and better adventures, and make you stay with a 'hobby' which, if you're lucky, becomes your work. Those cuttlefish let me in to their world but also gave me the break to make wildlife films about the sea.

It's mid-March in Babbacombe, South Devon, and that's a good time to dive with the cuttlefish that are only a starfish day's walk offshore, which is to say not very far, and easy and low-cost diving without a boat. I'm here for fun, as these are the days before I even realised you could actually have a job filming marine creatures. Well, I probably realised some of *you* could – I'd watched Cousteau, after all – but I wouldn't stand a chance. I wasn't even French.

I float slightly above the seabed in only about 6 metres of seawater, 8 at most (18–24 feet), and I'm a voyeur of a really important part of their lives. These black and white animals, 'underwater zebras', come by all the time. When you see a lot of them it's likely that you've stumbled across an underwater arena where cuttlefish males come to court females and females to choose a male. Today I'm not sure, though, because in the usual green-grey, algae-filled fog of British temperate seas I can't see the full shape of it. In fact, you can't see beyond your toes, even if it were easy in the thick rubber suit to bend to look at them.

We're in dry suits, which are light years from the T-shirts and jeans of the surface. When they don't leak through the seals around your neck, wrists, ankles, zip or through holes in the suit itself, they are very warm and comfortable. Even so, a thick fleecy insulating liner under the rubber called a 'woolly bear', and an extra inflation pipe to keep air in the suit, adds to the clobber, and makes movement a little stiff. It's great when it works, although because your cheeks, forehead and nose are exposed, your face freezes off. That's not too troubling, because after about thirty seconds of agony all exposed areas go numb and you never think of them again. You can't feel yourself smile, though. If you get your buoyancy just right, you can hover and make slight adjustments up or down just by breathing in or out. This way you can stay almost still and just watch, without alarming the cuttlefish – if it lets you spot it in the first place.

In the mid-1990s I used to go to Babbacombe every March with dive buddies and spend hours in the water watching the cuttlefish. Chief among them was Alan James, a legend in the marine still-photography world. He'd started an underwater photography shop in Bristol, but had previously been a builder. With sky-high interest rates at the end of the 1980s, Alan had to sell his land and quit the building business, and didn't know what to do. That was when his partner, seeing his obvious interest in diving, gave him a Nikonos underwater camera. The camera developed a fault and Alan fixed it; probably no big deal to him, but his diving mates took note and were soon offering their broken and sometimes flooded underwater cameras for him to repair. In his typical hard-working style Alan would get up at 5 a.m. and by lunchtime have salvaged half a dozen cameras. This was a business opportunity he could put all his heart into, and couldn't miss.

I was introduced to Alan by Richard Bull, a dive safety adviser for the BBC and many other filming companies. Richard was famous in the business with a fantastic way of making sure that even the most hair-raising dive operations could be approached safely. At the time he also owned a dive shop in Bristol, not too far from the BBC Natural History Unit. It was there, buying more dive kit than I could afford, that I stumbled across Alan for the first time. Richard had kindly given Alan a counter towards the back of his shop, and I can remember a heap of camera stuff and various underwater camera models around him and stacked up under the counter. We got talking, and I realised how great it would be to be able to take pictures underwater. Sounds a bit dim, doesn't it? But, like all things we gravitate towards, it seems to take us by surprise in some way, and if you're like me you don't fully realise at the time what's happening. The borderlands to the future are fuzzy. Either that, or Alan is one of the world's greatest salesmen.

Alan gently explained to me that if you put an ordinary camera underwater it was likely to get wet. So you have two options. One: waterproof the camera entirely so that every orifice is sealed, and of course make sure the controls still work despite being potentially jammed with resin (something only a factory could do at the design-and-build stage). Or: put a normal camera in a sealed underwater box. The trick is to make this underwater housing control the camera inside it, and since that must be done with rods, or nowadays electronic links, you have to have holes in the housing. Holes eventually tend to mean leaks, even if they are cleverly sealed with rubber glands. And of course, there is one very big hole, which is the joint in the casing that allows you to take the camera out to reload, originally with film, now with computer cards, and to charge its batteries.

It seems when filming underwater all roads lead to Cousteau, and in 1961 Nikon took on Cousteau's and Belgian engineer Jean de Wouter's original design for an underwater camera called the 'Calypso', and improved it to make a range for sports divers, called Nikonos. They were brilliant, fully sealed stills cameras (without housings), and manufactured until 2001. Inevitably though the digital revolution largely killed off those purpose-built underwater cameras, and nowadays the way to go is to have a housing for a high-quality land camera, because they are more versatile and their housings have become so well machined that they are almost part of the camera itself. The best of these housings are well balanced in the water, their controls are responsive and light and don't jam when you see a tiger shark, and enable you to see directly through the lens, often with a big screen at the back too, which is a great help when looking through a dive mask. I do feel nostalgic though when I see a beautiful old Nikonos and remember how I counted the 36 shots of film trying to find the discipline to stretch them out over a whole dive, when now it doesn't matter how many digital frames I take.

Alan sold me a second-hand Ikelite housing for my Nikon F3 stills camera, a housing which even a quarter of a century ago was from the Stone Age. But when you had learnt its religion you might occasionally get an excellent picture. It was, by the way, the only housing he ever sold me, because my stubbornness matched his stellar sales ability.

When you come across a cuttlefish it seems to be looking at you as much as you are staring at it. Sometimes it takes flight, but when it stays it often signals to you. One of the most common is a couple of raised tentacles above the head, which I used to think was very cute until I discovered it is the molluscan equivalent of 'Get lost!' Actually, probably more like 'f–off', though there's likely to be a lot lost in translation between mollusc and human, and the idea of it being offensive, rather than just a simple protective response, is mine also (though cool if I'm right).

If you read *Octopus, Squid and Cuttlefish: A Visual, Scientific Guide to the Ocean's Most Advanced Invertebrates* by Roger Hanlon, Louise Allcock et al. (as I do) you will discover that there are fifty-four recorded colour changes, and thirteen different shape changes for the European cuttlefish, *Sepia officinalis*, suggesting it's a brilliant communicator. It does this with its skin layers, using colour elements and intricate shape changes a bit like the 'letters' of a language. But its 'words' – the patterns it makes using those elements – are consequently very varied. Hanlon and Messenger painstakingly catalogued them all, condensing the information in just a single table (this and their composite drawings are presented on page 90). So you might see a white-splotched, dark-mottled, smooth-skinned, arm-raising, hovering cuttlefish, or any number of different combinations. The cuttle truly does wear its heart (actually three of them) on its sleeve (actually all eight arms, and the entire top part of its body).

How cuttlefish and their kin use their skin, for camouflage and as a biological semaphore, is nothing short of miraculous. Like so many things invented by nature they far surpass our

TABLE 1. BODY PATTERNS AND THEIR COMPONENTS IN *SEPIA OFFICINALIS* L.
(See figure 13.)

chromatic components

light		dark
(1) White posterior triangle		(17) Anterior transverse mantle line
(2) White square		(18) Posterior transverse mantle line
(3) White mantle bar		(19) Anterior mantle bar
(4) White lateral stripe		(20) Posterior mantle bar
(5) White fin spots		(21) Paired mantle spots
(6) White fin line		(22) Median mantle stripe
(7) White neck spots	mantle	(23) Mantle margin stripe
(8) Iridescent ventral mantle		(24) Mantle margin scalloping
(9) White zebra bands		(25) Dark fin line
(10) White landmark spots		(26) Black zebra bands
(11) White splotches		(27) Mottle
(12) White major lateral papillae	head	(28) Latero-ventral patches
(13) White head bar	or	(29) Anterior head bar
(14) White arm triangle	arms	(30) Posterior head bar
(15) Pink iridophore arm stripes		(31) Pupil
(16) White arm spots (males only)		(32) Eye ring
		(33) Dark arm stripes
		(34) Dark arms

textural components	postural components	locomotor components
(35) Smooth skin	(41) Raised arms	(49) Sitting
(36) Coarse skin	(42) Waving arms	(50) Bottom suction
(37) Papillate skin	(43) Splayed arms	(51) Buried
(38) Wrinkled first arms	(44) Drooping arms	(52) Hovering
(39) White square papillae	(45) Extended fourth arm (males only)	(53) Jetting
(40) Major lateral papillae	(46) Raised head	(54) Inking
	(47) Flattened body	
	(48) Flanged fin	

body patterns

chronic patterns	acute patterns
1. Uniform Light	7. Uniform Blanching
2. Stipple	8. Uniform Darkening
3. Light Mottle	9. Acute Disruptive
4. Dark Mottle	10. Flamboyant
5. Disruptive (weak, strong)	11. Deimatic
6. Weak Zebra	12. Intense Zebra (males only)
	13. Passing Cloud

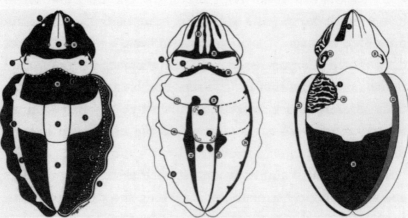

FIGURE 13. Diagrammatic representation of the components of patterning. See table 1 and text (§4.2).

own technology. In fact, nothing equals their ability to change appearance rapidly. They all but have the legendary invisibility cloak, cleverly using what's called a three-layered system in their skin. All the layers are controlled by some of the biggest, fattest and fastest nerves in the animal kingdom, which explains how quickly they can change colour. The top coat has a system of changeable coloured pixels called chromatophores, and in cuttlefish these come in yellow, red and brown. The chromatophores are altered by circular muscles that make a kind of iris around the pigment to hide or reveal its colour. Incredibly, those muscles can expand to 500 times their original size: we have yet to engineer a material with that elasticity and on such a tiny scale. The middle layer contains particles that reflect and refract light, like drops of oil making rainbow patterns in puddles, and they are wrapped inside cells called iridophores, after the iridescence they make. The final base layer is a background white, and contains reflective crystals within cells called leucophores, that throw back the ambient light. All three layers combine as though in some living Photoshop project.

This combination of pigment and reflection gives the animal the flexibility to blend into almost any background and, when it wants to, to make itself visible and communicate fiery intentions of love or war. Not only that, but cuttlefish, and its other squid-y friends, have special tiny muscles that can pull their skin into bumps to give a malleable 3D texture, which helps make its mimicry of the background complete. Wouldn't it be strange and great if people could do this, and suddenly disappear by matching the pattern of kitchen cupboards or brick walls? What fun children would have surprising their parents!

Roger Hanlon has made it his life's work to study the communication and camouflage of cephalopods: squids, octopus and cuttlefish. I have talked with him a couple of times and been fascinated to read his work, but we have never met. I should say thanks now in case I forget, because all wildlife film-makers owe a debt to the scientists whose research helps them understand what's going on in the natural world. Curiously, one of the things Hanlon is known for is his 'scream of excitement'.

Like the scream he made after sneaking up on an octopus with his video camera and capturing one of the best examples of camouflage and colour change ever seen (google 'Hanlon + octopus changing colour'). At first we see what looks like a fluffy clump of seaweed, but, as we get closer, the bottom of the clump becomes white, and we see the outline of an octopus, which promptly squirts black ink and disappears into the distance. The whole thing happens in less than two seconds, and in his YouTube video Hanlon also plays the sequence in reverse, so we can see how the octopus faultlessly executes a transition from smooth white to a swiftly rearranged and intricately sculptured brown seaweed-lookalike. His scream of excitement after filming this was so loud when he got out of the water that his colleagues thought he'd had a diving accident.

Even if he'd seen this sort of change many times before, this one was a perfect, clean example, clearly showing the sequence of the rapid shape and colour change. Fascination with such encounters led him to thirty-five years of intensive cephalopod study, in an attempt to answer such questions as how these clever relatives of the slug can look at any background and reproduce it almost perfectly with their skin.

The cephalopods may be clever, but what's happening is also so complex that even they must be taking short cuts or 'guesses' as to how to match their background. Even in a biological brain there's not enough power to calculate how to change the millions of elements in their skin in a fraction of second. Hanlon and his team have shown, however, that there are only three to five basic patterns octopus, cuttlefish and squid use to make their camouflage on any background: uniform, mottle, and disruptive – and in milliseconds they choose which one is most appropriate for their background. Then they modify them to make them even more perfect. This explains why, as we see when the video of their colour change is played back slowly, many of the camouflage elements come together in stages; they don't all happen at the same time.

Of course, the cuttlefish brain is not doing this for fun: it's doing it to save its life when a large predatory fish, or seal could bite in two. So to trick those predators it must make patterns that are relevant to how they see the world. Cuttlefish, however, cannot see colour. So what is also mind-boggling is that they have second guessed how to camouflage themselves from species that do have colour vision. For Hanlon's next generation of research his team have built specialist cameras that imagine the world from the point of view of a seal or other predators. Yet his research could go on forever, because the mysteries of the sea will never be fully understood. At the very least they will gift many lifetimes of work to even the most cunning of marine biologists that follow.

Like an apprentice military codebreaker I stare at two cuttlefish courting. Discarding all camouflage, the male and female are dressed in black and white. The male is a stark zebra pattern, right across the body, while the female is more blotched. He's clearly guarding his mate, and trying to impress her with his best suit. Both move with careful precision, with small waves of locomotion travelling across the fin-skirt around their body. The male sometimes manoeuvres himself right over the top of the female, skin touching skin with what seems remarkable tenderness.

Suddenly from nowhere there's an explosion of water-dust – the silt from the seabed is kicked up – and for a while everything goes cloudy. A smaller male has tried his luck and darted in to lunge at the female. The first, bigger male has quickly seen him off with a super-fast, aggressive counter-strike. He's also got darker, but quickly went back to the female and became a slightly lighter zebra – females have a preference for only moderately aggressive males and don't like them to be too cross for too long. Sometimes the male will show his best zebra pattern to the female on one side, and a blotched female-type pattern on the other, with a definite 50:50 split between the two patterns on either side. This is thought to help the courting male not be disturbed by sudden attacks from other males, like the one I witnessed.

Mating looks like two hands kissing: the male and female manoeuvre face to face and push their tentacles[1] straight out at one another, the male inserting his into the female's mouth. First, he blows water through her mouth to flush out previous male sperm, and then he stabs his own banana-shaped packet of sperm, called a spermatophore, into the back of her mouth, where with any luck she will also place an egg. When they are doing this, they seem not to care if the diver is only a nose-distance away; sex is universally a major distraction in the animal kingdom.

---

1 Technically, the term 'tentacles' is reserved for the feeding appendages of a cuttlefish, the other eight appendages being called 'arms', but that would royally mess up the simile about the arms being 'like kissing hands'.

If I come back to Babbacombe slightly later in the season, maybe a week, I can see the females egg-laying. It's a methodical if mysterious process, because it's not clear what's going on inside the mouth cavity from where the eggs come. But if you keep quite still, the female will let you see her egg-laying up close. She lines up with some brown seaweed, a type that has air sacs on it for buoyancy and that covers many patches of the bay in Babbacombe, and, pushing black eggs out of her mouth, sticks them to the stalk of the seaweed. Soon the seaweed clumps resemble a weird underwater vineyard, as the black eggs are just like black grapes, and arranged in bunches of about forty, the female being able to produce up to 200 eggs altogether. Soon after laying, the females and males die, and within a little while all that remains are their cuttlebones. Soon after that, the tide washes this fragile skeleton to the strandline and, walking down the beach, you pick it up, unaware of the extraordinary life form it was part of, or the little dramas under the sea that make up its story. If you're a hoarder you might put it on a shelf in the bathroom, which our consciousness of water and the sea seems to think the right home for it. We've got a cuttle bone that's been on the bathroom windowsill for fifteen years.

Cuttlefish don't live very long – only two years – which is unusual for such clever creatures. In the mammal world intelligent animals like us need a lot of programming – learning for the life ahead – and therefore long lives to fit it all in and reap the returns. Cuttlefish are born with a lot of learning pre-programmed, and studies of young cuttlefish show they learn rapidly up to their first sixty days of life, and then become more set in their ways. So that's my mistake: expecting these sea-aliens to be like mammals, and bringing to them my land-based ideas. It's that 'flip' in our point of view that's necessary to understand marine creatures and gives me one of the biggest thrills. They are differently beautiful.

We are still in the realm of coastal animals that live in, as I've called it for easy reference, 'the brown planet'. My colleague Miles Barton, who made the coastal programme for *Blue Planet II*, was naturally not very flattered when I mentioned I thought of his programme as 'The Brown Planet'. However, it is indeed the place where the majority of sand and sediments washed from the rivers and estuaries settle not too far out to sea, and these are generally a shade of brown. Cuttlefish and the like, certainly animals that need shallow, light-filled water and a place to rest, would find the open sea too difficult to navigate, but that's because modern cuttlefish evolved on the coasts, and over evolutionary time it's often the habitat that shapes the animal. Likewise, sperm whales adapted to deep waters, and hawksbill turtles to feed on coral reefs.

In the sea, even within one habitat there can be a million places to live. Along the coast of Sulawesi, Indonesia, there's one of the most diverse and beautiful habitats I have ever encountered. When I first saw it, though, it reminded me of what a city friend once said when a group of us got together for a holiday on the small Scottish Isle of Coll: 'Why have you taken me to *Doctor Who*'s quarry?'

To be fair that Hebridean island does look a bit barren, as it has only a handful of trees, and those are small and stunted. Yet very soon you realise its beauty – that you can clearly see cuckoos, or the rare corncrake, and that this bare island, this 'barren quarry', lets the sun, sea and its fabulous swathes of white sand register in your very bones. And that's the case when you go 'muck-diving', as it's called, in Sulawesi, Indonesia, too.

It occurs to me we could go on this next exotic dive together. After all, there is supposed to be a 'buddy' system, where one diver looks after another. First, you'll need the briefing: we've come to the northern part of Sulawesi on a diving holiday with ten others, organised by the aforementioned dive-photography-shop owner Alan James and his partner, Heather. We are on one of the arms of Sulawesi, a large octopus-shaped island, looking out onto the Lembeh Straits towards Lembeh Island, about a fifteen-minute boat journey away. As you cross the ultramarine water, passing brightly coloured fishing canoes, with palm trees behind you and on the island ahead, and a light breeze in your hair, you've every expectation that you are in a classical and romantically gorgeous tropical paradise. You're in for a surprise.

Listen to the dive supervisor on the boat telling you that she expects you to be in the water no longer than fifty minutes, and to go no deeper than 25 metres, to ensure you don't have to do a 'decompression' stop before you come up – a more complicated type of dive, not usually for beginners. Get your dive kit comfortable: good diving is all about being comfortable in your kit. It's easy diving, because you don't need the clunky, thick dry suits of cold seas: this is water at 28 degrees centigrade, with a baking surface sun. You could just wear a T-shirt and shorts, but thin wetsuit dungarees will protect you from scratches and minor stings. Now would be a good time to make sure you have your fins on, but if you get them on too soon people will step on them, which makes for slapstick comedy when you stand up and then promptly fall over, but if you put them on too late you'll have to wiggle like a marine worm to fight the others for the space you need to bend and pull the fin heel over your foot. If there's no room at the moment you'll just have to do it a little later, with all your clobber on.

Now make sure the straps on your air tank, aka 'dive bottle', are tight onto the 'stab' jacket: the 'stability jacket' or piece of dive clothing that controls your buoyancy with air pockets, and on which everything is held together on your back. Make sure you have your weight belt on. Make sure too that an air line is fixed into the stab jacket. Then sling it and your bottle onto your back. I say 'sling', but it's an awkward process, finding one arm hole and then feeling for the other, often inexplicably blocked by some stubborn fold in the material. Veterans among you might be able to do the funny manoeuvre which involves holding bottle and stab jacket upside-down and lowering it over your head and both arms simultaneously, so it somehow ends up in the right position in just a few seconds – something I have never mastered.

The boat handler is about to drop you and two guides in the middle of the shallow Straits, so make sure you've turned your air supply on, press a button in the middle of your 'demand valve' to whoosh some air and push out any water, and put it in your mouth and check you can breathe. Check that as you breathe the pressure gauge doesn't move rapidly, which is the sign of a leak. Take the demand valve out of your mouth to save air until needed. Be particularly careful that you have put your weight belt on, and on properly, otherwise you're about to make a good impression of a cork. But also feel the buckle to make sure its latch is easily opened with your right hand in case you need to drop it fast. Now get your buddy to look over your kit.

The captain tells you to wait until he tells you you can go. He's got to be sure there's nothing or no one you will fall on, and of course the propeller of the outboard must not be turning, the engine in neutral or turned off, in case the propeller slices you in the water. Make sure your camera housing is switched on, and in a place where it won't get knocked but will be easy to hand down when you are in the water.

Now you're perched on the rubber shoulder of the RIB, sitting with your back to the sea, and the heavy bottle of air trying to pull you over. You're almost ready to go. Make sure you've squirted a little air into your stab jacket for a little buoyancy on the surface. Spit in your mask and smear it about, then turn sideways and, carefully holding onto its strap, wash it in seawater just below the line of the boat's hull. That will stop it from steaming up. A good dive is all about being comfortable, as I think I've already mentioned, but it's worth saying again. Put your mask on your head, but don't pull it down just yet: if you have it on too long on the surface then it will steam up as the sweat from your face evaporates into the mask and the colder wind on the glass cools it down and condenses it again on the inside. You're trying to estimate when exactly you'll be told to go, so you can do all these things in the right order at the right time. OK: pull your mask down now; put your demand valve in your mouth, you're nearly ready to get wet. Picked apart, step by step, it sounds convoluted, but like explaining cricket, the explanation is ridiculously more complex than the execution.

Go! Go! Go!

Glancing quickly to confirm it's clear and, holding your mask with one hand so it doesn't rip off, you just give in to the weight of the air bottle and tumble backwards. It's a relief to lose the weight and get into the cooler water after the steamy struggle on the surface. The tumble itself I always find wonderful, falling into a haze of white bubbles and entering another world, with a full tank of air and the enticing possibility of encounters with strange life forms. You're momentarily disoriented – you probably went down about two metres and maybe did a full 360 backwards – but as the bubbles scatter you pop up to the surface and everything is clear again. You reach up to the boat and a colleague or one of the guides passes down your camera gear. If it's a high-quality video housing with a lot of good glass and a fancy camera inside, then it's probably quite heavy. Less so in water, of course, but then again you want a bit of solid mass to get stable shots. Keeping an eye on your buddy, you dive together, vent hose held upwards; you push its valve button and the air escapes from the pockets in your stab jacket. You start to descend, checking your air gauge is at about 200 bar: that's about 3000 psi – pounds per square inch if you're still imperial. Glancing at the dive computer, the watch-like gadget on your wrist, you're soon down to 6 ... now 10 ... 12 ... 15 metres, say 50 feet. You're not vertical any more but tilted head down.

Now here's the surprise: as the seabed becomes visible it's completely black. It's *Doctor Who déjà vu*, and you can't even see the sides of the quarry. The floor is made of granular volcanic pumice, about the same gauge as dog kibble. What are we doing here? There's nothing to see, and we've come halfway across the planet not to see it!

This is the realm of the coastal animals, living in a warm shallow bath of seawater buzzing with life. The kibble-like pumice isn't dead at all. Though it puts the 'muck' into 'muck diving', it's probably the reason there's so much life here in the first place. The marble-sized pumice pebbles don't fit perfectly together, and below the seabed there's probably at least a metre of pumice water-spaces before their own weight crushes them more tightly together, and even then there's still the bubble voids within the pumice itself, made when hot lava met cold water and steam infused the stone. That's surface area right there, just as surely as if your lungs were spread out on a tennis court: surface area for microbes to live on, for algae to feed on, for the 'catfish mobs' to extort a living, and for the prawn to graze and be scoffed in its turn by a sneaky frog fish. The pumice is at the centre of a giant food web, sending strands in 360 directions to connect the lives of unimaginable numbers of dining creatures, some on each other's menus, in this, the richest of coastal restaurants.

So stop; look closely around the grave-black gravel; 'get your eye in', as they say.

There – at the entrance to an old paint tin: an octopus. It gathers up a plastic lid in its arms and hides behind it as if it were reading a newspaper. A black and white eel pops out of a hole and meanders across the sediment; a stone fish, camouflaged like a commando, seaweed clumps on its head, turns on little leg-like appendages under its head. A leaf fish – looking like a long and dead, indeed, long-dead leaf – flops realistically in the current. A wall of yellow-and-black-striped catfish comes towards us stacked ten by ten and twenty deep: 2,000 of them in a tightly packed pallet, each the size of your finger, rummaging along the floor and throwing up a sand storm of particles as they search for food. Look closely at the sponges lying on the seabed: not so different from a bathroom sponge, but more orange and knobbly, so it's a surprise when one of them moves. You can just make out an eye, and above it a feathery lure I call a 'dangle', also sponge-coloured but with a fleck of alluring blue on the end. As you try to peek beyond its sponge screen you can just make out two little feet – well, hybrids of fins and feet. These little splayed-out feet-fins form a kind of bipod for what looks like a big face, cracked with a very wide mouth. Further body parts seem to be missing, although the rest of its fins look like a badly cut-out school project.

This is an orange frog fish, one of nature's 'uglies', its pock-marked face mimicking the pores of a sponge. But that is to be quite unkind, because it's beautiful at the same time, and the resemblance to a sponge can only be applauded. I would say, 'its mum loved it', except that she had 179,999 other eggs, and even if she did guard them until they hatched (as some frog fish do), she would quickly have run out of names for all her offspring and become confused as to who was who. And if she did have any affinity for them it would only have been out of a sense of evolutionary-instilled duty. Then again, that's probably the origin of 'love', albeit in paler shades.

Frog fish are very endearing, actually, especially when they realise the game's up and they have been spotted. That's when they let go of the seabed and do their Mr Tumble act, turning cartwheels across the black dust, bouncing on every rotation like spacemen on the Moon in 1969, and finally stop when they crash into another clump of orange sponge. It's a very cute escape response, especially since their perplexed, rotating faces seem to send out 'help me' looks as they go. Frog fish are also available in red, white, yellow, brown, purple, blue and green, and combinations of all of the above. They are a type of angler fish – that's what the dangle I mentioned earlier was – so their sponge mimicry is also about camouflage for hunting as well as being hidden from other hunters. I imagine a little prawn comes upon the sponges merrily thinking it has found something lovely to eat – and that's the last thing it ever thinks.

From your first thought that there was only black gravel to having your mind blown by a shopping catalogue of marine wonders has been just thirty minutes. And time seems to have stood still for us while we took it all in. But look at your dive gauge: 110 bar (1,595 psi). If you're not too extravagant with your breathing that means you've got about 15 minutes left until you need to return to your world. By convention and for a good safety margin you always need to return to the surface at 50 bar (725 psi). It's a good rule, so stick to it. I often have to remind myself in case I get carried away with the water's wonders.

We haven't got much time now, so look for the dive guide from the resort whose local knowledge will give us a short cut to finding more creatures quickly. We start to go towards shallow water, maybe just a crab's carapace below 10 metres (multiply by three, imperialists). Now we're among heads of coral, a whiter contrast to the black seabed, but again teeming with life. Something like a brightly coloured rat scuttles by your feet. It stops and looks up at you, two eyeballs on stalks, naked and hardly in sockets, swivelling up and down, side to side, and staring at you from several different directions at once. It's absolutely stunning: a ribbed and mottled green tail, red and green peacock-eyed paddles at the front, and a vibrant blue head. Its eyes, moving all the time, give it comical look as if it were a cartoon animal, and for a second I think we're extras in a Pixar movie.

This brilliant distraction is a peacock mantis shrimp, colour-co-ordinated and walking the runway of the seabed. Not only is this creature the height of fashion but it's a great 'looker' too, in the sense of having probably the most sophisticated and weirdest of eyes in the animal kingdom. These are compound eyes, common in insects and the like, and made from hundreds of tiny lenses which you can just make out with your own naked eye. But that's the only familiar thing about them as, constantly swivelling and rotating, three vertical black dots look at you from inside the eyeball. These dots are pupils, or something like them, and all three are linked and move together. Then there's a band around the equator of the eye that looks as if someone has scratched fine parallel lines on its surface. This seems to be like a scanning-machine sensor, as it moves up and down taking in the detail of the world, line by line. Not only that, but research has shown that mantis shrimps have the potential to perceive many more nuances of colour than we can, with up to sixteen different colour receptors against our three. It seems they can detect six kinds of ultraviolet too, not to mention various kinds of polarisation, and their visual range extends further into both the red and the blue than ours.

No one seems to know why they need such visual acrobatics, but of course it has got to be something to do with the two main drivers in all creatures: food and sex. Maybe that's why they are so intricately coloured: it allows them to be exceedingly precise in how they market themselves to their fellow crustaceans. I doubt whether all this intelligence-gathering was intended to be comical, but I can't help thinking they look like disapproving librarians, twitching over reading glasses, and waiting for you to cough up the fine for returning your books late.

Luckily, because our air is getting low, the peacock decides it's time to go and, just as you're beginning to feel slightly embarrassed by its attention, the super-arthropod blasts off from the seabed and jets towards the safety of its burrow. These shrimps seem both curious and cautious about us, trying to guess whether we mean them any harm. We were never meant to meet like this, of course, two creatures from very different backgrounds, yet such brief encounters linger with us the longest.

Heading towards the shallows, we float among the coral heads, through clouds of glowing yellow and violent blue damselfish that hang above them, passing tomato-red clownfish, pearl-dotted cardinal fish and psychedelically coloured sea slugs, to where a guide is pointing at a sea fan corkscrewing upwards from the seabed like a bonsai tree. The guide is using a small stainless rod that telescopes like a classic radio aerial, and he needs it because what he's pointing to on the sea fan is very small indeed. Sea fans are a type of upright coral, also called gorgonians, branching like trees and covered in knobbly bumps that look like cut-off stumps and are in fact coral polyps. Look closely and you can see little tentacles in them. Just in case you still think you're not in a unicorn's garden, this bumpy tree is several shades of bright pink.

The tip of the guide's pointer rests in a narrow branch of the gorgonian, and it's a bit tricky to see why he's finding that so interesting – until you just make out a pink-and-red-striped face, exactly matching the colours of the sea fan, and with exactly the same spacing of polyp-like bumps as the coral. It's a pygmy sea horse, hardly a centimetre – about half an inch – long. Its tail is wrapped around the branch of coral, and it doesn't seem to suspect you've seen it at all. There is of course absolutely no way you would have if it hadn't been pointed out by someone who dives here every day. They are such amazingly petite and fragile creatures, and the only defence they have in the whole world is their camouflage. It's undeniably cute as it pecks at microscopic food particles that have landed as current-borne dust on the sea fan.

Now your pressure gauge reads 50 bar (725 psi), and it's time to go. With a two-minute safety stop at 6 metres (26 feet) to make sure any nitrogen in your blood doesn't bubble to give you the bends, you gently ease to the surface. You extend one arm fist-first above the water and break back into the air-filled world.

This has been a special dive. I didn't make it up: that's exactly how many creatures we saw on one fifty-minute dive in the Lembeh Straits. The coasts are often rich, but here there's an orgy of organisms among the black volcanic 'muck': so rich that many scientists and photographers have made it their life's work to document the marine creatures of Sulawesi.

We stayed at our diver resort in Kungkungan Bay on the Lembeh Straits for ten days, diving three times a day and clocking up a number of night dives too. Each one was as varied as the first. A special mention must be made of the flamboyant cuttlefish, a mauve, yellow and flame-red animal about as long as your thumb. It crawls on its arms, moving like a tank on the seabed. This species has the most extravagant changes of patterns, and as it hunts tiny shrimp rapid pulses of colour shoot down its sides like waves of flame. The pulses are thought to mesmerise its prey before it strikes with its two feeding tentacles, that pop out explosively from under the skirt of its body like a deadly party whistle, snatching the shrimp out of the water with their sticky ends.

Since they are so small they are not easy to find, but after a long search we found one. Typically I had also just found a leak in the housing of my video camera. I could see a small drip of water in the viewfinder, and the right thing to do is to get as quickly as you can to the surface, because seawater kills electronics stone dead almost instantly. Yet I was so excited to see the little dragon-like cuttlefish blowing its flames that I stayed with it to get some footage, all the time watching the drips grow bigger. Luckily the camera and the images survived.

Of all the animals I wanted to see in Sulawesi the 'mimic' octopus was at the top of my list. In fact, there are two species, one more active at dusk and the other a daytime species. Both are beautiful and surprising. They have strong, brown-and-white, concentrically striped and very long legs, giving them a thin and elegant look. But that's just their 'default' colouring. The mimic octopus has been seen to copy the shapes and colours of at least fifteen other sea creatures. It does this particularly when threatened by predators like large fish, or even over-sized frisky crabs, impersonating more fearsome beasts to fend them off. It can do great impressions of banded sea snakes, copying not only the bands but splaying out groups of tentacles in two directions, and wrapping them into tubes like a snake's body double. Other venomous creatures it copies include the lionfish, swimming in mid-water and raising several legs to look like the lionfish's spiny, venomous fins. At times too it can quickly pretend to be a flat fish, scuttling off along the seabed in a speedily arranged flat-fish oval shape that must bewilder its pursuers. But although I looked and looked across the black muck of the seabed, and although some of my colleagues found them, I never saw even the sucker of a tentacle. I was so disappointed, which is unfair considering all the other wonderful muck-dive surprises I had.

9

Swimming with Seadogs

Filming seals in shallow forests

Monterey in California is famous for its aquarium, but visitors might not know that the bay around its pier is one of the most interesting parts of the ocean in the whole world. Less than a winkle's burp from the shore the kelp forests start, thicker in summer than winter, like the leaves of deciduous trees. Kelp is one of the most gigantic of all green things in the ocean. I would say 'plants', but strangely, like other seaweeds or algae, scientists mostly lump them together with things like water moulds or even malaria parasites than plants, and so kelp is the largest member of the large and diverse group of life called 'Protista' - even having spores that can swim. They look like plants to me though and they do photosynthesise. The Californian kind is called 'giant kelp', with huge, flat blades streaming off a whippy super-strong stem. It is the proverbial beanstalk, albeit growing underwater. When you are in the water with kelp over you there's a warm light all around, as the sun reflects from its orange brown-green fronds, somehow managing to face towards the light in a swirling current.

In a world where few people are given the time to study the sea, Teri Nicholson has one of the best jobs ever. She has studied common or 'harbour' seals for much of her life, and in particular the ones that live along a strip of coastline just out of Monterey and into Pacific Grove. These are places hard not to love, still holding some of the gritty romance of John Steinbeck and his marine biologist friend Ed Ricketts, who together feature in the epic Steinbeck wrote almost accidentally about the sea, *The Log from The Sea of Cortez*, recounting their 1940 journey south along this coast and into Mexico. Reading it gives me both hope and sadness. It was not that long ago, really, but back then the Sea of Cortez (Gulf of California) was humming with life. Nowadays, though significantly diminished since Ricketts and Steinbeck's time, it's still a mecca for whale-watchers and beachcombers between Pacific tides.

Ricketts met a sudden end on a railway crossing not far from here, but his ghost still haunts, even in the daylight hours. At 810 Cannery Row his lab remains, a surprising wooden-shack throwback. Looking through its cobwebbed-cornered windowpanes onto old bottles of chemical reagents, test tubes and formalin-filled jars, I distinctly remember a big bottle filled with a lemon-curd-coloured substance. It looked like picric acid to me, used as a yellow dye, and in early explosive shells during the First World War. I imagine Ricketts might have used it for fixing microscope samples, but by now it ought to have started to crystallise, which is when it begins to become dangerous. In 1917 a military supply ship full of picric acid took out half of Halifax, Nova Scotia. I didn't tell anyone, of course. Probably was lemon curd.

I'm looking west from Archie's Diner a few blocks along

from the Monterey Aquarium. There is the constant shimmer of the Pacific reflecting ocean life back at me, and an ionising smell of water, salt and sea fog. In my mind's eye I can still see Teri running along the recreation trail out of town with her dog, Wander, for morning exercise along the marine nature reserve that extends southwards all the way from Monterey aquarium, past the famous Hopkins marine laboratories to Lovers Point about a mile away. Cyclists and runners, dogs and roller skaters weave patterns on this track at the top of the sand dunes that defines Teri's patrol area for harbour seals.

Getting to the sea from the road isn't always easy. A vast, plump carpet of ice plant, a succulent introduced from South Africa to stabilise sand dunes, has to be crossed. It's doing so well that this green band now stretches from here along the west coast all the way to Baja Mexico. The plant's introduction went as well as most biological introductions, which is to say not very: it turns out its fat leaves hold lots of water, and their weight and the shallow roots actually make the sand banks *more* unstable. Still, no getting rid of it now: it 'grows like fun', as my Dad would have said, and although as a member of the conservationist church I know I should be grumpy about it because it kills off native plants, its yellow or magenta daisy flowers and its verdant, tufted carpet are very beautiful. I remember asking Teri what it was called and why, and found out that sometimes when the sun is low it shines silvery like ice because of the tiny hairs on its leaves.

Beyond the fat ice plant swathes the sand and then the sea. Hauled up here in special places – cracks, gullies and just nice patches of warm sand, large herds of harbour seals. They look funny, especially as the tide comes in because they don't want to wake from their nap, and as the water sploshes over them they lift both head and tail to keep dry, looking for all the world like giant bananas.

For at least a decade Teri patrolled this patch, studying the seals almost every day, and had two- or three-letter names for every seal haul-out site:

PLP, Past Lovers Point
LP, Lovers Point
BLP, Before Lovers Point
WB, West Beach
CV, Cove
BR, Bird Rock
SR, Seal Rock
MBA, Monterey Bay Aquarium

PLZ, Plaza
ELT, El Torito
RMP, Ramp
HBR, Harbor

Her mission was to see if it was possible to recognise individual seals by their pelt colours, which are spotty white and grey and sometimes rusty, to figure out how they interact with each other, whether they were here year round and from one year to the next, and how they grew up together.

It's what's called, in zoological terms, a 'longitudinal study', like the ones done by Dian Fossey on the mountain gorillas, Jane Goodall on chimpanzees, Birutė Galdikas on orangutans and Joyce Poole on elephants. Longitudinal studies are just ones done across generations, rather than a snapshot over per- haps only a few weeks. They're most often done on long-lived, intelligent and social mammals, and so increasingly these days for marine animals too, as well as their more famous land-borne cousins. They're good for identifying long-term family relationships, or at least blood lines, even if not of the same family group. Studying such clans over the years slowly teases out life stories: what's happened to so-and-so, the daughter of so and so. Detailed observations slowly write what is a kind of animal soap opera, or at the very least a long-running series of *Love Island*.

Teri doesn't just study the seals on the shore. She dives with them too, mostly at just one particular place: what was once Monterey's shanty Chinatown and is now home to the famous Hopkins marine laboratory. In front of it, looking towards Monterey Aquarium, there's a tiny white rocky island, just 55,000 barnacles from shore. Here a fraternity of seals dog-nap uncomfortably on rocky perches above a splashing low tide. This group are well known and have been intensively studied in this little bay for at least forty years, and the laboratory is part of Stanford University, so I guess these seals are Ivy League. Hopkins is pretty important as the first marine research station on the west coast. Even Bill Clinton and Al Gore have awkwardly trodden these shores to visit Hopkins, with an entourage of special agents, black regulation socks getting wet in the rock pools as they stand guard around their precious charges. The seals don't worry who you are, though, president or pauper. It's more *what* you are: a moderately threatening standing ape – though they obviously have not grasped the full story.

The German for the common or harbour seal is *Seehund* or *Seadog*, and that's right, because they seem very close to dogs in their behaviour. I dive off the shore with Tom Fitz the cameraman, and cross underwater to the Hopkins Island seal-study site SR (Seal Rock), and I feel as if a lot of eyes are looking at us. And they are: big eyes brimming with welled-up tears, like black pools that somehow never drain; mammalian and flat-faced, they have an achingly sorrowful stare that appeals to our parental instincts. One survey found that many of the most successful wildlife films are about animals with just such cute, round faces and forward-facing eyes – like meerkats – presumably because we see them as childlike, even babyish.

It's really beautiful in this shallow water. Tall green eel grass (not kelp) ripples like wheat, dapples of light reflecting from its green sword blades at every swell. It's perfect, but Tom the cameraman is being uncharacteristically annoying. He's pulling hard on my fins. 'What the heck?' – I turn around to look at my feet. It's not Tom, but the doe-eyed face of a harbour seal looking right back at me and, it seems, is wanting to play. It's pulling hard on my black fins as if egging me on. It could easily bite through them but, like a gun dog, can be very gentle with its mouth and is holding the fins in a gummy grip. It lets go and just looks at me; then it fins off very fast indeed and, a few seconds later, comes back with a friend. Just a few feet away, they both look at me. Perhaps it's my turn to show them how I swim? I make a few feeble fin strokes and turn again in their direction. 'Oh dear!' I can feel them thinking: 'poor, crippled animal with strange bump on back – can't swim at all. We feel sorry for you . . .'

For *Blue Planet* series one (in production 1996–2001), we were filming mostly on what was called Digibeta, a Sony-trademarked camera, and a great video format for its day, having many of the characteristics of high definition. For surface, or so-called 'topside', shots we often filmed on real film

– Super 16mm. I remember when I joined the *Blue Planet* team in 1998 and at a meeting calling the underwater filming 'bottomside', which for some reason seemed to illicit great hilarity, though it seemed logical enough to me! In any case, the last time I went out with film crews who actually used film in earnest was in 1999, also on the first *Blue Planet*. Looking at the series now on Netflix, I can clearly see the much grainier film sections compared to the electronic video, although maybe the grain somehow gets amplified when transmitted via the (relatively) poor quality of streaming. Yet Super 16, shot mostly on the Arri HSR2 camera and sometimes the Aaton XTR, had its uses, chiefly in allowing us to take slow-motion shots by running the camera at double speed and playing back at normal speed – something we take for granted now with video cameras, and even our smartphones, but not then generally available on any video camera.

It seems counterintuitive that running the camera at high speed is good for *slowing* motion down. Filming is about sampling the world, focusing images on light-sensitive chemical or electronic surfaces many times a second. The more times a second, the more 'time detail' you will capture. Human vision starts to believe it's seeing motion when shown about 12 frames per second (FPS) and, just to be on the safe side, film camera manufacturers decided to roughly double that to 24, 25, or even 30 FPS depending on their mood, nationality and the frequency of the local electricity supply, which could be used to time the camera. Going higher than 25 FPS, you start to take in more samples of the world than normal, and if you go to say 60 FPS and then play it back at the standard 25 FPS, you appear to be slowing time down, and our eyes start to see novel things they otherwise wouldn't.

Film is expensive, though, and even more so when you are running it through the camera at high speed. But Tom decided he wanted to catch the expression of those mischievous harbour seals at high speed and slow them down. There are various kinds of film stock for daylight or indoor tungsten lighting, the chemicals in the film being optimised for either case, but Kodak's most commonly used Super 16 stock was called 7245. A 400-foot load, or 'can', standard for the cameras mentioned, would last 10 minutes. So at the time that stock cost about £60 a roll in the UK, plus another, say, £100 for shipping and development, and a further £400 to transfer it back to video in a 'telecine' machine, a kind of giant video camera that filled a whole room. Although by this process it eventually ends up as video, since the telecine was the best part of a million pounds it was pretty good video! In all, therefore, that's a total cost of £600 for ten minutes filming, not to mention camera rental costs, etc., I once paid for some for my own film: I stopped after only four cans.

During that period of transition in moving over fully to video, I think I might have thought it an indulgence, to say the least, when Tom asked to film the seals. Still, we had the film, he had the underwater film camera as well as the Digibeta and, sceptical as I was, it made for a most beautiful under-water sequence.

The grace with which harbour seals move through the canopies of kelp takes your breath away. But if you are filming at higher speed you've got to choose your moment, because of the cost, and because if you use too much you will run out. That's where the art is, apart from all the usual things of exposure, focus and framing. It's true of all good filming, of course, but more so with film as the margin of error is much less than with video. That, by the way, is probably the main reason people still like film: yes it has a certain granular and wistful look to it, but it's mainly that you have to be careful what you film, and much more selective than with video. The result can be an altogether more considered movie than just 'hosing' everything with hours of digital media. Of course, you could be disciplined with video too, but most people aren't.

Wildlife photography is all about noticing. Noticing what the animal does just *before* it does the thing that you want to capture; noticing how shy or curious it is; noticing places it comes by – that it usually stays in this place at this time – and noticing when it is distracted by food, love, or just playful mates. We had noticed that harbour seals are curious about the camera – they particularly liked looking at the image of themselves in the large acrylic domes or 'ports' of the camera housings. Seen from the right angle they are like mirrors. I've seen all kinds of fish, including big sharks, and especially puffer fish, come up to the port and admire their reflection – so much so, indeed, that the puffer fish becomes a pest (unless your film is about puffer fish, of course). Most of these creatures, though, think they're looking at the image of a rival, curiously approaching them at the same speed and with the same look in its eyes. Only a few animals understand that it's a reflection of themselves, although that's hard to prove. As a boy I kept Siamese fighting fish, and marvelled at how they would extend their beautiful fins, making a multi-coloured dreamcoat, at the slightest hint of a reflection.

Working with chimpanzees, the psychologist Gordon Gallup invented the clever but simple 'mark test', which can help us understand if the animal knows what and who it is. He painted a red mark in the middle of the chimp's eyebrows, and if they noticed and tried to groom themselves or remove it, then it seemed likely they understood the image in the mirror was themselves. Harbour seals, you would imagine from their inquisitive looks, would also pass the mark test splendidly, although I know of no current research team that has proof. A few have tried, but I think it has proved too difficult to come up with a 'mark' that seals would care about enough to show grooming behaviour. Even so, I am pretty sure that they are in the 'self-awareness club', right up there with chimps, dolphins and, more surprisingly, magpies. But we are getting ahead of ourselves. Long-term studies of social animals are just that: long-term. In the meantime there is more basic stuff to do: for a start, can we recognise individual harbour seals just by their fur pattern?

One of the very first things Teri Nicholson knew she had to do was to prove that she could identify individual harbour seals from their pelts, from hour to hour, day to day and even year to year. That would then allow individuals to be identified and enable us to say something meaningful about how they navigate both the ocean and their social world.

For three very focused years, from 1995 to 1997, Teri patrolled the seal beat along the shore from Hopkins to Lovers Point. The pelage of a harbour seal, as I've mentioned, is a complex pattern of splodges, in various shades of grey, black, white and occasionally rusty brown. You would certainly have to be paying attention to remember which is which, or even to distinguish individuals from one another when they are right in front of you. But, as with every group of similar-looking creatures, if you spend a lot of time with them, you will start to notice their differences. In her three most intensive years of almost everyday seal study, Teri was able to repeatedly recognise

444 individual harbour seals from the unique markings on their coats. There were about another hundred or so too that she counted that were not resident to this patch of coast. So that showed attentive humans could succeed in writing the *Who's Who?* of harbour seals. Before her study it was generally thought that harbour seals, or common seals as Europeans call them, were only a little bit social, mainly when they hauled out on the beaches but not at all when they were in the water, where they would just go off and do their own thing.

As I glide over the seabed with the current I over-fly a small canyon: a kind of underwater rock garden, surrounded by spears of eel grass flickering in the sunlight of shallow water on a bright day. I almost miss the white fat underbelly of an overturned seal beneath me on a sandy patch in a hollow. It starts out of sleep at this unexpected intrusion to give me what I can only interpret as a filthy look, blowing bubbles as it barrel-twists to the surface to breathe, and darts off to the borders of visibility, looking back to see if I'll follow. Curious that an air-breathing animal should sometimes choose to sleep underwater, don't you think? For us it would invoke fears of suffocation and drowning, perhaps, but for the seal, I suppose, this waterbed supports its weight and, unperturbed by anything except wildlife film-makers, it can dream on. It does dream, I am sure, and, just as your dog dreams of catching rabbits, so in its whiskered mind it replays the hunt for fish.

On a filming visit to Köln Zoo in 2002 for a series about animal perception, we filmed some research involving a remote-controlled model submarine, a swimming pool and a very intelligent harbour seal called Henry. It was to prove a breakthrough in the understanding of how harbour seals use their whiskers to sense tiny currents, such as that made by a trail of fish. Even a goldfish makes a little turbulence as it swims which, it turns out, can be a life-threatening betrayal of where it is – not the goldfish, you understand; that's in an unrealistically safe bowl, but the kinds of fish harbour seals eat; let's say rockfish or flounder. Since seals don't have the sonar that dolphins do it was speculated they might be using their whiskers to track fish, particularly in murky water. But how to prove it?

Henry was a rescued seal, I was told, although I can't remember his back story. Maybe he had gone up a river and got stuck far from the sea, as some harbour seals can do. Certainly his life story would make an excellent version of a story like *The Tiger Who Came To Tea* or, more exactly, a kind of reverse *Stick Man*, with Henry swimming away from the sea rather than towards it like Mr Stick.

Showing his inner *Seehund*, Henry was certainly up for representing sealkind and showing what could be done with whiskers. Previously he had been trained to follow the model submarine for a reward of fish. Now, waiting patiently on a diving board just above the pool, he was gently blindfolded with a sleeping mask, and had some ear defenders placed over those little holes that are the harbour seal's lobe-less ears. Then the model submarine was motored away from the diving board and randomly turned right or left. It was then quickly fished out and, blindfold and ear mufflers now removed, Henry was allowed to go into the water. Without the submarine, and not having heard or seen where it went, Henry turned in the same direction that the submarine had gone. He got this right 95 per cent of the time if only 5 seconds had elapsed since the submarine went by. Obviously this required a fast turnaround, whipping the sub out of the water and removing Henry's blindfold, but even thirty five seconds after he was still able to follow its invisible wake correctly at least 70 per cent of the time.

So seals are extremely sensitive to tiny water movements and have the ability to sense the ghost of a fish thirty seconds or more after it has passed, tracking it down until it does indeed become a ghost. Sense organs, like those of the spider I once studied, are connected to the brain by nerves, and the more nerves the better. Seal whiskers, it has been found, have about 1,500 nerves, each one plugging into the brain like the cable looms from the stage going back to the mixing desk at a massive rock concert. It's usually cats we associate with sensitive whiskers, but they have 'only' 200 nerves per whisker; they don't much like water, either. And in the harbour seal there seem to be (I've counted) twenty whiskers on each side of the face, plus three curious ones where the eyebrows should be, like the one hair in mine that grows fifty times faster than all the others, so that's 46 x 1,500 nerves telling the brain all about water movement. That's what you need to follow water sprites: 69,000 nerves – but how can we imagine what these ghostly traces of passing fish appear as to the seal?

How animals perceive the same world differently from us is fascinating, and if we can get even a little inside their heads it gives us another view on our world, too. That's why the harbour seal's *über*-sensitive whiskers are so interesting. How can we imagine a fluid world in which you can see the slightest wake from a fish that has passed almost a minute ago? Maybe it's like the shimmer of hot air in a mirage, only all around you in water. The seals take it for granted, though, just as we do our extraordinary eyesight.

It's likely you know about synaesthesia in humans – a sound evoking a colour, for example – but actually it refers to any sense being indirectly triggered by a response in another, presumably with crossed wires somewhere in the sense organ/ nerve/brain pathway. Not surprising, really, because nerve fibres are way more complex even than the shocking spaghetti inside those roadside telephone junction boxes, that unfazed repair technicians seem to want you to marvel at as you pass in the car.

Researching a show on *Human Senses* I discovered that paint manufacturers prefer to choose women for matching paint shades, because women's colour vision is better than men's. Also, one woman in 40,000 perceives *four* primary colours, not three. Who even knows what that means? But for the person who has that condition reality must be especially colourful, as it is for the mantis shrimps, who, as we've encountered, have the ability to see in many shades of visible light and ultraviolet.

I mention these conditions because it always causes me to try and understand what it's like to be inside another mind with another set of sense organs. It would make the world different, and your mindset very different, and unless you lived in that body you wouldn't really understand. You only have to take a dog for a walk to know what I mean: it obviously lives in a much more smelly world than we do, with the joy of smelling the stale urine of colleagues that passed by a month ago (and up to *five* years ago, apparently).

When you spend any time in the company of harbour seals in shallow water you soon realise, as Teri did, that, despite what was often written, they are very social. In the many years during which she got to know the 'Hopkins family' of seals she saw them communicate with splashing, bubble-blowing and grunt-ing vocals. They would play and fight with each other by rolling, mounting and biting with varying intensity, and even signal intentions by 'head-thrusting', scratching their body with their fore flipper, and growling. It's all part of a rich seal repertoire that speeds up learning, reduces over-all aggression, helps them get on in the social world and, as each knows its place on the social ladder, keeps the herd together.

Large males are pretty obvious underwater by their huge bulk and generally confident behaviour, but as we drift towards one I can see something most peculiar is going on. It's upside down with its neck bent back on itself, exposing the throat, and making a series of gurgling grunts. You can see the muscles flexing in its throat and its chest is expanding and contracting, as we do when we whistle. As you get near, the sound becomes very loud and deep. Some people have called it 'singing', but in reality it sounds like an indecisive old man taking his time to clear his throat, though the sound has a rasping rather than a mucal overtone. Suddenly two smaller males come over to see what all the fuss is about, and start to hold their heads next to the big male, touching whisker to whisker in a most intimate way.

It was in the early 1980s that this startling addition to the male harbour seal's vocal repertoire was discovered. Teri was the first to document such behaviour as essentially sociable. She showed me footage she had taken of *six* other young males gathered around a calling male – a kind of underwater vocal scrum around the monotonous bass solo of the mature male.

What's believed to be going on is that the male is calling out for females, or at least proclaiming his territory; presumably the more noise the male can make, the larger and fitter he must appear, and therefore the sexiest. However, it's been difficult to confirm whether the female actually warms to this kelp forest karaoke to the point of agreeing to mate, because the 'singing' mostly happens at night, and few have ever seen an underwater mating.

So it was that I spent the spring of 1999 in Monterey filming the seals with Teri and cameramen Tom Fitz and Florian Graner for the first series of *Blue Planet*, and that footage appears in the film on 'Seasonal Seas'. It includes a short bit about the male singing, but we only see two young males at a time 'attending' a bull, as it is called, when they touch whiskers. Oddly, just a couple of years later, I find myself back in the same place filming the same thing in a different way for a different film. It's a strange feeling, because you revisit yourself too of course, forced to confront accumulated changes in mind and body, but one I am now familiar with in a longer career.

We came back because we realised there was enough about the seals for a whole film. It was to be a *Wildlife on One*, Sir David Attenborough's returning series which ran for 253 episodes until it finished in 2005, and was often a portrait of just a single animal. We wanted to tell the story of a seal pup growing up, and of course needed to start that at the beginning, with a birth. No one back then had filmed a seal birth, but Florian was up for the challenge – if we could give him enough time. *Wildlife on One* needed a fresh look too and so we came up with the slightly whacky idea of comparing the harbour seals with US Navy Seals, both 'training' in the same Californian waters. Identifying with the human suffering of the troops was a way of showing how brutal it can be for young seal pups growing up in the sea.

Harbour seals are known to forage as much as 60 miles a night, and during their immensely tough training the Navy Seals do a paltry 5½-mile swim along the coastline of Coronado near San Diego, the Navy Seals' training base. Not 'paltry' for *Homo sapiens*, of course, as the water is very cold, your wetsuit chafes, your legs ache, and it's the week after the notorious Hell Week, an assault test from Hades that all elite soldiers do. With all the calories you're burning you're so hungry you'd pull limpets off rocks with your fingernails and eat them raw.

To do the part of the filming with the Navy Seals we went to their base in San Diego; I had arranged permission via the cameraman, Florian, who conveniently, was a friend of the local admiral's family. When we turned up, the officer in charge was not at all impressed, and it took what seemed like hours before the message must have been confirmed from on high, because then we were allocated three Navy Seals who were very helpful. We explained we just wanted to film them in close-up crawling along the beach and through the surf, and then in their swimming pool, which had glass sides so you could film their swimming technique, giving the signals they make to each other when attaching limpet mines to warships in a war-torn harbour (I imagine, but they do have a very impressive range of underwater signals). I explained the parallels between real seals and Navy Seals: how they both did long-distance swimming; how the design of the fins the Seals were using to swim with had actually been copied from the fins of harbour seals; how they both survived in cold water, and so on. The sailors nodded sagely and seemed very understanding and gentle as only trained killers can be, and then one asked, 'What about the suckling?'

For the natural history of the seals, we made a base in the hallowed Pebble Beach area of Monterey. It was cheaper to rent a bungalow at Pebble Beach than have the film crew in a hotel, plus it would have been tricky to give the dive boat and underwater kit to the valet every day. The area is, surprisingly, more famous for its golf course than harbour seals, and the US Open at Pebble Beach is obviously more famous than the Navy Seals because we weren't allowed to film near the course. That didn't stop us, though: we have scuba gear, remember! Just off Pebble Beach's 7th hole, at the edge of Stillwater Cove, was the chosen spot, and we came from the seaward side on a boat. It was only a one-off to see if the water was any good and our harbour seal chums would turn up. They did us proud. All along the seabed, you'll not be surprised to hear, are thousands of golf balls, and a harbour seal came right up to our camera and picked one up in its fins as if juggling. I have to rub my eyes, but it's in the film.

Following individuals in a mammal society like the harbour seals makes for many unexpected discoveries. One of the most notable was a seal with the most appalling scar. It had been almost entirely cut in two with a tell-tale shark bite completely around the circumference of its now not so fat waist, as if it had a cummerbund of flayed flesh. For a great white shark an adult seal is a Thanksgiving turkey. Harbour seals are aware of this, and even take deliberate anti-shark action when returning from a hard night's forage to the haul-out beaches or rocks in the shallows. They are seen to stick close to the seabed as they come into the coast, making sure they don't silhouette themselves against the surface and present the great white with a target.

Jacques Cousteau recommended never being complacent around sharks, as sooner or later they need to feed. Yet there are times when would-be living meals seem to chance their luck: I've seen massive whites at the surface being mobbed by seals when, like crows spotting a buzzard, the seals swim up to them to shoo them away. Tuna, too, will come up to the surface to rub against the sandpaper-textured skin of the greats to remove their parasites, which seems like a cheeky thing to do, until you realise that animals understand context. They have remembered, and are keenly tuned into, the behaviour that's a warning of imminent attack, and know that everything else you can relax about, because you have to get on with your life.

A great white at the surface is not hunting but just ambling around, and exploring or even just resting. When it wants to hunt it is perhaps 300 feet (100 m) below, looking for hapless silhouettes of sea mammals. Launching for the kill, it becomes a deadly missile rocketing up and taking out its victim on the surface in a single decapitating strike. It needs to make sure it's a swift death and catch a seal or sea lion unaware, or else the shark will get some pretty serious teeth in its own skin as the pinnipeds bite back. One of the things you may have noticed on programmes like Shark Week is that there are some pretty serious lacerations, bite marks and scars on great whites, and while those scars are often inflicted by others of their species, especially during rough sex, many of the deeper dagger wounds are from the teeth of seals in attacks gone wrong.

We can only image the battle between the great white and our scar-bellied seal almost cut in two. A rookie pilot navigating home south of the Farallon Islands towards Monterey from a hard night's fishing on one of his first solo swims, he wasn't, for once, hungry: just having fun at the surface, incautiously splashing, full of the flounders of life in the morning sun. It was probably a Friday, as that's the most dangerous day of the week for commuters. Crunch, bang! The sky goes inexplicably black, but you can just make out a triangular, razor-edged tooth big enough to cover your whole eye, though you don't yet realise you're partly inside a shark's mouth. I'm not making this up, by the way:[1] just listen to this slightly worrying encounter, as widely reported by the *LA Times*, other Californian journals and Discovery Shark Week:

> 'All I heard was a big crunch, kind of like a garage door closing,' abalone fisherman Rodney Orr, 49, said. 'My head was in its mouth, and I could see the teeth at an angle. The shark had me up out of the water, and the sea was kind of flying by. Then all of a sudden it just let me go, and I just popped out of its mouth. It was very frightening.'

'Very frightening' – are you kidding me? Shitting yourself hardly begins to cover it! But there you have it – a first-hand account of what it's like to be a swimming mammal hit by a great white. Obviously, for his story to be told, Rodney survived. He has a massive scar on his face, but luckily it is coinciding with his wrinkle lines as he gets older (he says). I interviewed him for *American Shark* on Shark Week, 2005, and it's clear that on the plus side he has probably made a small fortune in appearance fees from the Discovery Channel, BBC and National Geographic. However, it does prove you can be bitten and survive a white bite.

---

1 Except for the bit about Fridays – doesn't apply to marine mammals, only car drivers. Rodney Orr's shark attack happened on a Saturday morning.

Our young male seal too is likely to have been spat out in a similar way, or at least somehow struggled free. You'd think such a big bite would leave him fatally wounded, but the plucky harbour seal healed well, and no doubt being able to recuperate in a somewhat supportive seal society helped him defy the odds to live another day. Bet he never mucks around on the surface of deep water again!

When you first get into the water with the harbour seals of Monterey Bay, they play with you for a while, nipping at your fins and even staring square-on into your face mask. Then they all seem to disappear, bottling off at high speed out of sight and not returning, as if bored with you and moving on to more interesting things. Novelty is a universal stimulant, it seems. You might come across sleepers or even singers doing their own thing, but they are not so interested in you. After an hour or so, the water is empty apart from a few rockfish, some crabs and the blowing eel grass fronds. Because it's only a few metres deep you could stay for longer, but reluctantly you signal to each other that there's not much left to film, and you turn around for the shore just half a football pitch away. You come to the sandy ledge that's the underwater portion of the beach and start crawling out with the heavy camera gear and your diving clobber.

Frustratingly, that's exactly when the harbour seals appear again. They have been 'watching' you all along from the edge of your visibility, but well within whisker range. And when you stand up, they pop their heads up above the water too and all stare in your direction – once I counted as many as six doing this. 'Hey, funny crippled swimming animal with a bumpy back!' they seem to be saying. 'Why are you leaving us? Where are you going? You sure are ugly, but we'll miss you!'

10

Green Planet

Forest seas

The RV *Cormorant*, our filming ship, scoots out along the tidy rows of motor yachts lining the five miles or so of canal that straights its way to the sea from the Californian harbour of Newport Beach. For the whole length there is hardly any space between the long ships sitting pretty at their marina jetties. Here, to have one less than 60 foot is a pointless waste, having not quite reached the required threshold for a status symbol. If you are going to go for it you need to be over a certain size, it seems. I am reminded of a well-known rule of inverse proportion.

When I first started at the BBC it took me a year to save up for a dilapidated Mini, my first car, which, like all British cars made in 1960s to mid-1980s, rusted to bits from the subframe upwards. A parking fine I got once cost more than the car. With its sideways-on engine, a revolution in its day, it exposed the spark plugs and its electrics directly to the water spray from the road through a flimsy grille. Which would be fine for a country where it never rained, and honestly who could have predicted that it would rain so frequently in the UK? When the plugs got wet the car just stopped. With a stroke of genius British Leyland came up with, yes, a *cardboard* spray cover for the plugs, which did nothing but to make the Mini's reliability slightly more unpredictable. When one of the doors rusted away it was replaced with one my dad found at a scrap dealer's. Only the 'new' door was yellow, and the car was red. But this slightly rusty red Mini with one yellow door on the driver's side was my first car, and one I loved for all its faults. It never occurred to me that some people saw it as a sign of 'lack of success' in life and treated me accordingly. What exactly is it about new cars or big boats and anything meaningful?

We pass a particularly big multi-decked ship with all the chrome fittings, in showroom condition, its hull painted in glossy battleship grey, with gleaming white superstructure, only slightly smaller than an admiral's flagship. And there on the poop deck reading the Sunday paper is the admiral, but I don't think it's just because it's a Sunday that he's not going to sea. This vessel isn't unusual either: there are perhaps two billion dollars' worth of ships here that don't get out much. I sigh at what we could do with that to explore our oceans, as our slightly battered, faded-yellow research vessel rounds the corner of the sea wall past the lighthouse and we head out towards the Channel Islands.

For a Brit the Channel Islands mean Guernsey, Jersey, Alderney and Sark, and a few others no one has heard of (sorry, Brecqhou). For an American they mean a scattering of odd shapes off the southern coast of California, all with Spanish prefixes: San Miguel to San Clemente. Until my late thirties I had been blind to their existence, which is a shame because the eight big islands are fab places, and five of them form the Channel Islands National Park.

Thirteen thousand years ago indigenous peoples lived on these Channel Islands, but prehistoric travel to the mainland was easier then as, during the last ice age, sea levels were quite a bit lower, and the four northern islands were all joined together. One piece was only 5 miles from mainland California. That's swimming distance for a Colombian mammoth, apparently, which before the sea-level rise of 10,000 years ago came to the islands and promptly evolved into an oxymoron: pygmy mammoths. Presumably only such scrawny mammoths could survive on poor food, and there's evidence that they once lived on Santa Rosa, Santa Cruz and San Miguel. Maybe it's the contrast with the not-too-far-off cluster of Los Angeles, but when you climb such places as San Miguel Hill and look down across the spiky grass and ice plant-covered dunes to the sea, there's tranquillity amidst the ghosts of ancient elephants.

We're not here for the history, though: we've come to find some bat rays, of course. It's for the 'Seasonal Seas' episode of *Blue Planet*, the first series, and the only one we thought would ever happen at the time, or else we'd have put a '1' after it.

Many species of rays come together in huge schools numbering thousands. For example, the cow-nosed rays have been seen in such large groups that estimates of their numbers could only be made from the air. In one report over 150,000 individuals layered three to ten rays deep were seen migrating in the Gulf of Mexico. Why they come together is a bit of a mystery. It could be that it's a kind of ball where they can find a mate. Or it may be that migrating groups this large are looking for new feeding grounds with fresh supplies of clams and other shellfish that are their main diet. Certainly, coming together in large formations, like flocks of geese, saves them energy as they move behind the slipstream of the ray in front.

Whether like geese they swap the hardest, pole position at regular intervals I cannot find in any research to date, and the few times I have come across huge schools of rays they seem to have a broad front, rather than the backward-V pattern of high-flying geese or swans. I guess you'd have to be a great swimmer to keep up and watch, and the yellow mobula ray swarms I've seen are very skittish, so a scuba diver would have a hard time to get close even if they could.

Bat rays are, like all marine creatures, very beautiful, if you are inclined to that point of view. Others will think they are hideous monsters, and might be afraid. One of the biggest creatures of the sea, a bat ray can grow wings 6 feet or approximately 2 metres across, and the biggest weighs as much as us (also one of the world's biggest animals). I hardly need tell you that a bat ray is so named for these big wings, but they are indeed bat-like, in both their flapping movements and the dull matt-brown and slightly wrinkled skin of a bat, an animal that always seems old before its time.

We were here to catch the kind of 'spectacle' we wildlife film-makers seek, namely the summer bat ray festival. As usual before our visits we had done extensive research, calling scientists and fishermen, talking to our network of camera people from our base in Bristol. One of the likely spots was near Willow Cove, just off the resort of Avalon. Likely for bat rays, that is; not for a resort. Avalon, San Catalina Island's casino town, was financed by the chewing gum that made its sponsor, William Wrigley's, fortune, and probably in places sticks to its marble. A congregation of bat rays had been seen schooling here on 10 June 1998, the previous year but, as you can guess, as with shares, 'past performance is no guarantee of future growth'.

An unexpected pleasure of writing this down is that I can capture a scene I thought was long lost, because the camera was never switched on or looking in the right direction. Not relying on technology, now I can replay the neural recording I have of the dive as if it were happening right in front of me . . .

Our big yellow research vessel, RV *Cormorant*, is lubbering at anchor in Willow Bay, the current making it point seawards from the shore. The sky is a bit cloudy and threatening to drizzle like an English day, unusual of course for California. On deck an underwater film crew are gearing up, having left their tepid breakfast coffee on the plywood shelf of the plywood-lined galley, part of a cabin that extends 30 of the 50 feet of the ship. I can hear the hiss of air as high-pressure hoses are connected to diving bottles and systems checked. There's laughter and some gentle joshing, particularly between diving buddies. We've had the dive-plan talk. I can see from my dive logs that it's 9 June 1999, and I am diving with first camera Tom Fitz, second camera David Reichert, and marine biologist Jack Engle, from UC Santa Barbara. My role is to double up as a trained health-and-safety diver, imperative when diving for work, and as the BBC producer in theory I lead the team. Although in practice, since those with me have far more experience, we have a democratic but sensible discussion of what we want to film, the sea conditions, and the type of 'no-stop' dive we are going to do. That's the kind where you are not in the water long enough to need decompression stops on the way up to release blood gases slowly, and although it will need a safety stop for 10 minutes at 6 metres, it's pretty safe. There's no need for any other kind of dive here, as it's usually no more than 60 feet, 20 metres or so deep, tucked into the coastline of Catalina.

It's a clumsy business getting into the dry suit, and its neoprene rubber smells like an unloved medieval church. The bendy material seems to fight back when you pull it and, even with the help of talcum powder applied to the head and limbs, which lets the suit slide over you, you're pretty much exhausted, and by the time you've pushed your limbs through its black rubber seals, with your talcum-white hair you look older too. Then you sheepishly ask someone to zip you up, because for reasons decided by some committee, dry suits are reversed, and the zip is down your back where you can't reach it.

Why wear a dry suit? It protects you from the cold. The warmest it gets here is 21°C or 70°F, and that's at the surface: deep it's more like 16 in the summer, and even that will be uncomfortable in a wetsuit for any length of time. Naturally, it's what you're used to; the Victorians probably would have dived in tweed plus fours and not complained.

The light in the water is the most stunning thing about the Californian seas. Near the coast and around islands there are beautiful forests of the orange-green, not to mention brown, kelp – what most people might call 'big seaweed'. It seems to flavour the colour of the ocean, like a kind of weak tea, filtering and dappling sunlight very gently on its way to the seabed. The sun must have come out now, because I can see shafts of light, like the ones that catch you unawares in dusty rooms and between trees on foggy-sunny morning walks. My father used to call this, the light escaping between gaps in clouds on stormy days, *God light*, and its soft touch enters this fluid world too. Dramatic on land, underwater these rays are even more amplified, and intruding into these enchanted woods, embarrassed by their beauty, religious or not, you sense something has shifted about how much you love this world.

Here among the stout arches of seaweed, opaleye and blacksmith flutter. Although mostly plain – some would say drab – these fish have a gentle seduction. The olive opaleye has blue eye shadow, and the blacksmith fish hasn't been undersold either: stout black, but turning silvery green when the light catches them the right way. The blacksmiths are members of the damselfish family, and the young ones shoal in their thousands through the kelp leaves. Tentatively, when all is calm, they move out from the seaweed's protection and peck at the plankton that hangs around in open water, but at the slightest sign of trouble they move as one shoal back into the umbrella of leaves. Is it a coincidence, or are all the damselfish family skilled at playing hide-and-seek? On coral reefs, blue, white or yellow damselfish shoals do exactly the same thing, darting into branched coral heads for cover.

Perhaps it's the darker palette of colours that makes this place so striking. Against the green and the blue there are also red and orange fish. In the middle of one of the seaweed trees I spot a Garibaldi or golden trout, the official state fish of California. It isn't huge – about as big as your hand – but it's bright orange and proud of it, and dominates the stage in front of the green curtain. He's the biggest of the world's damselfish, and maybe his size is something to do with the need to survive in cooler water. They are called 'Garibaldi' after the flamboyant general Giuseppe Garibaldi, who helped unify Italy in the mid-1800s, and who with his followers wore bright reddish orange shirts. What a life: to have a biscuit *and* a fish named after you . . .

As Italian fathers are known for their attentiveness towards children, so with this fish, I know, the males look after the young, guarding the nest of yellow-white eggs for almost a month and fanning the water around them with their fins.

Suspecting this one's a male, I look for the nest, often to be found in cracks in the rocks or near the base of the kelp, but no luck. He's still a flamboyant general to me, though. I continue through the kelp-lined corridors, aware that around every bend there's likely to be another surprise.

I can see David, Tom and Jack on various sides in front of me, silhouettes moving through the undergrowth. It's dark near the seabed, because the seaweed grabs the light, but those illuminating shafts still poke spotlights through the gaps. Tom Fitz has the main camera, and my role now is to help scope out what's here, to make a cracking story from the pieces Tom will catch. It'll be a mix of what we came to film and what we can actually film, as planning meets serendipity. How could it be much else in the blind 'lucky dip' of the sea?

We come to a clearing in the water forest, and a small expanse of muddy-brown sand stretches out before us. On the other side of the clearing I see a cloud of mud being rhythmically stirred up by a big black object pounding the seabed like a jack hammer. It's a bat ray. I try to attract the attention of the team ahead of me, without success. I'm inching forward now, floating just above the sea's floor and trying not to stir up sediment. Now I'm almost touching the back of the bat ray, although not yet in range of the toxic barb on its tail. The lip around its head, like the fringe of a giant sucker, seems to make a seal with the sediment. It moves its head up and down vigorously, drilling into the sand in its quest for shellfish, who must have got the message by now and are digging down faster than Fantastic Mr Fox. And how right they are, because you would not want to be crushed between the sharply ridged plates of that flat, bony mouth, like interlocking steel tank tracks regularly sharpened by new growth.

Now the moment only recorded in memory: out of the green a Californian sea lion duck dives from the surface 20 metres above, from where it might have been spying on the bat ray and me. Maybe it only saw me, the bubble monster, clearly staring at something and, as everyone wants to know what you're looking at, it came to check it out. Right in front of me the sea lion touches the big wings of the ray with its flipper, then turns and stares me in the mask as if I'm insane: 'OK, it's a bat ray. What's the big deal?'

People talk about the improvements in technology making for better wildlife films, but really one of the biggest changes has been that the world is fuller than ever of experts, and wise wildlife crews go with them into the field. Although we'd seen one or two bat rays, and they were indeed impressive, they weren't playing ball, or at least they hadn't come to the ball as billed. The following story was not planned, wasn't known about in the office when we went out, was not the piece we'd come for, wasn't written about in any script, and yet it ended up as a great little sequence in our film.

We were now on our plan B, codenamed '*Navanax* and *Janulus*'. To be honest, I hadn't heard of them either. It was our resident marine biologist, Jack Engle, who told me about the intriguing behaviour of these colourful mini creatures, and said they were right under the boat. I was instantly sold on recording the drama of their lives.

Navanax and *Janulus* are types of sea slugs, and they're also deadly enemies. Technically, *Janulus* is a nudibranch, but the zoologically astute among you will know that *Navanax inermis*, although similar, is in fact a marine opisthobranch gastropod mollusc, from a more ancient lineage than nudibranchs called cephalaspideans or head shield slugs. I am joshing you, as the number of people who know that can be counted by an octopus that's lost seven legs, but I've always wanted to simultaneously flatter and patronise with the Victorian phrase 'the astute among you'. It would be an understandable mistake though to lump together similar looking kinds of animals, especially in the sea. Zoology has a funny habit of putting lookalikes in very different groups, and very different-looking animals in the same group (see also bug and beetle, hyrax and elephant).

Nudibranchs, and related sea slugs, have probably the most psychedelic colours in nature; poison dart frogs, eat your heart out. They also come in a great variety of shapes and styles, but many are a bit like upside-down scrubbing brushes with feathery bristles. These are the gills through which they breathe, and it's also where the 'nudi' bit comes from, as they are naked gills without any body structures to cover and protect them. That vulnerability is also likely to be why they are so colourful, advertising to would-be predators that they have powerful toxins and will make an upsetting meal. Nudibranchs get the material for this chemical warfare from their food, such as sponges, or even in some cases by stealing the weapons of jellyfish, their intricate mini organs, called nematocysts. Although the closely related *Navanax* is pretty too, with thin yellow lines on a blue background, if it was bigger than its 9 inches, 23 centimetres, it could be one of your worst nightmares. It's a frightening predator, with a retractable tubular mouth that it can thrust from its head in a fraction of a second to suck the life out of its victims: one that even the draughtsman of *Alien*, H. R. Giger, might have considered a bad dream. Just like the spawn of his imagination, this ocean alien is intelligent, and it's going to track you down . . .

At school, I now remember, the term 'sea slug' was sometimes used unfairly to describe some of the Year Sevens, treated like lower forms of life by seniors who'd forgotten what life is like in the lower form. They are in fact extremely cunning (like Year Sevens), and a fantastic example of how resourceful nature is in exploiting every available method for survival.

One of the things peculiar to slugs and snails is the way they get about, as you will know if you've ever got up at 3 a.m. and caught the slug that's made a slimy slug line to the dog bowl, but only after wondering as to its whereabouts for three days. Slugs glide on a conveyor belt of snot.

If that's where the story ended it would still be amazing. I mean, who would have thought that a lubricated path made from a never-ending line of mucus would be a practical way to travel? It obviously is, as all 'footed' molluscs use it, and it must have advantages, such as being able to get over most surfaces efficiently without harm, like a train that lays its own tracks and laughs at the idea of 'leaves on the line'. But it's not where the story ends.

For a start, the mucus itself is very clever. There are several types produced by molluscs, but the one we're interested in is the one secreted under the foot, a mixture of lubricant and glue. Mucus is not much different from water, as Julian Vincent, my 'biomechanics' zoology lecturer, once told us in his excellent talk, 'Snot and Slime'. It has a small percentage, less than 9 per cent, of chemicals called glycoproteins. As with wallpaper paste, you only need a bit of powder to make gel.

I suspect that said mollusc also mixes the amounts of 'powder' according to the job it needs the mucus to do, getting various consistencies from not-very-sticky trail slime to very adhesive stuff for rock climbing. That would be how nature does things: use the same material in different mixtures to get different properties. Spiders do it, producing different silks for egg cocoons or webs by altering the speed at which they push out liquid silk from their spinning organs, the spinnerets, which changes how the silk mixes with oxygen. Someone has obviously copied that, because in 3D printing there are now machines that can change the mix of the same raw materials according to the need for lightness or strength. Even if we stopped there, snail slime would be pretty wonderful, but that's not all.

Like many of its kind *Navanax*, the predatory sea slug, has been around for millions of years. Naturally, if you invent a way to get around on mucus, making trails everywhere, and you also can't see or hear very well, something else happens. As well as easing locomotion, the mucus can potentially send snail mail to whoever stumbles across its sticky path. So the slug group, from garden snails to *Navanax*, evolved chemical signals to mix into the slime. In *Navanax* these chemicals are pheromones called navanones. Three kinds have been identified: A, B, and C, mixed together from a gland just below the anus at the back of the foot. Presumably the percentages of each can be altered for different messages. And of course, there are organs to detect pheromones too: on either side of the mouth of *Navanax* are highly sensitive 'taste buds' that sample the mix of mucus and its chemical signals.

Depending on the mix, when *Navanax* discovers another's trail, it responds in different ways. When previous slugs have been alarmed by a predator the trail contains warning navanones, and the next slug to come by will turn around (hello? – have we hit on an eco-friendly garden slug deterrent here?). When there are mate pheromones *Navanax* follows – sometimes a perilous course because, mate or not, many bigger individuals have a cannibal side to their personality. The pheromones deteriorate in light too after only a few hours, so as not to leave too many confusing signals. Clever old sea slug. And that's still not all.

Navanax also uses the slime telegraph to find its prey. That's where our second character, *Janulus*, comes into the picture. It's a beautiful, vivid, yellow-flecked nudibranch, but to our fearsome predator, ignoring these warning colours, it's a meal. It's not really understood how the slug hunter knows which way to go, but perhaps it senses the way the mucus trail flows, just as we see the way a river flows? Whatever, it's very effective, and for once it's easy to see it happening on the seabed right beneath the RV *Cormorant*. We soon capture the slimy stalker, *Navanax*, as it sneaks up on its prey and makes a decisive lunge to embed its jaws in the yellow flanks of *Janulus*.

As with all good natural history sequences, though, there's a twist: *Janulus*, having been bothered by *Navanax* on many previous occasions – over tens of thousands of years probably – knows just what to do. It rolls into a ball, hits the ejector button, and blasts off the seabed, leaving a bad taste and a few yellow feathery gills in the alien's mouth. That'll show him (and her, actually, because sea slugs are mostly hermaphrodite). There you have it: in episode 5 of the first *Blue Planet* series I count it as 1 minute, 59 seconds, with less than a paragraph of script, but here detailed over several pages – and if you want the detail, read a book – a television voice over is more sketchy by nature.

That scene was first broadcast in November 2001, but it still resurfaces in peculiar ways online, such as in a blog about 'Apprehension'. I kid you not: *Janulus* escaping imminent death has been used as a metaphor for getting rid of apprehension and emotional burden:[1]

---

1 Abusethekeyboard.wordpress.com /2014/07/06/the-janulus-sea-slug/

'It's not good to hang on to such burden and, rather than dwelling on it, let it go. You might lose a few feathery gills, but at least you won't be consumed and destroyed.'

Yeah, right, 'apprehension' – that's what I'd feel if I had an alien on my tail. Though secretly I believe the blogger is right. Good advice, in fact. Just let go.

When you go diving, what you see occurs in a small snapshot of time, and that's why no two dives in the same place are the same, even if you go in again, say, an hour later. We are brief visitors to this underwater world, and our view is coloured by the short time we spend there. It could be like only visiting London at four in the morning, for forty minutes or so, and then you have to leave for an urgent appointment. You would think of the capital as a relatively empty place where traffic lights change for no particular reason because there isn't any traffic, and yet it is of course one of the biggest cities on Earth. It's the same with the sea, although ocean nightlife is better.

I can see from my dive log that our night dive in the Channel Islands was on 15 June 1999, at Torqua Spring Reef, 4 miles north of Avalon on Santa Catalina Island. You may be thinking, 'Aren't you afraid of diving into black water where there might be sharks and other things out to eat you?' Not really, because we were probably too close to shore to encounter sharks like great whites, and they usually don't go through a kelp forest, which may act like a natural shark net. Besides, if it came near us, we'd thankfully film it! Yet there are of course big sharks here, and recently I saw great pictures of a magnificent sevengill shark lurking in the kelp. These 'cow sharks' are pretty much the only living representatives of an ancient Jurassic group called sevengills, growing to 8-plus feet (3 metres), and I might have given my right arm to meet one. Actually, there's a decent population of sevengills under the Golden Gate Bridge in San Francisco.

In fact, what you are mostly afraid of, for yourself and your team of night divers, is getting lost in the dark and swept away forever. That's why we use a lot of lights – everyone attaches a Cyalume (other brands are available), one of those glow sticks you break to make a lasting chemical light, which young children enjoy on fairground nights. They're mostly green, but it's best if you have a different colour for each person, so you know exactly who you've lost. Putting a big beacon on the recovery boat so you can see it immediately you come up, and everyone having torches, whistles and lit marker buoys – inflatable tubes that you erect when you surface – all makes it safer.

As soon as I back-flip into the black I can see there has been a radical shift change on the seabed, and the day staff have all clocked off. The blacksmiths, opaleyes, assorted rockfish and Garibaldi have all gone to sleep. In fish terms, sleep means staying very still and hiding among vegetation or in cracks between the rock – unless you are a coral-dwelling parrot fish, in which case you build a translucent sleeping bag entirely out of mucus, but there are none of those here in colder waters. Now we see the night crew: several small horn sharks, in brown, cream and spotted camouflage like some sort of desert tank, and with sloping, tank-like heads. They're not very threatening, being maybe 2 feet at most, and pretty much like a European dogfish. Just before each of its two dorsal fins, and sticking out vertically from a small turret of skin, is a short but sharp spine.

Until now I always thought that those were the horns in question, but you learn something new every day, and it turns out that people think the ridges over the eyes are like horns. Doh! I always thought those spines were pretty rubbish horns, but they would surely stick in your mouth if you tried to swallow a horned shark whole. Horn sharks also eat shellfish, and maybe they're on the nightshift while the bat rays do the day, but although I can't see any bat rays just now I think they moonlight too.

Probably more interesting than the brown tank is the swell shark, so called because it can double its size by filling up with seawater, a trick it uses to limpet itself into crevices. Swell sharks live here too in kelp city, and they're only slightly bigger than a horn shark, and sometimes found in groups. I'd seen a fantastic photo of about six swell sharks all rammed into a small gap in the rocks on top of each other, having a sleep in the day. Tom the cameraman and I discussed whether we could capture such a cool thing on video and make another little sequence, because it is amazing that a shark can inflate. If I remember, he did find one or two swell sharks, but they were so rammed into a gap you could hardly see them. I think from their perspective that was the point.

Ahead of me I can see Tom. He's being lit by David with a large generator-fed underwater light from the boat, and the shadow Tom casts in the cloudy water behind him starts to explain sightings of Bigfoot in the snow. As I pull up alongside he immediately seems to contort out of his neoprene skin, and through his legs shoots something that looks like a high-velocity orange cricket ball which promptly lands on the rock next to me, and for the few seconds that it stays still I can see is a gigantic Californian spiny lobster. We've just witnessed its impressive escape response after Tom almost stepped on it, and Tom's impressive escape response too, not having thought to pack a ball guard in his dry suit.

The strong filming light is attracting lots of little shrimps and various, somewhat microscopic, marine life like arrow worms, translucent with arrow-shaped heads. Fish larvae and other zooplankton in their millions, too. Their reflections of our light make a mesmerising underwater firework display as the bugs chatter and dart in the limelight. I've been on filming night dives where this plankton soup is so thick you can't see anything, and you just have to give up. We hardly know why these tiny marine creatures come to the light, any more than we do moths. Perhaps it's a sex signal, and we've suddenly created a giant red-light district in the sea, or perhaps, as I have read, it is because the plant life the tiny animals eat itself gives off a faint green or yellow light, which we've amplified massively, and the hungry zooplankton has gone mad for it. Once the little animals are here, though, it isn't long before something bigger will come along to eat them.

As we get back near the surface a huge silver mirror glides right across my face mask, lunging at the illuminated meal buzzing around us. The large scales, like elements of a solar panel, identify it as a fish, and one that has huge fan-shaped fins tucked up against its missile-shaped body. Maybe it's the angle and closeness with which it glides around me, but I've never seen one this big before. In fact, I've hardly ever seen one underwater at all, because it's a flying fish, and the Californian one is king, sometimes growing to almost 2 feet, 60cm, it's the biggest in the world. Looking around I can see there are about twenty circling me, but something spooks them, and immediately the silver sides vanish into the black. So apart from the poor old, drab old horn shark, who is not that far from Hollywood, but still a bit player, all the exciting creatures have proved too fast for us, and we must dive another day.

Looking back now I'm not sure why we didn't continue with the night dives in the Channel Islands – following up that magnificent flying fish, for example. We did, I remember, experiment at night with a remote camera on a wire that I bodged together back home with the cameraman and inventor Jonathan Watts. Jonathan is a story in himself, but his ability to put unlikely bits of kit together for unlikely filming jobs is legendary. This camera was inside a housing that had a small round acrylic dome at the front, about 4 inches in diameter, also 'home-made', by a friend in my underwater photographer group, Ken Sullivan, an engineer who forms them with a vacuum cleaner on home-made rigs in his garage.

It was not long after the spiny lobster incident when we deployed this remote system, right underneath the boat. Since the cable to the camera was nearly 150 feet long, we could watch the seabed on a monitor in the comfort of the ship's cabin. We'd set up the camera on a dive during the day, and buried some bait, a small tin of fishy cat food,[1] in the seabed just in front of the camera. Nearby we'd also put two underwater lights cabled from the ship. At about midnight we switched the lights on, to embarrass six startled spiny lobsters. For a few minutes we saw them so close we could see the facets of their eyes, but they weren't happy with the light and soon crawled

---

1 Bait is used in certain circumstances, such as with remote cameras that cannot roam the seabed like divers, and most often to lure in sharks, but I don't like it much as it alters behaviours. You can be sure we cleaned up the seabed and took the buried tins away afterwards.

back into the night. I was delighted, as I still am, to have this freedom to experiment, but now also surprised I was allowed to do this sort of thing, which sometimes came to nothing. I'm grateful that people like Alastair Fothergill, the original series producer of *Blue Planet,* were confident enough to trust my filming methods in an ocean thousands of miles from the office. Yet innovation almost always pays off. That same remote camera system was later used to get pictures of a storm underwater, in a situation far too dangerous for a camera person, to film what looked like the inside of a washing machine on its intensive cycle.

From 28 May to 16 June 1999 RV *Cormorant* was our home, and we did fifty-three dives in total, to record sequences that helped to explain the underwater forests of our blue planet. The most magnificent of that set of dives took place fifty miles south of Avalon, off the southernmost Channel Island, San Clemente. Here you can find the tallest kelp, the redwoods of the ocean, triffids of the seas. Deeper than a normal scuba diver can venture, these specimens rise 200 feet, 60 metres from their holdfast, a clever labyrinth of finger-like roots that holds the whole green tower to the seabed. Strictly speaking, they're not roots, because they don't take nutrients from the 'soil' of the seabed, but they are still amazing structures. No more than a seal's flipper across, it's a miracle how the 'holdfast' bears the strain of the massive kelp swinging in the current, but its strong fist will hardly ever let go, even in the heart of a winter storm.

With a view to redesigning boat anchors and finding ways to implant tidal generators into the seabed, there's been a twitch of interest in understanding how the holdfast works, especially because they don't go either wide or deep into the ground. It seems there are some clever forces at work: the stubby disc at the end of the 'roots', the haptera, grows over rocks like a sucker, and has extensions that grow into every tiny crevice. This creates the same kind of tensions found in mountaineer's rope clamps knocked into the cracks of rocks. After attachment, the tiny branches shrink, grabbing the seabed even more firmly. The spread of a holdfast looks chaotic, as if the mountaineer's lines have become hopelessly tangled, but its confused mass is just a way to increase the surface area and find new holes. The stems of kelp and its holdfasts are very flexible too, and less likely to break than rigid poles. Finally, as you might also have guessed, the kelp has its own glue, although scientists hardly understand its chemical composition. I laugh when I see 'thoroughly clean and dry' in the instructions for household glue: kelp sticks to pebbles in over *50 metres* of seawater. That's superglue.

You haven't asked, how come the kelp grows upwards to the surface? Why doesn't it just flop around and fall across the seabed? It's because each leaf, the blade, has a large swelling at its base, an air bladder, like a fishing float, that holds it up, true and taut in the water column. Those questions go on and on, though don't they? What is the gas inside that air bladder? Where does it come from? How does the seaweed fill this balloon under pressure, and where is the metaphorical valve hole through which it is filled? As with a lot of such questions in marine science, the answers could best be described as 'incomplete'. The gas inside the bladders comes from the seaweed's metabolism. Its composition is similar to air, but sometimes has more or less oxygen, and a little trace of carbon monoxide too, which seems odd. It's likely that the kelp can reabsorb the oxygen at night when it isn't making any in sunlight through photosynthesis, which probably comes in useful, but, then again, that would alter its buoyancy – so does kelp sag in the dark? I think you should become a marine biologist and find out.

From my dive log I see we were at Pyramid Head, on the southern end of San Clemente, about 41 miles from mainland California, on 29 May 1999. It is here, if I remember rightly, that the tallest of the tall 'redwood' kelp grows, and where we filmed it in all its magnificence.

Kelp can look very different depending on depth, current and light conditions. So different that Victorian seaweed biologists described seventeen kinds, based on various shapes of holdfasts and blades. I'm afraid they have egg on their classification because now, with DNA analysis, we know *Macrocystis pyrifera*, giant kelp, to be just one species, albeit with remarkably flexible forms. That's not just the taxonomic reality; I've experienced it physically too: once, off Monterey, I became hopelessly entangled in the dense type of fronds that spill across the surface of shallow water. Held in this seaweed web, I fought to stay calm and ease my way through its slimy knots to the surface. Sometimes I wonder at the absurd epitaphs I might have had (and might still) on my tombstone, such as:

GUILLOTINED BY THE CLAWS OF A
GIANT LOBSTER

but

STRANGLED BY SEAWEED

is right up there. At least it alliterates.

Yet in the deep, clear and sheltered water of San Clemente the jolly green giant grows into huge columns, tall and straight, and is unlikely to hold you there for long, except to wonder at its beauty. As the sunbeams shaft down between the foliage and stems disappear into the abyss with the perspective of railway tracks, they mix up your sense of height and depth; a vertigo peculiar to this fluid forest. In the first series of *Blue Planet*, the graphic designer, Mick Connaire, picked up on the striking images of kelp we had stolen from the sea, and framed their towering columns in a glass orb, which became the series logo.

The green, aquatic forests of this planet are truly beautiful places that support so much interesting life. In the holdfasts of giant kelp alone over forty species of animal have been counted, from sea urchins to hermit crabs. We haven't even talked about the fantastic giant octopus, the sheep's head or the 500-plus other species of fish that live here. Kelp forests are awesome. Don't take my word for it – this quite well-known bloke even came to the same conclusion without scuba gear:

> The number of living creatures of all orders, whose existence intimately depends on the kelp, is wonderful. A great volume might be written, describing the inhabitants of one of these beds of seaweed . . . I can only compare these great aquatic forests . . . with the terrestrial ones in the tropical regions.
>
> Charles Darwin, *Journal of Researches into the Geology and Natural History of the Various Countries Visited by the HMS* Beagle (1839)

Although giant seaweed is among the fastest growing organisms on Earth, with its blades growing towards the sunlight above at 2 feet a day, it's more ephemeral than the land's trees, and lives an estimated seven years at most. It is fragile, too, in a more delicate balance with the ocean's creatures than its stout columns might suggest. Several times in the last few decades the kelp of California has died back extensively, and as far as is known still hasn't returned to its historical abundance. Again, the culprit is likely to be climate change. Kelp likes relatively cold water, but that's only part of the story. The control of its major enemy, the sea urchin, depends in turn on the sea urchin's predators being on top form, but they are, sadly, mostly sick. Sea-urchin-eating starfish, like the beautiful sunflower star that preys upon red and purple sea urchins, have literally melted away: since 2013 such sea stars have caught a wasting disease, thought to be a virus, exacerbated by the warming seas. Their arms start walking in different directions and their bodies just become goo. Without their check the kelp is ravaged by hordes of hungry urchins.

Other predators, like sea otters, might also step in and eat the pesky urchins, but they are being hit too. Availability of prey, entanglement in commercial fishing gear, oil spills, contaminants, disease and even shark predation are all to blame and, despite the best efforts of marine conservationists, the sea otters of California are in decline, and what's called urchin barrens, where underwater deforestation has occurred, become the new norm. It's difficult to reverse, though not impossible. I do hope those tall kelp fronds still grow off San Clemente, and that if you dive there you will see them too. Don't let us allow their only remembrance to be through old documentaries streamed to your living room.

11

Islands – Mountains of the Sea

Important dots in the open ocean

Many islands are just the tops of mountains peeking through the sea, though somehow it doesn't seem like that to us landlubbers, enjoying the solid touch of earth and the sea views. On an island you can be an ocean mountaineer, reaching the summit easily and looking down on clouds of liquid blue. Islands are also waypoints in the Saltwater Country, and the most distinctive features on maps of the sea. 'Land ahoy!' sailors may cry; underwater there's an equal cheer among marine creatures finding food and shelter in the ocean expanse.

It's the new century, about three years into the filming of the first series of *Blue Planet*. I've been given a shopping list as long as an oar fish of things to get off the west coast islands of Costa Rica and Colombia. It's crunch time, as in any long television production, when you must *just get on with it for goodness' sake!* Three different producers, Alastair Fothergill, Martha Holmes and Andy Byatt, have sent me off, the delivery boy, to get the stuff they need for their films. But it's not bad to have to run errands like that, and soon I'll be in the Pacific in charge of a

65-foot ship with a range of nearly 3,000 miles, with three film teams, and £15,000 cash as 'float money'. I have a company credit card too, not that many people take Visa 400 miles offshore, or so I thought. It's just before the days of universal internet, international calls via satellite are like caviar, and WhatsApp is still nine years in the future, so once I leave the office, apart from emergency, we're on our own, *going solo*.

Of course, I'm not really in charge of the ship. Heinz, our captain, reminds me that people come in at least 57 varieties, all unique. His ship, and our home for over a month, is called the *Inzan Tiger*, an exotic-sounding name with visions of daring deeds from Antigua to Zanzibar in the time of pirates, but is in fact just a combination of the 'in' from Heinz and his wife's name, Zan. I can't remember where the tiger comes from, but no doubt it summons up the courage you need to face the Pacific in such a sturdy but relatively small ship. There are eight berths, plenty of space for cameras and a great back deck to dive from, and it does indeed have very sturdy engines, so reliable that you forget their existence. It also has its own water-maker, an osmosis purifier that means you can far exceed the distances you might venture at sea with only a limited water barrel. It smells in equal proportions of varnished plywood, saltwater and diver's sweat. That last is putting it politely, because in a big tub at the back (or stern, as you should call it), are a load of soaking wetsuits with more diver body fluids than just sweat, if you know what I mean.

Mostly fine, those aromas do sometimes get out of balance on hot tropical days in the doldrums. Once the smell became so bad I got up and shouted, 'OK, bring out your dead!' and everyone had to wash their dive suits again in fresh tub water while I poured in a whole bottle of the mild French antiseptic, TCP. I can highly recommend it if you need to make sweaty divers sweet, even if it's harmful to cats and should be disposed of responsibly.

Heinz is a large man, dressed in what looks like a long silk dressing gown, with bare feet, and gold rings on his toes, standing proudly at the wheel of his ship. He made his fortune in the brewing business, finding markets that others couldn't reach. Selling out, he and his wife decided what they really wanted to do was have their own ship and dive-tour business; that or buying a brothel in Arizona. Or so he told me, perhaps as a joke, though a convincing one. Anyway, they obviously settled on the boat, and not any old dive business, because they could take *Inzan Tiger* to some of the most unvisited places on Earth, for diving tours that would blow your mind. It would be true to say that I was somewhat wary of Heinz. 'Maverick' perhaps describes him. And yet everything he said about the sea – his observations of the clouds, where the birds flocked and the sea currents stirred – all made great sense, and I knew I could learn from his ocean wisdom.

To be fair, there weren't many other competitors for the diving business where we were going. Even today there's still only a handful of dive operators that can take you to all the places in the 'hammerhead triangle', the wonderfully shark-infested seas off Costa Rica and Colombia. So how, actually, do we choose which people to go with on these expeditions? Well, it's at this point that I must credit those who make these fruitful, and frequently fantastically surreal, filming trips possible. They are the people that find out what support is available for filming crews, often book it at short notice, and make the best deals they can to keep within budget. They are known as production co-ordinators and production managers.

THE WHALE IN THE LIVING ROOM

PCs and PMs make everything happen. Let's name check them as we go. On this one it was Amanda Hutchinson and Samantha Davis as PCs and Katie Walker, PM. Mindful of time zone differences, Amanda and Sam would be my first port of call should there be a problem. Their neatly laid-out tables of flights, car hires, contact lists, customs procedures and where you're meant to be and when are known as schedules or call sheets. If only we had a call sheet for our life.

The decision to go with *Inzan Tiger*, rather than anyone else, was because it allowed us to have exclusive use of one ship. We could have gone with a larger commercial dive tour, but that would have either involved hiring a massive vessel for its whole cost, or sharing with tourist scuba divers. While I am often on such ships myself, it isn't really fair on either filming crew or tourist divers. In fact, it's a nightmare. Pleasure divers are usually on an ocean tour, and that means seeing as much as you can and in as many dive sites as you can, spending a little time at each and quickly moving on. Underwater film crews, on the other hand, find something good to film and try to stay with it for hours, often days, dive after dive as necessary, making sure it's well filmed and that the video can be cut well with all the angles to tell a story. It's frequently painstaking work, and you absolutely don't want to be hurried. Having said that, it was the advice and camerawork of some tourist scuba divers that really helped us on this trip, as I will explain. One should never be too proud to learn from someone who obviously has something to teach you.

How we get to these locations is something of a blur when you've done a few shoots. It usually involves a carbon-guilty flight, always in economy for max value, not max legroom. It involves a huge amount of kit precariously navigated through airports and customs. It involves crews meeting up for the job from all over, as most are freelance and not long-standing teams. Who is chosen depends on their skills of course, but also availability, and indeed whether they want the job, though most do.

Good underwater camera people float to the surface of their chosen career, if you pardon the pun. But perhaps the only qualification they share is a passion for their subject. With me on this Central American epic, and each obsessed in their own way with diving, filming and the sea, were the Californian cameraman Bob Cranston, British maestro Peter Scoones and, on second camera and dive assisting, Florian Graner from Germany and Peter Kraig, originally from Denmark but now Californian. Please don't be put off that these were all camera-men if you are a budding camera*woman*, by the way, because there is absolutely nothing that should stop you, and the next generation does indeed have many more female underwater photographers. I prefer the American term for camera people, though: DOP – Director of Photography, which is gender-neutral, although it also has some hierarchy associated with it as it implies you are the top-dog photographer.

Those credits for the crew, with phrases like 'and on second camera', sound like the spiel of Jazz DJs, but perhaps, as my teenage son would say, 'No one cares, Dad!' They're squashed now into a box after the show or simply disappear after five seconds as the next autoplay episode kicks in. I guess they matter mostly to us TV and film folk, whose careers depend on the last good credit and a mention on IMDb (Internet Movie Database). But those names mean so much more to me – Cranston, deGruy and Scoones. There are many others, but those three in particular, because they are no longer with us, and it's true you don't know what you miss till it's gone. They brought more images of the sea to your living room than you know, and taught me so much with an ocean of enthusiasm that infects me still. I'm so lucky that, at a few times and in some very strange GPS co-ordinates, I was with such hallowed people. They wouldn't want me to get maudlin, so let's just keep going and dive on.

Cocos Island, Costa Rica
5°31′4.79′ N -87°04′10.80′ W

Bob Cranston is standing on a cliff above Chatham Bay on the north end of Cocos Island, looking towards Costa Rica, 550 kilometres, 341 miles away. Red-footed boobies soar like mini-pterodactyls around him, although you could be forgiven for thinking that their blue beaks are more striking than their red feet, but then the blue-footed boobies would complain. I'm standing with Florian behind the camera trying not to step back too far and become fish food. What we are recording is for the 'Making Of' pieces at the end of each *Blue Planet* episode in the first series, called 'Making Waves'.

Bob looks to camera and throws his arms out wide to signify the expanse of the sea:

> This is a place, in this vast ocean, and the deep water currents come in and hit this island, sea mount, whatever you want to call it, and it *upwells*, brings all the nutrients up. So the little fish can feed on the nutrients, and the bigger fish can feed on the little fish, and the sharks feed on them. The whole food chain is right here, and we're here to film it!

Bob is a natural on camera: he's bright, clear and warm in his delivery. Warmth, I think, is the main characteristic of a good presenter, not that he often did presenting, because his first love was working with an underwater camera. He did the piece in one take, and it just flowed out as though he was talking to you personally and all he wanted to do was to explain the sea as he experienced it. He was an American but, working as a diver on oil rigs in the North Sea out of Aberdeen, he had obviously developed a soft spot for the Brits. Then, I think some time as a tour guide, showing people the blue sharks off California, and he settled in San Diego. Here, with some other famous marine film-makers, Howard and Michele Hall, he began to make ocean wildlife films, including IMAX 3D, lugging around underwater cameras the size of a small car. Bob knew Cocos well because he'd spent about six months in '97 and '98 making *The Island of the Sharks* with Michele and Howard in Cocos, a great IMAX film. Bob was a tall cowboy of a man, a cowboy riding the plains of the ocean frontier, a gentle giant who loved sharks.

That shopping list was starting to burn a hole in my pocket. I look back on my time at Cocos with wonder, but I can honestly say I'm much calmer writing about it, mixing images in my mind with images on playback from *Blue Planet*, than I was when I was responsible for several expensive sequences I had to get for the series. That's the mindset of a wildlife director in the field. You need to work out every cunning way you can to get the footage before time and tide run out on you, and you might come back with nothing, and you'll have to explain to the team and your boss why, knowing that you're only as good as your last shoot. It's as much about people as fish: how to help the team and keep them going when it's all going wrong.

So what form did this shopping list take? I sometimes read with interest those little pieces of paper that are a crib into other people's lives: lists unclipped from abandoned trollies and floating in the breeze begging to be noticed. No doubt Sherlock Holmes could have told you a lot about people from their shopping lists, but even I can see that you don't buy a family-sized washing powder if you're single, although you might buy a family-sized bar of chocolate if you are. Such lists are plans, simple ones of course, but plans nevertheless, evidence of strategy and forethought, an intention of necessity and staying on track, of not going off-piste and buying the whole shop. And that's the essence of film lists too. It's not a good idea to film everything; it is a good idea to know what you want before you get there, and, of course, if you see a great special offer, a steal in season, you might take it, even if it's not on your list.

There are levels of detail, naturally. It starts with a conversation. Sometimes very brief, and often, in the old school, extremely brief. John Sparks, a legend on the BBC Natural History Unit in Bristol, the director who was with Sir David when David was with the mountain gorillas, probably the most famous Attenborough scene of all, once said to me, 'John, I think you should film some fish in Africa!' and that, bar a jolly word and a slap on the back was that, leaving you with a thrilling freedom.

At another level of detail Alastair Fothergill, the original series producer, would discuss the general concept he wanted to show. In one case we had a chat about how to show upwellings and currents underwater, so that we could talk about how islands are ocean cafés supplied with food by nutrients served up from the deep. Tricky, actually, as some of it is 'filming the invisible'. We went through the ways it could be shown: a haze of water like a mirage could reveal a cold-water current coming up from the deep and mixing with warmer surface water; particles like snow in the water might donate nutrients; flapping seaweed, fluttering schools of small fish riding up on the currents, although that also looks like they're just swimming too; and then the abundance of life in general reveals the productivity of the seas around islands. Shots which started by looking into the deep, to the base of underwater cliffs, and then slowly tilted up to the underwater sky of the surface, showing the volcanic island walls and suggesting how they stop and force the deep water up to fertilise the surface.

'Do some shots of different lengths so we can have flexibility. Give us a good hold on either end,' might be the sort of brief a director would get from a producer sending them out into the field. That's a good tip, in fact, as moves with holds give you three shots for the price of one: start in one spot and count to ten, move the camera to another (still recording) over say, eight seconds, and then hold for ten again. Now you have three shots, and if the move is no good you still have two different static ones. Of course, you knew that, but it's still polite to go through the rituals of a briefing and also (note to self) it's a good idea not to think you know it all and keep your ears open.

I'm afraid the producer/director thing gets muddled in TV wildlife documentary, because most often they are the same person, but here, on a big series, I am talking about a senior producer sending out a newish acting producer and director (me) with instructions for what they wanted in the film. It just boils down to the fact that there are all sorts of relationships inside production teams and a rough hierarchy of people in charge. I was somewhere in the middle. I still am.

* * *

As I mentioned, I was working to three more senior producers, and Martha asked me to get a sequence about whitetip sharks at night off Cocos for her coral film, and instructed me that it must not be over-lit and should look somewhat dark and blue like moonlight. I was all for that, because I agreed that too brightly-lit shots at night look artificial and spoil the mood, and we agreed it should even be darker than you'd naturally be happy with if you wanted to get the perfect exposure. I'd later have to explain that to Bob, who was used to full-on lighting and only got it when he said, 'Oh, so you want it to look crap!' and I said, 'Yes!'

Andy Byatt was the producer of the open seas show on the first series of *Blue Planet*. I didn't know that fourteen years later I'd also be making a similar episode for *Blue Planet II* – probably one of the more difficult ones of the series because of the vastness of the open seas and the cost of crossing them. I'd have had more empathy for what he was going through – gut wrenching worry that you weren't going to get anything before the money ran out.

As islands like Cocos are rare stopping off spots for large open ocean creatures Andy asked me to get shots of the cleaning stations where giant hammerheads come to have fungus and parasites removed by cleaner fish. The spots where this happens are quite well known on Cocos from previous film-makers and divers. In fact, on Chatham Bay's shoreline, not far from where Bob did that piece to camera, there is a stone plaque commemorating the visit of Jacques Cousteau and his team in 1987, and they must have surely seen such things. He was to return many times, and declared it 'the most beautiful island in the world'. That's the perspective of a diver, though, because it would take the whole picture, above and below water, to convince you of it being the 'fairest of all,' even if it is thought to be the inspiration for the island in *Jurassic Park*.

There were many other things discussed for the lists, such as the large schools of scalloped hammerheads we expected to encounter (there are about nine species), and how we could show they navigated to islands by sensing disturbances in the magnetic fields islands make. Simply put, the answer is: you need to see their heads 'wobble'.

These kinds of discussion produced a list of shots that might look like this:

Currents
1. Haze in water
2. Seaweed bending
3. Fish pushed upwards in big clouds
4. Huge variety of marine life – portraits of many different creatures
5. Tilt down to seabed and then upwards following volcanic walls to surface. Give at least three different shot lengths on this.
6. Be on the look-out for any other signs of current.

Giant Hammerhead shark
1. WS [Wide Shot] cleaning station. Reveal if you can by following a large shark to the station or tilting up from the seabed (that creates a nice surprise).
2. Yellow cleaning fish, CU [close-up] alert and looking for sharks to clean.
3. CUs of parasites and shedding skin on giant hammerhead.
4. Cleaning fish pecking off parasites

And so it would go on for a number of pages, until you had a small book of lists among all your other director and field-producer paperwork.

At another level of detail, you could go the whole hog and do a storyboard. It's really another form of list, but shows how the images fit together too, drawing the key stages in the progression of a visual story. When I moved from radio, where images are carefree and only in the mind, the 'grammar of film' took me longer than most to grasp. The thing is that in films or videos you actually have to show something while you are talking, and make decisions on behalf of the viewer as to what that thing is that you will show. An obvious and simple point but, it turns out, not so obvious or simple in execution.

I think you can learn the basics – camera angles, cutaways and some frills – in perhaps half an hour, but it may take a lifetime to perfect them. It helped me to understand the history of film, and that when the camera was first invented people took just one static shot, and let the action play out inside it. They had the model of theatre, where the actors did the work and there was really only one point of view, framed by the arch of the stage. Although hopefully you had the good seats. Then, through the eye of a magnifying lens, came a stunning invention: the close-up, abbreviated in shooting scripts and lists to CU. In the CU you could see all the detail that the mind craves to analyse. It's probably an artificial version of what we do in any case in real life: looking at a whole scene and then, as the fovea of your eye lands on something for a closer look, scrutinising the detail. The only difference is that the film-makers are choosing where your focus of attention lies.

You might be wondering how all this applies to wildlife film-making? Storyboards and drama scripts surely belong to feature films and theatrical direction, where people can be asked to say a line and move in a certain way? You can't direct fish, can you? Well, not really — only in *Nemo* — and so the process of directing in wildlife films is more by negotiation, even if I have often seriously tried to explain to blue whales that if you do this feeding thing we know you do then we'll be out of your slightly thinning hair right away, and we'll all be happy. You can, though, imagine what you *hope* might happen, and you can try and be alert to signs that what you want to film is about to happen, and it's surprising when you plan it all on paper (or a screen if you must) how many other ideas come to mind for cool shots that add to the bigger picture.

I think I must have arrived at the Natural History Unit in Bristol just at the tail end of the old days, with vague instructions from my managers like that 'Go and film some fish in Africa', or even 'Go to Canada and see what stories you can find'. Today the opposite idea reigns, and at the BBC especially. There was even a directive that you 'can't go into the field without a detailed script and storyboard'. That's probably very sensible: 'failure to plan is planning to fail', and all that stuff that *The Office* parodied so well. Why, then, does the famous German film-maker Werner Herzog, once called 'the most important film director alive', say that 'storyboards are for cowards'?

I met Werner once in the corridor of a production house in Hollywood, or should I say I saw the back of his neck, as I passed him stooped in thought. I knew he was making *Cave of Forgotten Dreams*, and even more could be forgotten if I disturbed him. I believe I know what he means about storyboards, though: they give the illusion that they will be your guide, your rod of certainty when things aren't going as planned, and then distract you from what's really going on. Werner is a fan of free spirit and intuition, 'intense life' – the full scope and exuberance of life – without which he thinks films become stale. So storyboards are stale friends, memories of what could have been but isn't, or even what can be and is: either way an unnecessary Zimmer frame for those who are looking, filming and living in the moment. Yet Herzog, if you read deeper, is only telling you what works for him, and he's not objecting if you want a storyboard, just goading you into thinking about what you're doing.

The truth is, it depends what kind of mind you have: organised and logical, a planner and a plotter – or a 'pantser', flying by the seat of your pants, and going with somewhat controlled intuition and happenstance. There are also 'plantsers' too – somewhere in between – and of course we can all be any of these in greater or lesser proportions at different times.

Where the problem comes is when the modern world puts a value judgement on these behaviours. Since I am mainly a member of the pantser division, I notice that it is the planners and plotters who are favoured, because they can soothe the concerns of those who need reassurance that the plans are going to work (even if they aren't). Woe betide you, though, if you are a pantser that doesn't come back with the goods, despite your fabulous intuition. Actually, I like to do both storyboards and lists before I go away for a film shoot, though drawing ability slows me down, and often it's only lists. Tentative scripts are useful too, as they force you to spell out what you are trying to say, although if documentary is about documenting, then meaning can only be understood after observation, not before.

Often, as I say, in current documentary practice, your line manager will make a clear written plan compulsory. It's best to just do it, even if it stays in your suitcase; it's quicker and less stressful than arguing. It's true, though, that lists, storyboards and scripts, or even just imagining what you will get, is good practice for success, and will generate new ideas to remind you what to buy.

Reflecting on the filming process now I can see it's all about *translation*. The translation of an embryonic idea into a possibility of filming somewhere; somewhere you might just stand a chance of seeing and filming what your research has said you might. Translation from the discussion among office peer groups and hierarchy into the tangible picture stories and lists that come from those discussions. Translation into what the camera people need: what the storyboards mean, the sort of things to look out for, and the preferred style of filming. You may wonder about the things 'lost in translation' – how everyone interprets instructions differently, mishears and mutates the message – but a good filming team is about the things *found* in translation: what each person adds because they're tuned in and looking out for it. Success lies in the final translation, from film to viewer, when the show is broadcast and you find out if you speak the same language or not.

OK: we've had our surface interval now – that's the time between dives when you let the remaining excess nitrogen seep slowly from your blood; the dive computer or, in this case, the word count of the chapter, tells me how long it should be – and hopefully you don't feel as tired as excess nitrogen or hot air can make you feel, and we're ready for our next mission beneath the waves.

I've just played back the scene in 'Coral Seas', in the first series of *Blue Planet*, where we're filming the whitetip reef sharks hunting off Cocos Island at night. I think that's me with the lights in the 'behind-the-scenes' show, 'Making Waves', at the end. You can see me in silhouette from above (fame at last) as the bubbles from my dive gear go glugging up to camera. Now it becomes some strange dream where mutable memories and permanent video combine to form a new story different at every telling. Below me I recognise Bob, still an iconic stick figure in his dive suit, and above me must have been Florian taking pictures of us taking pictures. The scene it portrays is somewhat professional and calm. Even though we are diving at night with lots of sharks about us, in a place few of us would recognise even during the day. Everything is going to plan. Except that's not quite how it happened.

For a start, this scene wasn't shot on one night but several – over about a week, in fact, if I remember correctly. That's just how it is, because you don't usually get all the shots you need for a complete sequence in one go. Yes, some of the main action will happen all at once on one dive, and you pray for that, but it usually takes a few goes to get there, to learn what's going on and what the sharks are looking for and why, and to notice the thing they do just before the thing you want to film happens, so you've got time to pull the trigger.

During the day we had seen single whitetip reef sharks in the distance, rummaging lazily around coral heads, usually a bit wary of us. Probably one of the first whitetips I had ever seen, and I couldn't fault the name: a gleaming white fleck at the top of its dorsal fin marked it out as if a careless artist didn't have time to shade in all the silver grey of its upper body. It's not too big – about 5 foot, tops (1.5 metres) – and seems placid. At night they are very different beasts.

Our first attempt at filming the whitetips in the dark had its moments, it must be said. Despite the request to film in dim light so that the scene looked 'moonlit', you can't usually film underwater on dark nights without using light, and certainly not with the video cameras of the 1990s we had. So Bob had brought his full lighting package, which consisted of two homemade rigs each with two large tungsten bulbs in underwater casings on a T-shaped bar and with about 200 metres (600 feet) of yellow waterproof cable that wiggled its way back to a generator on the small inflatable boat, launched from *Inzan Tiger* anchored in Chatham Bay.

On a test dive I remember one of these tungsten bulbs exploding with an ear-splitting bang, even underwater. The seals around the light's housing had leaked. Water and electricity, never a good combination. Perhaps that wasn't a good omen for what was about to follow.

It gets dark about 6 p.m. in the tropics, and that's it: no long, drawn-out summer evenings with a gentle sunset fade to black – just 'Lights out!' However, it does take a little time for the night shift to kick in underwater, so it's best to leave it a couple of hours. By about 9 p.m. we were four divers, a boatman and a generator, overladen and riding low in the slightly deflated inflatable, going out to sea like a car with a flat tyre. It was as dark as moonless nights at sea can be, the saltwater pulling the last photon from a sparkle. Somewhere in the dark, the stubby finger of Isla Manuelita, pointing northwards towards Costa Rica just outside Chatham Bay. That's where the whitetip sharks gather among the coral heads for their nocturnal hunting parties. We roughly knew the spot from daytime forays, and soon the boatman and Bob decided we were in the right place. We took a while to get our kit together and, in the darkness, like divers laying limpet mines on enemy ships, we slid into the water, our big camera and lights with yellow cable handed down to us, our weapons of choice.

In the time taken to sort our kit, and with the outboard of the inflatable switched off for our safety, we had obviously drifted quite a way in the dark even before we were in the water. The generator on the boat throbbed like an idle lawnmower, and the lights in my hands faltered and then came back with the warm intensity of tungsten. The current was strong, a clearly defined river in the sea, and soon we had left the boat behind. Holding the lights just below the waves, so they didn't get hot, I could see the swirls of water blurring the shine.

Bob hesitated, and all the while the line from my lights was unwinding from the boat. He wouldn't dive if it wasn't right. Best to listen to Bob. He told me to wait and did an exploratory duck dive, returning to the surface almost immediately, 'It's too deep – we're in the wrong place!'

As the first two divers into the water that night, we had become separated from our colleagues, as well as the boat. Earlier I had been amused to notice that the plug into the generator from the light cable looked like a standard two-pin domestic US plug. There was no other support to the cable and, as far as I could see, it wasn't tied to the boat, but just trailed off over the side into the water. I could see a torch on the boat in the slightly hazy distance viewed from my eye line bobbing on an increasing swell. The lights suddenly went taut and pulled in my hands as the yellow cable came to the end of its reel. I was exactly 600 feet from the boat. Only the friction of two brass pins on the generator plug held me against the current, and it didn't seem so funny now. Bob looked at me, noticing that the line was taut too.

If the number of things you do right exceeds the number of things you do wrong, on balance, then you stand a good chance. Bob calmly outlined his concern to me in a spluttered conversation over the water. 'So we're in the wrong place, it's dark, there's a strong current, 400 miles of sea between us and Costa Rica, and there's no coastguard.'

'And I'm hanging onto the boat by a plug,' I thought.

'I think we're in trouble, John!' said Bob.

Scuba bottles, in case you're not familiar, have a regulator that reduces the pressure inside. To breathe straight from the bottle or tank would make your lungs explode, but an ingenious mechanism inside the regulator's so-called 'first stage' sorts that and, by the time you've sucked in air from the 'second stage' or 'demand valve,' which is the thing in your mouth, everything seems normal. The bit in the pipe between the bottle and the demand valve still has a pretty high pressure, though: about ten times atmospheric, or the pressure of the stuff you're breathing now. There is a cunning little device, a whistle, that makes use of this and, as per BBC safety instructions, I had one inserted into the pipe from the scuba tank. Like a foghorn, it has an ample supply of high-pressure air, and when you press the red button on the whistle it makes ONE HELL OF A NOISE.

I pressed the button for about ten seconds to purge the whistle. Now my ears were ringing, and for some reason I also had a metallic taste in my mouth and felt dizzy. You could have heard that sound from the other side of the island, if there had been anyone there, though people on the warden's post, just above the bay, later told us they could hear it clearly.

'We're not in *that* much trouble, John!' said Bob.

I was reassured, but still waiting for the inevitable: the *ping* of the plug out of the generator and my journey to Costa Rica.

Bob seemed to be able to counteract the current without the help of a cable, but eventually I knew he too would follow me towards mainland Central America. I couldn't immediately see any way out of our situation. We hadn't dropped the camera yet, though – that really would be desperate. We were literally treading water, pausing, as our lives swam in the balance.

True tales of danger have a weakness: there's no suspense, because their telling by the people involved implies survival. That will take the edge off it a bit for those of you who'd like to see my legs nibbled slowly by sharks or drift off into the blue in some unresolved mystery, but you're not going to get rid of me that easily. Even so, it appeared no one had immediately noticed our predicament, and the lights of the distant boat appeared to get smaller every time we looked.

Surprisingly, my lighting line was holding, and so our support boat must be drifting with us, albeit 600 feet away, even if it already looked smaller. So we had time to think what to do. I don't remember any long conversation with Bob, though, who was holding his heavy camera with one hand and swimming around me with the other. That's when I saw the faint glow of a diver's torch flickering quite deep below us. A few minutes later the diver's head popped up between us.

It was Peter, one of the other two divers we'd left behind and he must have been looking out for us all the time. 'Hello!' said Peter, and I couldn't decide whether that was his Danish accent or a slightly amused analysis at finding his friends, and especially Bob, he of 181 days' diving at Cocos for *Island of the Sharks IMAX*, somewhat caught out. But if anyone knew this place better than Bob it was Peter Kraig – he'd even spent a few weeks living on the island working with the National Park.

'You've been dropped in the wrong place!' Peter explained.

(We know.)

'You need to come with me – there's a hell of a current running here – because you are coming towards the tip of the island out to the open sea.'

We knew that too, but were really grateful to see Peter. He suggested we dive with him right down to the seabed and then follow him back to the boat. The seabed was deep here, at about 40 metres (120 feet), but if we were quick we wouldn't have too much time at that depth and be able to get back to the surface without any serious decompression stops. Being very close to the ocean floor is one way to beat the current, because in the first few inches above it the water is slowed down by friction with the sediment.

A lot of our film work happens pretty shallow, so it felt disorientating going so deep. In the dark, in featureless open water, you only see a haze of bubbles and particles in the light: an insect in a glass of champagne. The 'floor' keeps falling away from you, and it's an act of faith that you'll bump into anything solid before your dive computer tells you it's too deep to go further. Like the hapless insect, too, you'll feel intoxication, as nitrogen is forced into your blood at ever greater pressures and you experience the dangerous joy of nitrogen narcosis: drunk on the bubbles.

When I remember those moments now, twenty years later, I can still see my hands pulling the seabed and clouds of brown mud and sand kicked up, sparkling in our lights like shaken snow globes, with nothing else visible in the background. There's the momentary fear we can't make it – and then the elation at surfacing near the boat and clambering back to dryness, where you wonder what all the fuss was about. That's the ocean for you: you soon forget how its beguiling beauty, serene and mysterious, suddenly changes to lethal attraction. I hope I said thank you to Peter.

So that was night one of our dive on Whitetip City written off. Sometimes you get everything at once, but more often it's the process of slowly chipping away at a story that gets the goods. I notice from my spartan dive logs that I was diving with cameraman Peter Scoones too, and that it took at least four more nights to get the images you see in *Blue Planet*, 'Coral Seas'.

Hunting with whitetip sharks is incredibly exciting. During the day they are mostly seen individually, maybe a pair swimming quite far away from each other. But at night they cluster together in groups of as many as twenty animals. It's because they need each other to catch fish. A good meal for a whitetip would be a medium-sized grouper, a wrasse or perhaps a parrot fish, around 18 inches (45 centimetres) long. Most of these fish would be 'sleeping' in the dark and they'd find crevices to hide away in, making sure they stayed still.

But in the dark sharks use their amazing array of sense organs, smell and especially electric sensing organs, to detect prey. Water conducts electricity well, and all animals make a weak electric field, even if it's only from their heartbeat, so it's logical that electric sense developed in water, and seawater in particular, because it conducts electricity really well. In distant evolution there may be a connection between hearing and electric senses, but that's about as near as we're going to get to understanding how a shark 'sees' the world through its electric sense, pretty much unlike anything we have.

When you catch up with a whitetip pack at night, they are often swirling around coral heads probing and searching the cracks, and quickly moving on if they find nothing. Sleeping fish stay very still, and even stiller in the presence of sharks. Several times I saw a motionless fish just a few feet from the probing snouts, and it's clearly the case that a shark has to be very close to a fish, or the fish has to be very active, for it to be detected. This electric sense has also been likened, as much as we can imagine, to having a kind of fuzzy vision that only resolves into something detectable close up. Even though the sharks might know the fish is there, they cannot distinguish it from the background coral heads until it moves, or they are right upon it. It has the horrific tension of watching *A Quiet Place* on Netflix by yourself on a Saturday night, a film, in case you haven't seen it, where making any noise gets you killed. I found myself sharing a paralysis of fear with the fish as the sharks came within striking distance of their prey.

I didn't feel fear for myself or our crew. These were relatively small fish-eating sharks. We know that because fish-eating sharks have pointy and thin hook-like teeth and because, well, we could see they were only interested in the fish. Even so, I knew to never be complacent with sharks, and in view too of the 'floating off to Costa Rica' incident, I now had a more general safety mantra I would sometimes mumble to myself underwater: 'Never be complacent at sea.'

As we clocked up our time and paid our dues to the sea we started to build up a great sequence of shots that told the story of the night hunters. If I remember correctly, it was a squirrel fish that got nailed first. They are a group of nocturnal coral fish, often with striking red bars on a silver background, and mean-looking serrations on their dorsal fins like pastry cutters. They've massive eyes too, for night vision, and when you stumble across them, under a rocky overhang or in crevices, you both look surprised. Unfortunately for them, squirrel fish are active at night, and perhaps more likely to betray themselves to sharks than sleeping fish.

When one of the whitetips bumps into a fish at night all hell breaks loose. Usually it doesn't catch the fish first time, but now the panicked prey reveals itself to the whole pack, with what must be a clearer electric picture as it tries to bolt. It's then that we see why it's useful to hunt in a pack this way, as the sharks circle the prey and cut it off, trapping it inside a corridor of coral.

Now the toothy noose shrinks, and the desperate fish tries to escape. Just as you think it will, another shark appears from the black, like a wicketkeeper, blocking its path. A lone whitetip couldn't do this by itself, of course, and that's why they need to hunt together at night. Whether you could describe this as 'co-operative hunting', or 'unintentionally co-operative and a bit grumpy hunting', is a moot point, because there doesn't seem to be any communication between the sharks ('Hey Jim, it's going around the back!'), and as far as a meal goes it's everyone for themselves. Suddenly one of the pack puts on a massive spurt, thrusts into the open crevice where its quarry is making a last stand, and shoots out the other side with the fish in its mouth, the rest of the pack following in a spume of silt and sand. If they do this together all night, the better players will get fat, but the chances are that everyone will get a meal. Even if they don't, sharks are used to getting hungry, and some say they go for weeks without a meal, though I don't think it's that long with the whitetips judging by how keen they are for a kill. For evolution to work there only has to be a slight advantage to hunting together.

* * *

After a few days we had the whitetip sequence and, with just another night to get 'pick-ups', like the point of view of a fish in the hideout of its crevice as sharks swim past, we'd decided that we'd finished what was needed. We had to get on with the list. Then it becomes a game of working out how much time to spend trying to get a sequence, to make sure you spend your time wisely, but at the same time you need the quality of filming, and you can't rush that.

Before we leave the sharks, though, there is one tricky issue we should talk about.

Sharks don't usually hunt with lights.

If you went to Africa and filmed a gazelle at night with lights, you would be alerting all its nocturnal predators pretty quickly. How, then, is it different underwater? Do our lights kill every fish they reveal to sharks? These are the ethical problems to think about when filming in this way, and there's also the issue of how the behaviours are changed by the lights: are we really showing what happens when it's completely dark?

Unless we could see like sharks see, with their finely tuned electric senses, we cannot film in total darkness. Yet strong light is something alien to sharks, and we tried not to blind them by shining it directly in their faces. As for the prey fish, yes, it will have caused some of them to be dislodged, and in their fright make themselves more apparent to the sharks, and maybe others that would have been killed in complete darkness were passed by, changing the fate of individual fish on a particular night. What it boils down to is: if you want to show these amazing behaviours at night, you need light, but you should be as careful as you can and use the minimal intervention necessary, and be off again as quick as you can, leaving the sharks and their prey to get on with it. As for altering the behaviours: perhaps somewhat, as sharks are canny beasts, yet what we were seeing were like set pieces in a football match, clearly learned way before we put them in the spotlight.

Many of the images from Cocos Island in the first series of *Blue Planet* are short but memorable moments. I remember being with Pete Scoones, looking up from the seabed into a tornado of maybe 2,000 large silver jacks that spiralled all the way to the surface. Peter was in the middle of the school and turned as the wall of silver fish went past him, and his shots recorded the awe of the moment as well as you can without being there, and almost as well as being there.

Then there were little moments we never expected to come to much, like the single little red swimming crab out in deep water that Bob caught on camera near the surface in a kind of dance. Producer Andy Byatt and editor Tim Coope made a joyful thirty seconds out of it in the 'Open Ocean' episode (it's about 17 minutes in), and when George Fenton put some almost comical music to its swimming, the clip that others might have discarded came alive.

There are nine species of hammerhead, apparently, but I've only knowingly seen three. The smallest is the bonnethead or shovelhead, that's found in mangroves and the warmer inshore waters of the USA and Central America. It's only as long as your leg, and looks like a cute puppy relative of its bigger cousins. Then I've seen the scalloped hammerheads, which are much bigger and named for the scallop-shell indentations on their hammer. And finally, I've seen the awesome giant hammerhead, growing to 6 metres (20 feet), and with a long straight cephalofoil, the wonderful scientific name for the wing on the head. They do use these foils as wings, too, giving them lift in the water and saving a bit of swimming energy. Giant hammerheads are solitary, nomadic hunters, but scalloped hammerheads are somewhat social, at least the females, and group together in shoals sometimes hundreds strong, some think as a way of attracting males. Whatever the reason, it's a really impressive sight when they 'fly' above you silhouetted against the surface.

It was these scalloped ones that we stood the most chance of filming in Cocos, because we knew they came here practically every day to be cleaned by special fish, and that one of those cleaning stations, Alcyone, was their favoured carwash.

One of the surprising things you notice first about hammerheads is that they seem scared of any unusual noise. If you accidently let your spare regulator hit your air tank with a clang, they will all scatter, and perhaps not come back for ten minutes or ever at all. They remind me of the proverbial elephants scared by mice, because compared to an awesome hammerhead we're like a mouse; anyway, they don't match the butch reputation people would give sharks.

Sharks, and many other marine creatures, find islands by detecting the disturbances they make in the magnetic field of the Earth, and often hang around near the shore, as for many an island is a handy destination for food and occasional sex. It's also a useful place to get a good scrub: these large hammerheads have clearly visible patches of shedding skin and sponge-like growths on their hide, which must itch like hell. So just for one moment the lives of some hammerheads and ourselves coincided at Cocos Island.

The film crew are lying in wait just under a ridge of large boulders, keeping still and flat like a platoon in no-man's-land,

and holding onto the rocks because this site is more exposed than most. Those with rebreathers, the diving gear that recycles your air and doesn't make bubbles, are ahead; noisy, bubbling scuba divers are at the back. Bob, in his pioneering military rebreather, is crawling slowly up to the ridge with his camera and stops. He keeps deadly still and, with no venting from his dive gear, you'd quickly lose him among the boulders.

I can't see anything at first, but then, over Bob's head, a silhouette of a hammerhead, so close that if he moves they will touch. It turns, a little at a tilt, to expose its flank, slows down and just stops. This is a signal for the pit-crew to come in, and six or so hand-sized fish, bright yellow, as though in high-vis jackets, deftly move into position, immediately finding the flecks of peeling skin and parasitic growths on the hammerhead chassis. These are the so-called barberfish, from another family of metaphors that reminds us of hairdressers and grooming, and from the biological family of butterfly fish that are specialist coral feeders.

Now I realise Bob has been cheating: all he did was wait among these cleaning fish, dotted along the ridge of the cleaning station, because he knew that pretty soon a customer comes by. The fish crew takes a little longer than those from Formula One – about ten minutes to service the shark – but they look just as professional and seem to do a good job, helped by their special scrubbing-brush teeth. Itch relieved, the hammerhead leaves the ramp, and bingo! Another sequence on the oar-fish-long shopping list ticked off.

It's not often you can get a sequence in 'the can' as quickly as that. Truthfully, I think we did go back to get some pick-ups – extra shots that will help the editor cut the scene – but the sharks didn't come as well as they did the first time, and most of it was made from the first encounter. But just in case you think it all comes easily, we spent many dives here not getting complete stories. In the underwater lucky dip, you can't always choose what you stumble across, and have to be somewhat opportunistic.

It's at this point I need to make an apology to an anonymous team of research biologists I've never met. While scouting off Dirty Rock, another of the Cocos dive sites, we noticed an unusual contraption on the seabed. It turned out to be a time-lapse camera system with a huge battery, obviously able to run for weeks on end. It was clicking, at least once a minute or so, so clearly working. Goodness knows what sort of experiment it was set up for; perhaps to see how many fish passed every hour on particular days, or even how the light changed.

So what do a tired team of wildlife film-makers do, finding themselves with a rival imaging system and a bit of spare air, and possibly slightly drunk on blood nitrogen? Moon at the science camera, of course! I can't remember who suggested it – probably Bob – or even how we understood the silent signals (PADI don't teach the one for 'mooning'), but we all understood pretty quick, well versed now in opportunism. In a row we lined up in front of the camera, and bent over in a professionally framed composition, though we didn't take our kit off, in case you're asking. Like setting a self-timer, we waited for the next shutter click, heard more clearly in fluid than air, and when it came we laughed so much we nearly drowned. So please forgive us, marine scientist, when you found a frame of five men with bottoms to camera in your research data, of 5 June 2000, from a remote island off Central America. Actually, if you did: can we have the picture?

After a week or so in Chatham Bay we had got used to living there virtually on our own. There were a couple of commercial sport diver ships from time to time, but we pretty much had the place to ourselves. So, I got a surprise one morning when the frosted glass of the miniature bathroom in the *Inzan Tiger* went dark, and a huge shadow of steel appeared outside. It was a ship called the *Quest*, as big as a warship and with a helicopter on its back deck.

We had looked into doing aerial shots of Cocos, but it required a lot of planning and expense. At about 400 miles from the nearest airport it would need a fuel dump for a small helicopter to do the journey from Costa Rica and then fly around the island for a few hours. It was just too expensive. So, like a dog seeing a squirrel, the first thing I thought about the *Quest* arriving was: 'HELICOPTER!'

Heinz, our captain, radioed over to them, and soon I was talking to Andrew Wight. It turned out, wouldn't you know, that they were here to make an underwater TV series called *Adventures of the Quest*, and Andrew was a film producer working with the Australian company Beyond. I asked him if I could use his helicopter and, in what I would find out was his typically generous spirit, he said, 'Yeah mate, come on over and we'll talk about it over some beers,' or words to that effect. No red tape, no cautious reserve: only a sense of fun and wanting to help. First, he showed me around the ship, owned I think by one of the founders of the Super 8 Motel chain, who made a fortune in the 1970s marketing cheap motel rooms for $8.88 a night.

You may have noticed that billionaires are often involved in marine research and filming – because it's so expensive. To keep a big ship like the *Quest* at sea can cost more than $40,000 *a day*. That covers the daily wage of thirty or so crew, with hopefully some left over for the fuel bill and running costs. The deep sea subs (Chapter 1) from Harbor Branch cost $20,000 *per dive* (in 2000), not to mention the cost of the support ship that carried them, and were in part funded by a pharmaceuticals fortune. Jacques Cousteau needed the help of Loel Guinness to buy his ship the RV *Calypso*, and the patronage of Prince Albert I of Monaco for much of his work. David and Lucile Packard of Hewlett-Packard fame funded the Monterey Bay Aquarium, and its associated research institute, MBARI, via the Packard Foundation. So it's fun to know that beer, monarchy, baby powder, home computers and motel rooms are part of the funding mix that brings ocean images to your living room. Although not *The Blue Planet*, of course: part-funded by the licence fee, the compulsory tax everyone in the UK pays for the BBC service, and also with 'co-production' deals from international broadcasters that wanted to show the series.

When Andrew invited me over to his ship we had a great chat about the filming business, and then I told him I'd come to bend my BBC credit card to get some flying time in that helicopter on the back deck. I had to call the office on the BBC sat phone for this one, as I knew there were insurance and qualification issues for the airworthiness of the helicopter, but really with very little fuss it was arranged, and we could fly the next day. I got the machine for more or less the price of the fuel.

Bob had decided to use his film camera to film the aerials, because it was possible to run it at double speed and so, when slowed down, would even out the bumps. In those days digital cameras couldn't do slow motion. There was no camera mount, either: he would just hold the camera steady and point it out of the helicopter window. This was one of the last times I was to work with film on a BBC documentary, and Bob, having seen the writing on the wall, already had his Aaton Super 16mm film camera up for sale. I remember Florian, the cameraman on this trip making the 'behind-the-scenes' video, asking Bob, 'Who would buy a film camera like that now?' To which Bob replied, 'Someone who doesn't know anything about the business!' I notice a similar camera with a good lens today is about $4,000 on eBay, so perhaps they're becoming collectors' items, although getting the film stock might be tricky.

At first light we were in the aircraft hangar at the stern of *Quest* and, after a safety briefing, we took off and flew low across the water. The Australian pilot was a Vietnam veteran, no doubt having flown those famous Bell Huey helicopters on thousands of missions, and had, it turns out, a slightly sadistic sense of humour. As we took off a red light on the dash lit up.

'Bloody hell, mate!' he exclaimed, banging the panel. 'I've never seen that light on before!' As he continued to hit it the light turned off, and all seemed well, except our heart rates. It was, we learnt afterwards, a routine test of some kind, like the ignition light that turns on briefly before you start the engine of your car.

It was important to fly early if you wanted to see Cocos without the clouds, because the island is covered with tall trees and dense rainforest vegetation. Every afternoon this forest reluctantly gives up its vapour and, as it rises and condenses in a cool sea breeze, a white head of clouds builds up over the whole island. In fact, that's the first sign you might see of Cocos as you approach from perhaps 30 miles away. It doesn't seem much to remark on, but it's a sign of thriving life: an ecosystem that seems to control the weather, and self-sustaining with the fresh water falling back as rain. I have seen many small

Blue whale surfacing with a mouth full of food, often shrimp-like krill or sometimes pelagic red crabs, in their millions. Baja, Mexico, where most of the *Blue Planet* whale shots were taken for the opening of the first series of *Blue Planet*. *(© Mark Carwardine)*

The Johnson Sea Link II being launched using the 'A' frame (the submersible was laid off in 2010). (© NOAA – National Oceanic and Atmospheric Administration, photographer Liz Baird)

Dan Boggess, one of the sub's pilots, doubling as part of the recovery team as he prepares to attach a restraining cable to the returning submersible. (© John Ruthven)

The author after diving in the submersible, hoping the photographer will not block his way to the loo! (© John Ruthven)

Hull section from a 600-year-old Polynesian voyaging canoe found in New Zealand in 2014 showing a turtle carving, a powerful symbol in Polynesian culture. *(Dilys A. Johns, Geoffrey J. Irwin, and Yun K. Sung, PNAS October 14, 2014, 111 (41) 14728–14733; first published September 29, 2014)*

Seaweed pressing from Amelia Griffiths, the Victorian Queen of Seaweeds – this pressing could be nearly 180 years old and yet keeps a brilliant red colour. *(Royal Albert Memorial Museum and Art Gallery, Exeter City Council, RAMM)*

Atmospheric diving suit by Alphonse and Theodore Carmagnole. In the late 1800s there were experiments with diving suits of all kinds. The two brothers from Marseilles came up with this one that had 25 glass viewing ports spaced at the average distance of human eyes. Musée national de la Marine, Paris *(© Rama Creative Commons Attribution-Share Alike 2.0 France license)*

(above) Miranda Lowe, Curator at the Natural History Museum, London, has helped safeguard the precious glass models made by pioneering glass artists Leopold and Rudolf Blaschka in the late 1800s. *(© The Trustees of the Natural History Museum, London)*

The musky octopus – a Blaschka glass model. *(© The Trustees of the Natural History Museum, London)*

A Garibaldi fish, characteristic of the California kelp forests, with 'God light' shining through the fronds of the kelp. *(Michael Bogner/Shutterstock)*

(above) Blue Planet cameraman Tom Fitz looking for a seal to film. The big housing is made by Vince Pace of Pace Technologies who also co-designed the 3D cameras used on James Cameron's *Avatar* feature. *(© John Ruthven)*

(right) Young harbour seal, close enough to the camera to see its reflection in the underwater housing. *(Joe Belanger/Shutterstock)*

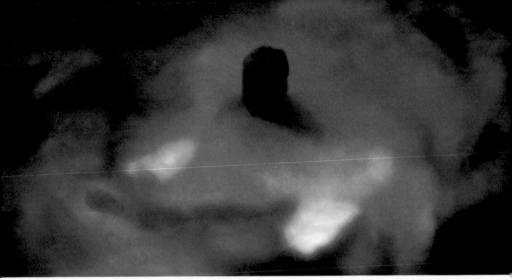

John Ruthven swimming in Bioluminescence Bay in Vieques, Puerto Rico. Dinoflagellates create this bioluminescence when disturbed – as seen by Martin Dohrn's Starlight cameras. *(© Martin Dohrn, Ammonite Ltd)*

(above) The peacock mantis shrimp in all its glory – with the swivelling eyes on stalks constantly looking at you. *(mantaphoto/iStock)*

(left) The eyes of a mantis shrimp have sixteen different colour receptors (we have three) – perhaps the most extraordinary eye in the animal kingdom. *(CHECHIN/Adobe Stock)*

(above) Malpelo Island, Colombia, from the water. A UNESCO World Heritage Site, it's like the real 'Tracy Island' of *Thunderbirds* fame! *(© John Ruthven)*

(right) Getting onto the island isn't easy as there is no gentle shore, just sheer volcanic cliff faces rising from the sea. *(© John Ruthven)*

(above) Huge shoals of sharks lie below, like these scalloped hammerheads. *(Janos Rautonen/Shutterstock)*

(left) The huge Colombian flag at the top of Malpelo dwarfs our crew. Left to right: Florian Graner, 2nd camera, the author, Colombian military personnel, and Bob Cranston, DOP, at the top of Malpelo. *(© John Ruthven)*

(above and left) Sir David Attenborough and crew at the bow of our rib as he does a piece about the blue whale for both *Blue Planet* and *The Life of Mammals*, off San Francisco, 2000. It was a moment of pure joy for him. You are not allowed to get this close to the whales unless you have scientific permits; we were with Bruce Mate and his team from the University of Oregon who were monitoring the movements of blue whales. (© *John Ruthven*)

(below) The fluke of the blue whale with water streaming off is an iconic shot in the first series of *Blue Planet*. From the side you can see the muscular powerhouse that drives this massive beast up to 30 mph (50kph) through the water. (© *Mark Carwardine*)

islands that don't have such a sponge of forest vegetation, and they are often barren. We flew around the north of the island for about three one-hour missions, and were able to get those rare aerials to highlight how such an island is the only destination in the wide and lonely open sea for thousands of marine creatures all around.

It's great that we got them, but it's not what I remember most about that helicopter. Andrew had told me that he flew helicopters sometimes too, but he wanted us to go with the Vietnam vet because of his experience. Very, very sadly, about twelve years later Andrew was piloting a helicopter to do some aerials in Australia with Mike deGruy, another of the top camera people on *Blue Planet*, and they crashed, and both were killed.

The two of them packed a hell of a lot into their shortened lives, putting passion into all sorts of underwater films. Andrew had gone on to write and produce the underwater cave movie *Sanctum*, highly acclaimed, and Mike, as well as many spectacular shoots, like the one we did in the Johnson Sea Link submarine, was an eloquent spokesman for the wonders of the deep, and became an environmental reporter and photographer of the marine pollution caused by the Deepwater Horizon oil spill of 2010. In a film about Mike's life and work with the sea called *Diving Deep: The Life and Times of Mike deGruy*, produced and directed by his wife Mimi, there's a classic Mike moment as he's winched off a ship in a 'Newtsuit'. That's a hard suit that keeps you at atmospheric pressure without the usual compression problems for the human body, and it's good to at least 1,000 feet (300 metres); it's chunky and painted bright yellow. We see a close-up of his astronaut-like helmet and Mike's chirpy face inside, and he looks just like Buzz Lightyear.

'To infinity and beyond,' he chuckles as he's winched off the deck into the water. He's a man that went 'beyond' all his life, and I hope he's exploring another watery planet somewhere else in the universe right now.

The sea is canny with its secrets, and sometimes – often – it seems as though nothing is happening. Nothing, day after day. Nothing, nothing, nothing: just waves. And then – *boom!* It all kicks off. That was happening right now in Cocos: nothing. We had come here with the promise of huge shoals of sharks, waters thick with massive hammerheads and silky sharks, the *Islands of the Sharks*. Maybe we were just spoilt? We had the whitetip sequence in the bag, after all, and the cleaning station. As ever, though, we were greedy for more: we wanted a massive predatory moment where the big sharks, tuna and dolphins would all pile in for a massive sardine snack: a gigantic feast on what's known as a 'bait ball': the Holy Grail – a tornado of swirling bait fish, like sardines or anchovy, caught at the surface.

The first time I'd ever seen one had been off the coast of Costa Rica, and the local fishermen had assured us, 'You'll only see that once in your lifetime if you're lucky!' It didn't inspire much hope, but don't look, don't get, and sure enough it happened for us twice in a week: millions of whirling bait fish forming a huge spinning ball pushed against the surface by a thousand fearsome predators. As the yellow-fin tuna attack they javelin right out of the water, hitting a large anchovy with such force that it explodes into pieces, a silver confetti of scales on the churning sea. When we got that it might have been one of the first ever filmed. This time, if it could look like World War III and last for about two hours, so much the better. But although we were seeing one or two tiny moments like this, they were just small 'flash in the pans': a few birds swooping at the surface, a couple of distant shark fins, then back to the 'empty' sea.

One time we found millions of green snappers in the shallows, and Bob was excited because he knew the sharks would follow them in towards the shore. But the water was unusually cloudy that day and we could hardly see what was going on, let alone film. Then suddenly the water cleared – maybe the currents had changed direction – and the weather became calm and still. On such days you can see whale blows or the slightest perturbation of the surface from miles. They are the best days to film wildlife at sea.

On this smooth and fish-scale-silver sea, we suddenly notice some massive ripples. It's a few boat lengths away, but we're soon on top of it, or should I say to one side, because you don't want to go straight over a bait ball and break it up; you'll need at least fifteen minutes to have any chance of getting in to film.

But these aren't bait fish. They are very dark black for a start and, from their shapes silhouetted against white sand, they look like well-rounded tadpoles. Two stubby flapping fins on their tails and an occasional flick of short spines on the head give me the name: black trigger fish, and they're spawning in their thousands. This is not nothing – it's a '*boom!*'

Trigger fish, I notice, are listed in *Reef Fish Identification: Tropical Pacific*, by Gerald Allen et al., one of the best and most comprehensive guides, under 'Odd-shaped fishes'. They certainly are – indeed, hardly look as if they could swim at all, moving forward in what seems like permanently unstable lunges. There are only about forty kinds, but obviously they're a very successful type, because they live in subtropical and tropical waters all over the world. The gun trigger spines on the head are used to wedge themselves into holes at night, apparently, but I've never seen this myself.

Spawning fish are oblivious of almost anything else but sex. White clouds of eggs and sperm tumble like dust as they mill in the column of water. Occasionally they do scatter as a whitetip splits the pack, their black curtain parting to reveal it. Lazy during the day, whitetips can be seen just sitting on the seabed (no, it's not true that 'all sharks have to keep swimming or else they die'), but there's nothing like the chance of a good meal to wake these drama queens. None seems to be able to pull a trigger, though, as the black hordes just dance around the sharks, a few shark-lengths out of reach. On the seabed we manage to get a few beautiful shots of the murmurating shoals, and the beautiful way the fish scatter at the arrival of the whitetips. Then, as quickly as they've formed, the black clouds disperse, leaving only some embarrassed-looking sharks still crouching on the seabed for no particular reason, a bit slow to realise their quarry has gone, but no doubt overcome by the smell of fish oil and eggs.

Over the next few days we diligently searched for more bait balls, unusual fish, strange happenings, but nothing much came up. Peter had a flood in his camera housing. He made his own housings, and was constantly tinkering with them. 'If you put something in water, sooner or later it's going to get wet,' he used to say. As you can imagine, seawater is the best thing if you want to instantly destroy a circuit board, but for him this was not too much to worry about, even though we are probably talking about $100K-worth of kit, because he had the camera standing on a frame about 2 centimetres (about an inch) off the base of its box, so the water collected underneath. When it flooded you could see it, because at that time his housings were made of Plexiglas, and at times about a tea cup of cloudy straw coloured seawater sloshed about at the bottom biding its time to murder the electronics, but if you kept the camera housing upright it never would. (Once, though, I was told, a nameless producer decided to have a look around a lagoon in the recovery boat while Peter was diving — something that's wrong for so many reasons — and, Sod's law, Peter's camera leaked. As Peter surfaced said producer was nowhere to be seen; he waited patiently with his leaking camera, trying desperately to keep it upright, for the best part of an hour.) Peter was gluing, soldering and adjusting his camera so often that you learned to ignore minor dramas, but his knowledge of how to get the best out of the vulnerable electronics of a submerged video camera was second to none, and his images were the best.

Cocos had been billed to us as having shark shoals that you couldn't swim through: proverbial 'walls of sharks', and certainly massive schools of hammerheads. When Cousteau and crew came here in the 1980s they caught fish for supper with their T-shirts. But the sharks we saw, although magnificent, were most often in ones and twos, and although we glimpsed a shiver of hammerheads in the distance one day, they took fright, and the hammerhead-count never reached its advertised level. Another testament to the not so slow deterioration of marine habitats perhaps.

Worse, we began to realise that a lot of the coral in Cocos had been killed, broken into rubble and smothered with green algae. When the water gets too warm the sensitive coral polyps start to die, in a process called coral 'bleaching'. Some of this is normal, but with climate change it's happening much more frequently. One of the things that exacerbates the warming is a reversal of the normal wind patterns, called El Niño. They've been occurring for thousands of years at roughly seven-year intervals and, although mostly mild, some are severe, killing everything on the reef and generally messing about with the world's climate. It's thought one such warming event may have been responsible for starting off the French Revolution, as it caused poor crop yields in Europe in 1789. Today such events appear to be more frequent and more severe than ever, although the exact interaction between global warming and increased El Niño events is still up for discussion. However, what we were seeing in Cocos was the aftermath of one of the strongest El Niños on record, in 1997 to '98, which is thought to have killed 16 per cent of the world's coral reefs. By the time we arrived in 2000 there were a lot of coral skeletons to show for it, but also some signs of recovery and new growth.

So despite what we had already recorded and the overall magnificence of Cocos, we were getting a bit frustrated. When nothing much is happening it's often a good idea to try something a bit left-field. I know this because I've watched *Men In Black III*, and there's a bit where the two main detectives have lost their way but, rather than do any more detecting, Tommy Lee Jones (Agent K) just says, 'We need pie,' and off they go to a pie shop to find inspiration. Just when we didn't know what to do next in Cocos we were invited to a barbeque on a big dive boat that had recently turned up, the *Undersea Hunter*. Although the barbeque was mainly sausages it turned out to be our pie.

That evening on the *Undersea Hunter*, about ten days into our Cocos diving, we met about twenty or so sports divers. Like all their wealthy breed they had great kit, and the latest semi-pro video cameras. During the meal they passed around a camera playing back some shots taken just a couple of days before on another island about 300 miles south, in Colombian waters. The little screen was filled with thousands of sharks: big ones, mainly silky sharks, but also massive groups of hammerheads and mixed schools of silky, hammerhead and Galapagos. Everything looked so healthy – the streamlined silkies, swift and inquisitive, hunting in deep blue and open seas – and the numbers were mind-blowing. It was as if this small video camera was a time machine and we were seeing the ocean as it was in the days before mass fishing, pollution and global warming. This was what we'd been looking for – images of these island hotspots that would take your breath away!

Without hesitation I knew we had to go to this island, and as quickly as possible, as we did not know if the sharks were just there this week or always hung around. This little spot, about two days' sailing from us, was called Malpelo. The name, ignoring the feminine and masculine forms, is two Spanish words put together: *mal*, 'bad', and *pelo*, 'hair'. I didn't realise at the time, or I might have wondered if we were about to have a 'bad hair day'.

It was time to get the credit card out again and bend some BBC dollars on the sat 'phone. Malpelo, being part of Colombia, had different visa requirements to Costa Rica and we had a multinational crew, all at sea and unable to go to any embassies. In addition, Malpelo has a secretive military base on it that understandably they don't want filmed. Once again, the office back home came up trumps. With a quick chat, maybe no more than three phone calls in total, I talked it through with the production team in Bristol and they passed on our request to the Colombian Embassy in London. Odd requests happen all the time in the TV world and everyone expects them, so by and large the team is unfazed. Even when I filmed elephant sex in the series *Battle of the Sexes*, no one thought it was anything out of the ordinary for a wildlife film-maker. I dare say there was a lot more planning back home than I saw from a coral reef 8,000 miles away. We were given the OK as we were already underway to Malpelo, and told to report to the military base on the island.

The journey took just over thirty-six hours in some pretty exposed seas. I did a rough calculation, and with the *Inzan Tiger* probably able to motor along at about 8 knots, that figures. It was almost non-stop except for stumbling across a very big tree. Yes, there are trees in the ocean – horizontal ones, that is, floating on the surface, getting gradually heavier with marine growths and barnacles and they're literally waterlogged of course.

Caught hundreds of miles offshore, marine debris, and even big things like trees, are often trapped in what are called 'gyres': gigantic bath-drain swirls of water spinning slowly across oceans. Depending on who you talk to, there are at least five, thirteen or umpteen notable ones in the world's seas. For example, Midway Atoll, at the north-western end of the Hawaiian Archipelago (but an unincorporated area of the USA, so not part of Hawaii state), sits in the middle of the North Pacific gyre, in what's called a 'convergent zone' – where stuff spins towards the centre of the plug hole. The shameful quantity of plastic here is a fatal problem for the beautiful Lysan albatross, but at least this is a place where plastic ocean debris have been extensively studied, for example by John Klavitter, a biologist of the US Fish and Wildlife Service. It's often difficult to date such debris but one piece, an identifiable olive-green tag found in a dead albatross chick turned out to have come from a US bomber shot down in 1944. That bit of plastic had been trapped in the gyre for perhaps seventy years!

So a large tree, perhaps fallen from a cliff and washed to the sea in a flooding river, may have been in the water a very long time, and in the process becomes its own little mini-hotel and waypoint for creatures of the open ocean. A micro-island of its own, if you like. Definitely worth a look at what's under it if you happen to be passing, and we were.

The hard surface a floating tree provides is rare in the ocean, and even rarer hundreds of miles from shore, and as such is always encrusted with barnacles. Predominantly they're goose-necked barnacles, so called because they were once thought to be the young of barnacle geese, whose nests had never been seen in Europe in the days before it was realised that birds migrate. What's more they thought they were part of a tree because they were often found on driftwood. These barnacles are also stalked beasts that grow a coin-sized taco shell on the end of their holding stem. In close-up you can see a brush of purple 'feet', which are the feeding tentacles that pulse from their smiling, yellow-edged gapes. We saw two hawksbill turtles come to nibble them, crunching and scraping the shells even though they'd tucked in their feet. The turtles quickly ducked their heads underwater too when they saw us. But a diver beneath this floating timber is in for even greater treats.

The following line expresses so well life in the open sea that I've found myself editing it out of this book twice already: *I once saw a small paintbrush floating in the middle of nowhere with perhaps twenty fish under it.* Imagine, then, a log the size of a forest tree. This one was no pine either, but a deciduous beauty with many branching limbs. Once shading animals on land, now it sheltered marine creatures, and where light once dappled through its leaves, now it dimples through the waves casting halos among the fish. We stopped the boat half a football pitch away from the tree, not wanting to bump into it. Engines idling, we drifted with the giant stump for about an hour to see which way it was going, and then snorkelled over with cameras.

The water is a slightly foggy blue – surprising, as you'd expect crystal-clear water so far from shore – but like seeing through thousands of sheets of clear glass, each one compounding the tiniest impurity until the furthest plate becomes smoky. That's possibly why the rainbow runners are cloudy blue, underlined by stripes of green, yellow, and neon blue, exactly mimicking the mild blue fog and flecks of sunlight at the surface. These torpedo-barrelled fish, some nearly a metre long (let's say 3 feet), are here in their thousands, but you would hardly know it at first. They're swimming in wide circles under the tree, using it as a reference point, coming and going, appearing like ghosts, then lighting beautiful flames of colour as they pass and disappear back into the blue. The precise point at which you lose them is hard to pin down, as when you watch an aeroplane and suddenly it becomes too small to see any more, although in theory it's there somewhere still and you can hear it, right in front of you in the blue. The rainbow runners get at least four stars, perhaps losing one because they have no red, surely an essential colour in any rainbow.

Then along came the five-star fish. Catching us unawares, a squadron of huge and unlikely-looking, brilliant-blue and but-tered-yellow fish fly by as if attacking, but they're clearly not interested in us, only each other. Two with curious rounded foreheads, like balding professors, are swimming in parallel at top speed, which someone once measured to be as much as 57.5 mph (nearly 100 km/h), a phenomenal velocity in the sticky fluid of water. These are sparring bull dorado, probably the most beautiful fish in open water; let's say in the top ten of all oceanic fish anyway. They're also called Mahi-mahi, meaning 'very strong' in Hawaiian, and they must indeed put up a fight on a fishing line, weighing as much as a small child and almost as big. Sadly for them, they have that fatal evolutionary flaw of being tasty to humans, and are a staple open-water game fish in the Pacific. I once saw one up close just after it had been caught and struck over the head, bleeding to death on the deck, its beautiful vivid-gold colour draining away to grey as it died, a gruesome metaphor for the way we treat the sea and its creatures.

Guilt can somewhat be assuaged, because Mahi-mahi, also known as dolphin fish, aside from the more romantic 'el dorado', are extremely fast-growing, and for the moment on a list of sustainable seafood options. It tells you something about their lifestyle that they can grow so fast out here in the blue. The speed and power make them an awesome predator as they catch up with flying fish and squid, destroy open water crabs and mash mackerel. Yet even they can't resist a good tree floating in the blue wilderness, and we see them alternatively displaying and hunting under its boughs as their spectacular fly-bys continue.

Close up under the tree itself, small clouds of tiny fish fry flitter in the sunlight. If we could stay here for days (something we attempted to do in *Blue Planet II*), we would find out whether such fish are loyal to the tree and grew up here over days, weeks and months. It obviously gives them a place to shelter, and the algae, barnacles and detritus on the tree provide food, and overall it could be a good spot for a kindergarten, as long as would be Nemos don't stray too far from the tree's protection into the fast lanes of bigger fish.

Who knows what turns up at this 24-hour ocean service station? No one has ever dived on an open-water tree like this at night. Even during the day, you get the idea that bigger eyes are watching – a hungry oceanic whitetip shark, for example, one of the few to be really concerned about if you saw it out here, perhaps gone days without a meal. This floating timber is a waterhole in the water, if that's possible, and a memorable flash of life in the blue as we passed, making us a bit late for our next appointment. It will be dark by the time we rock up to the rock of Malpelo.

It's a full moon, and the light falls on the sea and sparkles back in moonlight streaks thrown across the water as the sun does in the day, illuminating a black and faint-blue watercolour palette. At the horizon our satellite planet and the sea reveal themselves to be a close coalition, the Moon endlessly pulling on the ocean, and presumably the shifting mass of water pulling back. In the distance, even darker than the night, a dome-shaped silhouette, the island of of Malpelo. Here, about 17 million years ago, a massive volcano climaxed above what's now called the Malpelo Ridge to reach the surface world and make a tiny blip in the blue.

As we get nearer the island, we can hear moon-stirred birds: masked, blue-footed and brown boobies that must be sheltering on the cliffs, chattering like teenagers stealing extra hours of the night. The Moon's higher now, but as we reach our mooring it's suddenly blotted out by the cliffs 400 feet above our ship. Heinz, our captain, obviously knows this isolated place better than you might hope, and finds a white buoy he knew was there to tie to overnight. There's a slight anxiety of not knowing whether the rope will hold and we'll be dashed against the cliffs in the dark, but with a reassuring groan of tension the ropes tighten and the boat stays still, apart from a slow sideways rotation, backwards and forwards, in the current that's flowing still, even in the island's shadow. Hair salt-soaked, sleepy, we go gratefully to our cabins.

Light changes everything, and in the morning sun the baldness of the rock confirms the island's Spanish name. The strangeness of this place imprints more moments than usual in the everyday, and a rock like this sticking out from blue sea in every direction is a very vivid memory. It's only about a mile long, and there are three prominent bumps: bubbles of volcanic rock cooled and worn by the wind for millions of years.

Since it's a very tall island without any sloping shoreline it's difficult to get onto it, but we're required to report to the Colombian military base to confirm our presence. As part of the deal to come here (this was still in the tetchy days of revolutionary armed forces in Colombia), we had to promise not to film the base, which lay on a terrace, one hill along from the highest peak of *Cerro de La Mona*, 'Monkey Mountain', and to abide by any instructions we were given by the soldiers. Twenty years later I can perhaps tell you that with its angular red roof the base looked like a branch of Pizza Hut.

Getting onto the island inevitably involved climbing, although not the kind you might think. On the end of a gantry sticking out about 30 feet over the sea was an old rope ladder. Manoeuvring under this ropy ladder until it slid across the ship's deck, we grabbed it and made a hairy climb up onto the gantry as though being rescued by a helicopter at sea. A short steep climb up a scree path and we came to the army base, where some friendly soldiers greeted us and we signed their visitors' book. They were pleased to get the delivery of beer and chocolate Heinz had thoughtfully supplied. Some of these young men were on national service, I think, and pretty homesick stuck on this stone for several months. They were here only to provide a presence, really, as without a permanent ship they could not police fishing rights, although Colombia owning Malpelo greatly increases the area of its territorial waters. Slightly higher up from the base on a small plateau was the most enormous national flag I have ever come across – you could have made several family-sized tents from it and still had cloth to spare, although the yellow tents would be more numerous than the blue or red ones, if you look at the relative size of the yellow, blue and red stripes of the Colombian flag.

My radio days experience means I still record radio pieces whenever I find myself somewhere unusual, and so I did a short talk with Florian Graner, the cameraman who came with us on the top of Malpelo – it became part of a *Wild Tale* for BBC Radio 4. We sat on the rocks near to the flag and discussed the view: stones, mainly, but if you looked carefully among them there were peppered black lizards of various kinds: a slender, pointy-headed species which is a type of anole lizard endemic to Malpelo; a more chunky kind nearly a foot long with a blunt face; and a third species, thin and paler, a type of Colombian gecko, but only found here about forty years ago. Among them some fairly large land crabs, a shade of muddy tomato, and they too are a species found only on Malpelo, *Johngarthia malpilensis*, although pretty similar to those on the Colombian coast. Land crabs, you may have guessed, live on land, but still have to breed in the sea. They still have internal gills like underwater crabs, but on the land ones they seem to have more blood vessels and are effectively lungs.

So, apart from the birds, that's the list of larger creatures on Malpelo: three lizards and a crab. There are about eighty species of so called 'macrofauna' too – things like crickets, ants and beetles, many of them also unique to this little rock. It sounds exotic, but the evolutionary recipe for endemic island species, it seems, is just to maroon them on an island and leave them to get on with it for a few million years.

Although neglected until the last part of the twentieth century, the biology of the island has recently been more thoroughly studied, and some of the crabs and lizards even counted. In 2010 a team estimated there were 833,000 red crabs here, by multiplying up the average number they counted in a square metre, and a similar study was done on the geckos, which are nocturnal, and concluded there were 114,000. It must have been a hazardous exercise coming up with that figure, because the scientists had to walk near cliff edges with only head torches every night for a month, and you wouldn't want to get too distracted counting geckos.

All in all, that's quite a lot of creatures in a small space – barely a square kilometre, or less than half a square mile. When you come to think of it, they are all descendants of the shipwrecked and stranded, floating here on vegetation or maybe even stowaways on human craft. No one ever came to rescue these castaways, and they had to adapt or die. Even those that survived must have had a very tough time – something I am reminded of by a sharp nip on the bum that makes me cry out mid-sentence in the radio recording. It's one of those ravenous red crabs, and it really does hurt! I don't doubt that if you fell sick here these crabs would finish you off pretty quick, as would the larger lizard species, wonderfully called the dotted galliwasp, which eats the other lizards, crabs and even seabird poo; they're not fussy.

Ultimately the Malpelo food web starts in the sea, and needs the transfer of nutrients by the seabirds (mainly Nazca boobies) to the land to make it work. There are a few plants, some quite surprising ferns, but only in one or two scrubby patches. It's obviously an ecosystem balanced, literally, on a cliff edge. Anything you leave on the floor for even a few minutes is nibbled by the crabs, so you have to be careful on this very hungry island. Yet if you thought *these* creatures were rare, odd or misunderstood, we haven't started yet on what's underwater all around.

There is nowhere else in the world I have dived that is like Malpelo. In our first few days we split up into different teams. Bob Cranston and Florian Graner pair up, and Peter Scoones and myself make another diving team, not in the water simultaneously, but when one has finished a dive the other team descends, and that way we are working as efficiently as possible with the boat support, a six-person inflatable, running back and forth from the *Inzan Tiger*, crewed by three diver-support personnel, following us from the surface by monitoring our bubbles.

My first impression is that the sea is just fizzing with fish. As I descend with Peter our paths are blocked by a wall of silvery brown snappers, a massive shoal of interlocking fish, each bigger than two outstretched hands. We try to go around them, but the wall extends out of sight. We try to go through them, and for several minutes we are nosing past their silver sides as they slowly part. I have never seen fish schools so dense or fish so large and healthy, and again I am amazed by these visions of the sea before industrial fishing and pollution.

Peter has a way of suddenly disappearing, camouflaging himself against the seabed like a sniper crawling into position for his target, or hooking himself onto a crevice with his little grappling clamp that he always carries. And sure enough, before I have had a chance to remind myself to keep up and keep an eye on him, he's gone, lost on the other side of more fish schools. If you read the dive safety manuals they'll tell you to make a brief attempt to find your buddy when separated but then to ascend where you will hopefully rendezvous at the surface. In reality I knew there was no way Peter was going to do that, at least not for a short separation. Dive photographers are somewhat maverick too and don't want anyone close to them disturbing their subjects, so it's tricky following at arm's length. Coming up isn't great either because the rules say not to re-descend immediately, effectively aborting the dive. You just have to use sensible judgement, though you never completely stop worrying, even if the boat above is also closely following each diver's bubbles.

So for a while I am all alone at 20 metres in a fish fairground, and like fireworks their swirling displays go off all around me: little red creole fish in what seems like millions play in the current, yellow goatfish flutter like the flag of Colombia itself way above us on the cliff top, a grouper hunts among the whipper snappers, using their cover to sneak up on its prey. 'Whippersnappers' – I'm not sure if that is a name deliberately to christen cheekily confident little fish, or just casually given to common snapper species by a biologist who missed the pun. It's true that you'd soon run out of names for everything here and start to use funny ones. The varieties are further enhanced because, like the land animals on the rock above, many of the non-migratory fish are 'endemic': variants peculiar to Malpelo.

Only the life here underwater is a hundred times more varied than it is on the rocks above.

Like many small islands far out to sea this place is an oasis. Soundings only a few miles from Malpelo reveal waters nearly 2 miles, or about 3 kilometres, deep, and its volcanic walls block and push up deep-water currents that dump long-lost fertiliser from the sea floor around its cliffs. The effect is to attract 'pelagics': large open-water creatures, to the wealth of food this natural fertiliser promotes, and millions of 'local' fish too. The evidence is all around me.

I look down and suck another deep breath of amazement from my tank, because below me is a whale shark, blue and spotty, a smallish one only about three divers long, but as it pushes clouds of yellow fish out of the way it makes a stunning sight. I know its length because I can see the silhouette of a diver right by it to compare. Ah! That's Peter, hovering in mid-water, mask looking into the camera viewfinder and waiting patiently for it to come past him. I think that became a 20-second shot in *Blue Planet*, among a montage of wonderful fish scenes, to illustrate the abundance of life at sea mounts.

Although we had seen that video of thousands of hammerheads and open-water silky sharks around Malpelo just a couple of days ago, there were, typically, none to be seen here now, and the only notable shark so far was that plankton-eating whale shark. For the next couple of days we saw spectacular amounts of fish, but the big sharks seemed to have gone. I now got the familiar 'director's twitch of anxiety' in my stomach about spending large amounts of other people's cash without anything to show for it, and I had stuck my neck out like a goose barnacle to come here, even if the whole team had agreed.

We could only continue our daily plan and a relatively intense diving schedule to search for them. Again, Bob and Florian went in, and then Peter and I, together with a dive guide, Tina, swapped in rotation as they came out, doubling our 'down time' (in diving it means the exact opposite to what it does on land!). Bob and Florian were on rebreathers, and so were able to stay down longer than the rest of us, the 'open circuit' scuba team.

One such dive started relatively shallow near the shore. I sank down to the seabed, where there was what seemed to be a huge, dark-green tree with waving arms poking out from the rocks. As I descended it became clear that its boughs were not wood at all, or even coral, but the enormous muscular bodies of giant green moray eels, each as long as a man, with about six standing straight from a crevice writhing their heads into the current. They were about the circumference of a cyclists' thigh, and looked like they'd been working out in anticipation of just this opportunity for a good fleshy meal. Like one of those dreams where you can't get away, I found myself on a trajectory that would soon coincide with their mouths. If you've ever met such an eel you would know that they seem a bit humourless, and the dirty look they give you is not helped by their prune-shrivelled and peppered green skin that gives them 'something of the night'. This is not idle talk or a false reputation, by the way, because there are cases of divers being attacked by morays, having chunks taken out of their face or even thumbs and fingers bitten off, though usually only if you do something silly like feed them or land on them or something, as I was just about to do. As I got nearer, they started making faces at me, and showed their stunted but sharp teeth in a universal threat gesture, as if they were pirates lunging forward and shouting *'Arrrrgh!'*

I squirted a little more air into my buoyancy jacket and giving them the heave ho, landing gently on the rocks just out of eel reach. But one of the bigger ones still took exception and, as he wriggled out of the moray wedge, I knew I had better swim in the opposite direction, and fast. He followed me, and it was only by rising up towards the shallows again that I got away. I have never seen so many massive morays as at Malpelo, and it became a bit of a moray roulette every time we went down to the seabed as to whether you might land on their 'nest' – many eels together in their favourite spots between the boulders.

Usually, at the start of a dive, you do the deep stuff first, and then head for the shallows. This kind of 'dive profile' means you naturally decompress as you slowly return to the surface. Diving around an island, that often means you just let go of the seabed and slowly come up into open water. As you drift away from the shore it soon becomes only blue, any sign of land disappears, and at Malpelo, whose cliff sides plummet beneath the waves without any beach, you will be floating over very deep water, and possibly schools of large open ocean sharks.

It was towards the end of our fourth dive on day two, and Peter and I were just about to get out when we saw them. Only ones or twos at first, literally out of the blue. Then hundreds. *Hundreds* of sharks. We must have had about ten minutes of air left in our tanks, but I filmed them on my small video camera, something I'd found useful as an 'underwater film director' unable to talk directly to the main cameraman but who could playback grabbed shots to discuss back at the boat.

That evening, floating at our mooring on the *Inzan Tiger*, we had supper among an increasingly messy ship full of moist dive gear, cameras, batteries, lights, dive bottles and specialist parts for odd electronics like oxygen sensors and camera viewfinders. The cabin hummed with the noise of the air compressor on the back deck filling up our bottles for the next day. The others had been a bit dejected not to see any large shoals of sharks. Peter and I didn't say anything. After we'd eaten, I put my video camera on the table and flipped out the screen, rewound the last ten minutes and played it back to everyone, telling them the spot where we'd been last. The screen filled with the grey streaks of sharks and there was a silence. 'Right,' said Bob. 'We're going there tomorrow!'

The next few days of diving were a blur, but very productive for the whole *Blue Planet* series, and the silky sharks were the stars. They were very alert, and wanted to know more about you, but not in an overtly 'I want to eat you' kind of way, although no doubt that's never far from their mind. They have a magnificent gun-metal sheen that looks newly polished and pristine, their Greek scientific name *Carcharhinus* fitting well, because they have a pointy or sharp (*karcharos*) nose, and they generally look streamlined. At about 10 feet or 3 metres they look fit for long distances across the blue but, being not quite as big as great whites, tigers or bull sharks, they are perhaps training aircraft to the frontline fighters: perfectly formed, very able and with almost as much power as the real thing. I notice in one of our shots you can count seventy animals, and that's just a part of the silky shark school. The case is still out as to why they do this, and they've really only been seen in such large groups around Malpelo and another solitary stone pinnacle called Socorro, also called the Revillagigedo Archipelago, quite a bit further north from here near Mexico. The congregation seems social, with slow, parallel swimming in the same direction, as if it were important to size up your colleagues, but what function it has is unknown.

Obviously, as hugely strong fish, armed with the sharpest of teeth, silky sharks are potentially dangerous, but we never felt threatened by them even when we were right inside their schools with them streaming past us on all sides. Mind you, I would always listen to Bob Cranston, who, as a one-time tour leader for dives with blue sharks off California, had vastly more experience of big sharks, and daft divers, than any of us, and learned from his time with tourists to analyse human behaviour as well as that of sharks: how confident we were, and how likely to panic should the sharks suddenly change their minds about taking a nibble. So if Bob said it was OK to get into the water with these sharks, then I was confident it was OK, although I remember quizzing him about it a lot at first. He had an unfussy way which I liked of telling it like it is, and fortunately his comments are recorded directly in a BBC radio piece I did with him at Malpelo:

> The silky shark is a beautiful shark, and what makes them even more fascinating is that there're thousands of them here - I've never seen anything this *sharky* before. The silky sharks are sleek and sassy, they're a very curious shark, they come right up to you, which makes it good for photography, they bump you, they bite you, they push off your camera with their nose a little bit. I think they want to find out what you are and what you are doing here in their world.

Reading what he said literally now, it seems a bit more worrying than it felt at the time; however, it really wasn't. By 'biting'

I think Bob meant they only opened their mouths on his camera a couple of times to chew at it like a puppy, and of course that didn't affect the hefty aluminium box. It may have been that they could sense the electric current inside the camera too, which is something they'd go mad for, as the weak electrical signals might seem like those from the muscles of a crippled fish. On one occasion Bob lost a tiny bit of neoprene from his dive suit as a shark bumped him a little, but if these sharks were to chew on you properly or even brush their teeth on your skin you'd know about it for sure. Not to mention that in this dense pack all their friends would likely join in. Never be complacent with sharks.

Sometimes the water clarity was not as good as you might expect over 300 miles from any major coast or rivers, and the silkies in particular like to stay near the warmer surface where the sunlit water is often cloudier because of plankton. We had realised, though, that one of the more dramatic ways to film the sharks was from beneath, in silhouette, when the water clarity didn't matter too much. In fact, we got 'shark silhouette' shots more spectacular than we ever dreamed. We dived many, many times with hundreds of sharks. Most vividly, I remember lying on the seabed, quite deep at about 30 metres, and looking up to see a 'shark rush-hour' above me, as mixed shoals of hammerhead and silky sharks just kept coming by, with tailbacks to the underwater horizon. Once again, this planet was proving not to be quite the place I thought it was, and here was a scene that had been going on in places like this for more than a hundred million years.

The sharks we recorded at Malpelo are in the first and third films of *Blue Planet* series one, and are the pictures used on the front covers of the boxed set. We got hammerhead shoals, silky shoals, mixed hammerhead and silky shoals, and even Galapagos sharks in ones and twos among the crowd. These are similar to the silky, but bigger and beefier, and the Galapagos shark also goes deeper, but mixes with the other sharks too at times.

I have four small bronze models of hammerheads, bought in a seaside shop in Mexico, that exactly capture their graceful movement, the way their whole tail, almost a third of their body, bends and gently swishes from side to side behind their ridged hammer and stout pectoral fins. And despite the tail's rhythmic swaying, the propeller of its motion, the hammerheads somehow manage straight lines or even gentle and purposeful arcs, the whole shiver navigating in the same direction. As they come near you can see that the hammer's planes act like little wings, and sometimes they're not swimming at all, just gliding. Whenever I notice the bronze models in my office I have to make sure the little metallic shoal is all swimming in the same direction, following the same arc with exactly the right spacing between the sharks.

If you are trying to understand a social or semi-social creature, it is of course not only an individual animal but the group you must study, ideally in the wild. Usually, once you've seen them all together, the penny quickly drops as to what sort of being they are, and why they live together in the first place. For example, I never really understood elephants, kept only in ones and twos in older zoos, until I saw them in herds of thirty or so roaming free on the African plains. In the same way, social sharks are best understood by seeing them together in blue-water plains.

Sharks mostly appear to have an innocent grin on their face, but they are always on the look-out for the right moment to

find food, for a weakness in their prey: something that can't
defend itself or has become distracted and can be ambushed
unawares. I have often noticed how pristine the sides of sharks
look, and how generally healthy an open-ocean shark appears.
Though even at Malpelo the odd silky had a fishhook in its
side, they are all magnificent specimens, glowing with a silver
bronze sheen.

My theory is that, as with the mobsters of 1930s America,
there is a code of conduct among sharks: show any weakness
and you die. This means in practice that if you get injured in
any way you are immediately vulnerable, and therefore that
though you're attacking a smaller and more feeble creature, if
there's any chance it will injure you before you chop its head
off with your razor-sharp teeth, then other sharks will notice
you're injured and eat you too. This is possibly why few sharks
attack unless they can see they have absolute superiority, with
no chance of injury.

The only time the silky sharks became a little worrying, then,
was in the few moments when the support boat was picking
us up after a dive. Fragile invader into the ocean as you are,
underwater, as your head turns to track a moving shark it's clear
you're watching them and they you, in some kind of mutually
agreed stand-off. As you're getting out the rules change. For a
few moments your head is above water, and you can't see what's
around your little wormly, wriggling feet – which must be very
tempting for just a little nibble. Every time we got out I could
see the water boil in slowly diminishing circles around us, and
the only thing that would have made it a bit more edgy was if
someone had hummed John Williams' theme tune from *Jaws*.
They never did (we're professionals), but it did leave me
wondering if our feeling of safety around the sharks was an

illusion, and our fate was actually resting on a razor clam's edge. It might not have turned out so pretty.

The sharks certainly are opportunists. We'd been banking on it, in fact, looking still for that Holy Grail of marine filming, the bait ball. But it hadn't been happening for us once on this shoot, and that had been a big reason for coming to Malpelo. Around this gigantic rock sharks and other big predators from the open sea have a daily opportunity to whip up huge balls of fish. Being there at precisely the right place and time to film it is another matter. Always on the look-out, one morning we saw a commotion in the distance, about 2 miles off Malpelo: large numbers of birds and a froth on the water left us in no doubt. We raced towards this bait ball, hoping it wouldn't disappear before the cameramen, suited up and ready, could get into the melée.

Stopping short of it, we dropped Bob and Florian in the water. Often in Pacific 'bait balls' you get big yellow-fin tuna, many the size of a large family dog, but in this one there were the much smaller *bonito* tuna, with a delicate black banding on their sides and bright silver body, the biggest no larger than an expensive ornamental goldfish. What made it special, though, were all the sharks that came to the party, as of course they would around this Colombian shark capital. And so we captured another part of the *Blue Planet* jigsaw, a shot for the third show on 'The Open Ocean', that has a beautiful framing of a shark coming through this bait ball straight to camera in such an elegant arc I could play it back and watch it a thousand times. For all of human history and more these dramas played out in the ocean every day and, with luck, they still are. Yet only in the last twenty years or so have such stunning action sequences been brought to your living room.

I read now that people go to Malpelo and often don't meet the silkies in such numbers as we did. Perhaps we were just lucky and it was a coincidence they were around when we visited? They still can be found, I hope, but we known from satellite tags that these sharks can move fast when they want, covering 60 km (about 40 miles) a day, and although not yet proven, they could migrate from Malpelo to places like Socorro Island to the north, in Mexico, a distance of about 3,500 km (2,200 miles) in just under two months. Satellite tagging shows, too, that they will move to cooler waters if the temperature gets much above 30° Centigrade, as it can do in warmer El Niño years. And perhaps they are more sensitive to such changes than most, preferring the surface waters. That's about all that's known about their movements, because, like most of these fast ocean creatures, where they go, breed and grow up is still largely a mystery. If you think about how big and inaccessible their realm is, then it's not too surprising, really. I dream of being able to swim like a dolphin, fast and for days on end, to be able to follow such creatures and find out all about their lives. Anyway, we were very lucky to see so many, and I was grateful for the tip-off from the sports divers at Cocos Island that made us go to Malpelo in the first place.

Those are not the only mysteries of Malpelo, of course; in fact, the list is reassuringly endless. But it does have what might be thought of as its own Loch Ness Monster, which must count as one of the biggest. Heinz, our captain, had a proudly framed picture of himself swimming alongside one from a previous trip, and since no one has anything like that for Nessy I must concede that the mystery of *Odontaspis ferox*, the smalltooth sand tiger, isn't quite as big a deal as what lurks in that famous Scottish loch. Even so, it has got to be worth a look. In the picture it's probably about three times the length of Heinz, and he's not a small man. It's a bulky creature, too. These kinds of pictures are taken by divers on wide-angle lenses, which enable you to get very near your subject and yet still have it all in frame. A typical underwater-photographer trick is to put the subject between you and your fellow diver, who is on the other side of the shark. This apparently gives scale, but in fact the wide angle makes everything far away from the lens pretty small, so it seems that the shark is bigger than it actually is. This was the case with Heinz's trophy photo, but it was still impressive, and he was among the first ever to find them at Malpelo. Like many deep-sea species, they have a global distribution, but it seems they are more massive here than elsewhere in the world. They have been found really deep, too, around 1,000 metres (3,000 feet), and seem to like feeding on seabed fish and crustaceans. What's exciting about the Malpelo sand tigers apart from the fact that they might be a new sub species, is that they come up from the deep, especially in the winter months, to the limit of scuba diver depths. And even though it was June we badly wanted to include them in our filming loot.

I think the exact spot at which we were dropped from the *Inzan Tiger* to find these large and deep sharks was secret back then: only Heinz and a few others knew. Today it is usually at *Bajo del Monstruo*, 'Seamount of Monsters', which only adds to the awe with which you anticipate this massive shark and whatever else might be there in the deeply shelving seas off Malpelo.

As we descend we are deliberately going faster, so we can get deep more quickly than normal. I have the little 'behind-the-scenes' camera, and hope to shoot the moment the team ahead see the giant shark, or sharks, as they sometimes come in

212

groups of five or so. With the dive guide, Tina, I am on scuba, and Florian and Bob are on rebreathers, which in the hands of experienced people are in fact safer than the scuba tanks, both because they allow you to stay underwater for longer without running out of air, and because the oxygen mixtures can be more easily controlled to avoid toxic situations. The recommended safe maximum depth for scuba dives, you will recall, is set at 50 metres (160 feet). Not only is that easy to remember, in metric terms anyway, it keeps you out of the pressure region when oxygen gas becomes toxic. It seems strange that the gas that gives us life can be lethal under high pressure, but it's true. Too much of a good thing, perhaps, but too much oxygen under high pressure makes you convulse and fit – nothing good can come of that if it happens in deep water. Setting the safety threshold to the pressure of 50 metres is good because, with a normal air mixture, it's quite a bit above the point at which oxygen will kill you.

There's also the issue of nitrogen to worry about. Nitrogen at high pressures is a narcotic: it makes you feel drunk. So below 50 metres you can potentially die in a fit or in drunken delirium while breathing what you'd think is just ordinary air. It's the great pressure down there, forcing the gases into your body tissue in very high concentrations, that makes harmless air become something much more dangerous. Fifty metres is the limit, then, on scuba. The giant sand tigers, it was thought, didn't come shallower than about 60.

At some point when you go deep there comes a feeling that you can no longer get to the surface if things go wrong. It is as if a roof has been put over you and you are now effectively diving in a cave. This is mostly depth-related, but also depends on how much time you have spent below. At about 40 metres or so, I also start to feel the dizziness associated with too much nitrogen in the blood, but people are affected differently. I find it quite a pleasant feeling, really, getting drunk on nitrogen, too pleasant in fact, as its siren call lures you to ever greater and eventually lethal depths. I know I just have to say to myself, 'You're feeling like this because you're narked' (short for nitrogen narcosis – high on nitrogen). Mostly that works, but once or twice I have been tempted recklessly to carry on down. This has all the warnings of such a moment: the scenery is beautiful down here, long plains of white sand lie below me, dimly seen in the deep water. The big shark is nowhere, but we can feel the lure of mystery, and perhaps the stare of more experienced fish eyes looking back. As we get to 50 metres, still nothing, and the excitement and the drunkenness of nitrogen narcosis has become intense. I'm very aware I shouldn't go further, but before I realise it I've gone a little deeper, stayed just a little longer, for the chance to see and film a beautiful monster.

The light has gone very dim now – is it the depth or my chemically altered mind? 55, 56, 57 metres, and we pause. Every extra second I stay here my blood splurges with unwanted gases, supercharged under high pressure and potentially damaging my soft tissues. Soon, too, I won't have enough air to stop safely on the way up to avoid getting the bends. There's a lot to think about; parameters of all sorts are closing down my options very fast. 60, 62, 63, 64 . . . *Sixty-four metres*! That's too deep. Where's the bloody shark? Finally, I get a grip on myself and realise my buddy is now nearly 50 feet above me, because she's stayed where it was safe. I've been here now about two minutes and I've got to go immediately. Fighting the pleasant numbness of diving danger, I add a little air into the buoyancy jacket and bounce back to safety. I worry that this will set a bad example, but I want to tell the truth of what can really happen if you're being an idiot. It could make you safer I hope should you ever feel the lure of nitrogen. Florian and Bob go on together, able to go deeper and stay longer on their rebreathers, that allow more carefully controlled mixes of gas than the plain air of normal scuba tanks. As it happens, not seeing any sign of the leviathan, they didn't go much deeper, but it was a while before I saw them again, as they stopped to decompress before finally coming shallow and resurfacing.

So none of us ever saw a sand tiger, but all of us remembered that dive forever and the beautiful empty plains beneath Malpelo, with its mystery and the sense of something big looking at you, as though the abyss was indeed staring back.

From our first dive at Malpelo on 8 June 2000 to our last on 20 June we would have all done at least thirty dives a piece, with two camera crews working in tandem, equivalent to about three month's diving for a dedicated single person. So perhaps not that much really, but with such a spectacular location many of the shots would become iconic ones for *Blue Planet*.

When you are confined in small living quarters, like the six or so tiny cabins of our ship, with a group of people, and for several weeks, it's easy to fall out in unguarded moments of tiredness, exacerbated too by breathing copious amounts of high-pressure nitrogen, and sometimes because of frustration that there is never any peace from your fellows. Yet with the focus of our work to distract us we had all stayed reasonably civil. There was an incident when Tina, trying to be useful, insisted in helping Peter off with his dive kit, and Peter, hugely independent and somewhat old school, had struck out to fend her off. The smell of that misunderstanding lasted about forty-eight hours and was forgotten, but that was pretty much it. No one was bitchy behind each other's backs, because that was the point: on a small ship there is nowhere to go 'behind'.

I remember hearing that a colleague of mine on a long trip once had to ask to be put in the inflatable being towed behind the main boat, just to get away from everyone for a bit, and I can see why! Nothing like that happened here, and any arguments, like the 'discussions' over the crew member whose work permit had run out, or the concern over whether the deck crew would get their tips from the captain, and if they did whether they'd drink them on the first night, eventually dissolved in the huge expanse of seawater whose capture was ultimately our only goal. It may just have been luck with the way things went, but perhaps it was because we were transfixed by the ocean's 'lucky dip' and what the sea would offer up next.

On the last day, just before we left, Heinz the captain decided it would be a good thing to have a few more tuna in the ship's galley. We cruised about a mile from the biggest cliffs of Malpelo and he put out two lines, which soon went taut, as obviously a big fish had taken the bait. Then just as suddenly the line sagged slack again, and it was pulled in to investigate. All that was on the hook was a bleeding fish head, bitten off cleanly behind the gills. This happened several times before the crew gave up. Swirling around the stern of the ship, the tell-tale peaks of silky shark fins breaking the surface. We imagined that as soon as they saw a tuna on the line they seized their chance, always on the look-out for an easy kill, but how they knew to bite back from the hook and leave just the head we still don't understand.

The last note in my dive log, for 20 June 2000, says, 'Last dive in Malpelo', and adds in brackets, *'for now!'* That's optimistic because, although it's a magnificent place, it's not too often anyone ever gets here, let alone has the chance to visit more than once. If you have been, though, you will visit it again in your heart for the rest of your life. Most people never get to see Malpelo at all, of course, and I am humbled that in a way I was one of your representatives, helping to bring you images from places that are like the dark side of the Moon – on Earth. It might not surprise you to know there are still many such places to be illuminated in our ocean. Our world is not quite the place we all think it is, or at least has more mysterious parts than we may ever know.

Although we had planned as much as possible, and some of the things had worked out on our schedule – the whitetip sharks filmed hunting at night in Cocos Island, the hammerheads being cleaned – the majority of what happened was done on the hoof (on the fin?), and as our time on the mission grew longer our schedule became increasingly unplanned, or, if you like, our schedule had the flexibility that works well with an unpredictable ocean. How lucky we were too, in what we managed to film, and in our safe-keeping.

At the end of the shoot I finished off the radio programme I'd started in Malpelo. I've just played it back, and heard tones in my voice I had not noticed at the time. Recorded by a roadside ditch in the port of Golfito, at night, it sounds a little croaky, mainly because I'm recording a cacophony of Costa Rican frogs, but also because I'm tired and anxious to get home, to find out whether we've ticked off enough of our shopping list to constitute a good job.

12

The Glowing Planet and the
Hunt for the Giant Squid

Things that go 'blip' in the night

'For all we know that could be a giant squid!' Martin was looking at the grainy image on his laptop – a live feed from some very special cameras dangling in the current 500 metres below and in the middle of the night, in the heart of the Atlantic Ocean, 3 miles south of Pico Island in the Azores. No one but a spiritualist, perhaps, (and Martin) would have claimed that the slightly hazy and completely undefined pixels moving across the screen were evidence of a giant squid. Though as usual Martin was ahead of us.

Martin Dohrn is a very bright man. For him the world is clearly a place where stranger things happen in nature all the time and there's a way to capture them on film. I say 'film', but of course that's now shorthand for a mostly outdated medium, and what I really mean is 'video', but to say we were making a *video* doesn't seem so grand, and in any case that's out of date now too, and our images are all just numbers on computer cards. The distinction is more important in this case, though, because digital media can be electronically amplified and made hugely more sensitive than its chemical cousin. So sensitive, in fact, that we were picking up the traces of moonlight, half a kilometre down, in the middle of the night. Martin has spent much of his life perfecting such night vision with the invention and improvement of what he calls his 'Starlight' cameras.

When I was a boy, in rural North Wales, far from the light pollution of street lamps, I remember outstanding nights where the stars were ultra-clear, and the Milky Way was sparkle-dust across the sky. Those memories seem to be equalled today only on remote islands free from urban sprawl.

One night in Puerto Rico Martin was doing one of his famous night-time time-lapses, using a fairly ordinary stills camera and taking a still every thirty seconds or so to follow the dance of stars across the night sky. 'The sun comes up in the east,' he said, 'so if you want the stars to come towards and over the camera then you have to point the camera east' – and then several more filming gems would follow. But one of them in particular startled me. 'Look at the stars,' he said, 'and now look at the spaces in between. What do you see?'

I wondered what he meant, but followed his gaze to the unblemished carpet of stars above us. It's difficult to find the 'in between', because there isn't much between the teeming suns of our galaxy, but with a little concentration I could see what he meant. When you look hard enough into the black bits of the night sky you can see a tell-tale haze of very tiny red dots, similar to those you see on the back of your eyelids when you shut your eyes. 'That's noise,' said Martin. 'That's the noise in your visual system, in your brain.'

I'm not sure how useful that bit of information really is, but it's certainly peculiar, providing unnerving evidence of the biological machines we actually are, rather than the everyday 'higher beings' we assume ourselves to be. Yet it was spending some time working with Martin and trying to film in the dark ocean that would inevitably provide another insight into our planet and the ingenious way marine life has evolved. The majority of our planet, it turns out, is not a *blue* planet, but a *glowing* planet. In the sunless abyss of the ocean, and at night, nature has evolved ways to play with light, using it for alarms, distractions, lures and other types of communication. Sometimes subtle, this glow isn't always easy to catch on camera, but when you do it's truly awesome.

The bobtail squid has one of the most ingenious organs found in any animal, and it was one of my first introductions to the phenomenon of biologically produced light, or bioluminescence. I was making an episode of Attenborough's *Wildlife on One*, 'Gadgets Galore', on the clever structures that cephalopods (octopus, squid and cuttlefish) have evolved for life in the sea. I had read about how adaptable this group of animals were in evolving a whole variety of organs, and that part of their success came from the ability to 'mix and match' the genes from organs they already processed, from their advanced eyes – better in some ways than ours – to the colour-changing cells in their skin, or their ink sacs, or the muscular propulsion tubes that allow them to whizz around as if they carried jet packs.

In the back of the bobtail squid there is the ultimate example, a curious organ that is something between an ink sack and an eye. The central cavity of the sac has become a chamber that cultures a species of glowing bacteria found in most seawater,

Vibro fischeri. The eye part of this light organ, reversing its normal function, uses its lens to focus the bacterial light onto the underside of the squid. Inside the squid's special organ, *Vibro* bacteria reproduce in their millions, allowing the bobtail to illuminate its underside and match the level of light coming from the surface, at which point the little squid, looked at from underneath, is invisible to both its predators and its prey. This again is a type of countershading, as we touched on with whales, but of course occurs in many marine animals. Sharks, for example, have a light belly that matches the lighter surface from below, and a dark back that matches the deep water when viewed from above. Yet the sophisticated bobtail squid has taken the concept further and made an 'active counter-illumination' system, a glowing invisibility cloak it can adjust at will. Having lost the hard protective shells which their close relatives, the nautilus, still have, these squids must use intelligence, cunning and such 'high-tech' organs to survive; vital when you are tasty food for almost everything in the sea. What blows my mind, though, is that the bobtail can somehow detect and extract from seawater minute amounts of the one specific bacterium it needs, and exclusively cultivate it to produce light. In fact, concentrations of this *Vibro* bacterium are so low the bobtail's light organ must extract the equivalent of just one single tiny glowing cell per cup full of seawater. Somehow, too, it exactly matches the ambient light from the surface, otherwise the 'light camouflage' wouldn't work. It's a very elaborate system to have evolved, and it shows how important controlling light is for survival in the sea.

Even so, when it comes to filming the bobtail squid's light it's very tricky to show the counter-illumination effect. The squid seems to be able to adjust the light level of its underside almost instantly, and when it matches the brightness of the surface it will be almost invisible – that's the whole point. So how do you film the invisible? We experimented filming some bobtail squid through the bottom of a tank and quickly changing the surface light levels to see if the squid changed the light to match, hoping it was like a dimmer switch being turned up or down. But either it was too fast for us or something we were doing inhibited its natural behaviour, and I wouldn't blame it.

Bobtail squid are found all over the world, but there is one lab in Honolulu, Hawaii, under Professor McFall Ngai, that exclusively studies the Hawaiian bobtail squid. In 2003, when she was running a big research team studying the squid and the bacteria of its light organ, she kindly let us film there. It was purely academic research but, then again, an animal that has the trick of selecting one species of bacteria and rejecting all others obviously has a secret that may be vital in the search for new and non-resistant antibiotics.

I went out early to set up the shoot, aiming to film the glowing bacteria and the Hawaiian bobtail squid in the wild – but, for probably the only time in nearly twenty years at the BBC, the cameraman got sick and couldn't make it. For a while I filmed with a local person who was not a wildlife specialist, and we just couldn't get the same quality of shots. So apart from a few glowing images of laboratory petri dishes, in which the bioluminescent *Vibro* bacteria can be cultivated, we ended up with nothing.

Back in a displeased production office in Bristol I discussed options and the impact on the budget. I had known of a similar species of bobtail squid in Ireland, as similar kinds are found right across the world, and even though the Irish species was 10,000 miles from Hawaii, it also uses the special light organ.

So I suggested a much cheaper, three-day shoot to Dingle in Ireland to pick up the missing shots. Perhaps the budget was worse than I knew; in any case my line manager refused to sanction it.

I hope I am not too bloody-minded, although some stubbornness is needed in any film-maker, but my response was to take a week's leave and film and fund it myself. Altogether it cost £600. Together with two friends from Bristol, Alan James, himself a famous underwater photographer, and Ed Whiting, a diving buddy running an underwater image business in his spare time, I filmed the little squid in a shallow bay over three nights and came back with footage I now own and have sold to at least five different production companies.

Even if you didn't know about their wonderful light organ, the little bobtail squid, also called the 'little cuttlefish' in the UK, are fantastic creatures to watch and film. Their saucer-shaped eyes look back at you in a way that betrays their intelligence, even if they are only the size of your thumb. Also, their patterning is some of the most beautiful in the natural world: the Irish one is iridescent blue and gold with subtle greens on the underside.

Yet the intelligence of bobtail squids is indeed more fascinating than their beauty. You can see them constantly making small decisions – tiny to us perhaps, but massive for a mollusc – the greater zoological group to which they belong. They are mostly nocturnal, and as I dived with them at night in the shallows of a harbour they came to my filming light straight away, before concluding, it seemed, that I was on their 'big list of predators'- like flat fish and seals - and swiftly went into hiding. Using their jet siphon as a sand blaster they excavate the seabed and sink into the hole they've made, flicking sand over their heads with rowing movements from their two front tentacles. Soon only a beady silver eye looks back at you from between the grains, and if you hadn't seen them digging you wouldn't even notice that. But when they sometimes raise their bodies to peep out from their retreat, then you might indeed catch their eye. If they think they haven't been discovered they sit tight, but realising when the game of hide-and-seek is up, can hit the 'ejector button' and violently jet backwards in an explosion of sand.

The Irish bobtails live in very shallow water, where a diver's air consumption is frugal and you're unlikely to get the bends. You can stay underwater for hours in these conditions, and I enjoyed having the time to try and understand their behaviour. Once a female hovered like a little bumblebee in front of my torch, fluttering her two small rear fins like wings. I was astonished to see a couple of males dart out of the shadows almost instantly to court her in the limelight, and realised the bobtails had been watching me too from the shadows.

Until I met the bobtail squid I didn't understand the exquisite subtlety of living light. There had been one or two magic moments: the wonderful night I sat on the beach at Burnham-on-Sea in Somerset with my parents, every crashing wave making blue sparkles spill along the shore as trillions of pea-sized comb jellyfish tumbled in the spume. But it wasn't until I came with Martin Dohrn to Vieques, a small island off Puerto Rico, and swam at night in Mosquito Bay, that the penny fully dropped. It's a spot that's in the *Guinness Book of Records* as the 'brightest night-time bay' in the world.

This was Martin's project; he'd raised the money for it with National Geographic through his company Ammonite. I was another director-producer he'd brought along to help and for my marine knowledge. Although Martin was involved with every facet of the enterprise, as well as the camera work, usually, of course it's the other way around: the director employs the photographer. I was happy to do whatever was needed, but the simple act of employment changes the power dynamic, and Martin, as the cameraman employing me, was calling the shots, and my 'directions' became 'suggestions'.

As well as being the cameraman and main director, Martin had developed the amazing cameras we were using. I chipped in some design thoughts, but I couldn't match him for sheer practical engineering and determination to do what seemed like impossible things without the benefit of a company like, say, NASA. In his early career, he told me once, he had worked on a building site, but would often pass a photographic shop on his way home, and saw lenses he couldn't afford. But then it occurred to him that he could just *make them himself* from cheaper components. After all, a fully functional camera lens is hardly more than a collection of simpler lenses in a tube. So he made his first lens and it worked, triggering a lifetime fascination with camera optics, filming in the dark, and bioluminescence in particular. Thirty years later he had made perhaps the highest-quality night-vision cameras in the world, and had started to train them on the glowing world of the ocean.

The night-time glow of Mosquito Bay in Puerto Rico comes from the disturbance of plankton, and in particular trillions upon trillions of small single-cell organisms usually called dinoflagellates. These are beautifully intricate microscopic organisms that many botanists believe are algae, within the division Pyrrophyta, or 'fire algae'. But many zoologists too claim they are types of protozoa, like amoeba, noting two little hair-like structures that twitch to propel them along, called flagella. So not only do we not know many of the organisms in the sea, many of those we do know we cannot agree what they are exactly. It doesn't help that some dinoflagellates photosensitise like plants and some just eat like animals, breaking down our idea about the major divisions of life. It's not understood either why they glow, but the best, and most startling, explanation is called 'the burglar alarm theory': that it's basically a defence mechanism against getting eaten. If a tiny fish or other larvae gives them a nibble, they almost instantly glow, shining a light on it, and the feeding fish is now quite likely to get eaten itself when a larger fish sees it lit up. The dinoflagellate has activated its 'burglar alarm', and the predatory fish police are coming to investigate. It's a neat theory but, if you ask me, has a hint of the 'too good to be true', because why then do the dinoflagellates glow when disturbed by waves that do them no harm? Whatever the reason, it's very pretty.

In Mosquito Bay and other bioluminescent bays in Puerto Rico, dinoflagellates thrive, though recently there have been some years when they disappeared, and the lights went out. It's thought that the mangroves that grow around the bay, and the particular flow of the current in the bay, bring exactly the right nutrients and conditions for the dinoflagellates to grow. The truth is, though, that they are found in greater or lesser concentrations of warmish waters all over the world, and that the ocean is likely to be glowing everywhere to some degree. And you can see it if you have a sensitive Starlight camera, or even a sensitive eye.

The enormous eye of a giant squid was staring out of the giant laboratory pickle jar like a decapitated head. Through the jar's distortion I could see the face of Clyde Roper, an expert on these and other squid at the National Museum of Natural History in Washington DC. From this angle the eye looked considerably bigger than the scientist's head, which of course was a deliberate shot from our cameraman to emphasise its size.

'Giant squids have the largest eyes of any animal in the animal kingdom today, and possibly the largest that have ever existed,' Clyde was explaining in his precise New Hampshire accent. He was a lobster fisherman before going to study zoology at college, so you know his interest is genuine. Yet his explanation only leaves a larger mystery, because the giant squid, *Architeuthis dux*, with its massive eye, lives in darkness over a kilometre down (let's say a mile), and never sees the sun.

The giant, as the name implies, is at the other end of the squid spectrum from the bobtail. Twenty metres (60 feet) long, it is the largest squid of all, by length, although the colossal squid is bulkier. Giants are said to battle with sperm whales, although no one has ever seen this, and we only know of it through circumstantial evidence, namely the sucker scars around the mouth of sperm whales, the occasional morsel of a giant squid tentacle brought to the surface in a sperm whale's mouth and, from the days when whales were dissected on the deck of the whaling ships, the hard 'beaks' of the squid's mouth, which do not dissolve in a whale's stomach. On average around 3 per cent of the diet of sperm whales is giant squid (although it varies a lot geographically); the rest is made up of squid of many other kinds.

At least six TV documentaries I know of have tried to find the legendary giant squid or Kraken. So far, only one has succeeded, based on the work of Tsunemi Kubodera, the Japanese zoologist with the National Museum of Nature and

Science. On 30 September 2004 Kubodera and his team became the first to photograph a live giant squid in its natural habitat, after three years' work off the Bonin or Ogasawara Islands, an archipelago of thirty small islands some 1,000 kilometres (620 miles) south of Tokyo. This is a famous deep-sea area for Japanese fisherman, and one where sperm whales were known to hunt for large squid. The team's technique was to use very deep fishing lines baited with cuttlefish dropped down to 900 metres (3,000 feet).

In 2012, Kubodera and other scientists went back with a new team to film giant squid for the Discovery Channel. Again, they baited a deep fishing line with smaller squid, and waited nearby with a submarine, dimly illuminating the lure. Their patience paid off, and after almost a hundred attempts they succeeded in filming a little Kraken, 3 metres (ten feet) long, through the port of their research sub. 'Little', because dead giant squid *six times* bigger have been washed up around the world.

In truth, it's better to get some good pictures of giant squid first and then make a film about how you found it. But it doesn't work like that, because how do you pay for getting those very expensive images if you don't have a film budget in the first place? Hence the many failed attempts, in films that will tease you to the end and fail to show you even the slightest erotic hint of a tentacle. What these many attempts to film a giant squid do show is that we still have a fear of and fascination with the great voids of our ocean, and the monsters that might lurk there.

None of this, however, stopped Martin and the team I was part of doing another show in 2011 for National Geographic called *Hunt for the Giant Squid*. At least our show had come up with a very innovative idea to show the sea, quite literally, in a new light. Martin's theory, and increasingly many scientists', was that the giant squid has its massive eye (but lives in the dark) in order to see the bioluminescence. Specifically, that from dinoflagellates, and even more specifically that from its arch enemy the sperm whale, glowing with disturbed dinoflagellates getting out of its way.

The saucer-shaped eye of the giant squid is certainly unusually large, and most animals wouldn't evolve something so big, because eyes are very 'costly' in evolutionary terms, and just having them will require a bigger diet. So they must be vital. Sperm whales are known to hunt giant squid using sonar clicks that bounce off prey in the dark, in the same way a bat will catch a moth. From knowing the power of the click it has been calculated that the maximum range at which a sperm whale could detect a squid is 120 metres (nearly 400 feet), and it's not a coincidence that scientists have also calculated how far away the giant squid's eye could see light coming off a sperm whale from the bioluminescence it makes as it ploughs through the plankton: 120 metres. So the two animals are in an 'arms race' with one another, the predator continually evolving a sense to enable it to see its prey in the dark, which the prey combats by evolving a defence system to detect the predator coming.

I helped Martin develop the Starlight cameras for underwater use, first by sourcing glass housings (ready-made glass tubes good to 3,000 metres of water pressure: nearly two miles down). Glass, it turns out, is very strong, and a good, economical solution for filming in the very deep sea. As a camera housing it doesn't even need to be sealed with the usual rubber seals (O-rings), but instead you can use ground-glass surfaces that seal completely like the glass bung on a brandy decanter. It seems precarious but, as soon as there is any pressure on the glass tube and its lid, as happens immediately underwater, there isn't the slightest chance the container will break apart.

It was necessary to use off-the-shelf components as far as possible, because while lead times for engineers are sometimes in years, those for TV, when it gets a budget, are often measured in weeks. In the little time we had to develop the specialist low-light cameras for underwater use I was constantly asking engineering companies how fast they could supply the equipment needed. 'Oh . . . about eighteen months or so?' they would say, and I would reply, 'Ah. I was thinking maybe you could do something for us next week . . .' It was a bit of a nightmare, but with some queue-jumping and a little compromise we managed to make an underwater Starlight camera system and have it ready for our filming with less than three months of development.

Now we had something equivalent to the eye of a giant squid that we could use to find the giant squid itself. Everything that moved through plankton in the dark sea would make some kind of light, went Martin's theory, and the animal itself, the giant squid, would betray its presence by creating a dark 'negative space' inside this halo of bioluminescent light.

We chose to film in the seas off the Azores and Japan, where we stood a good chance of squid encounters. A week before we were due to leave the UK the Japan location had to be changed to Mexico and Belize when, on Friday, 11 March 2011, a mega-tsunami devastated the north east coast of Honshu Island. It would change what could be in the film, of course, but these sorts of random events are normal, despite all the planning documentary teams do.

The Starlight cameras were mounted on a small aluminium structure with stubby wings towed behind the fishing boat we'd chartered, also 'home made' by Martin. The signal from the camera was sent up a live feed through some fibre-optic cable so we could see instantly if we got anything. It was in the Azores, using this new rig, that Martin uttered the words that start this chapter: 'For all we know that was a giant squid!' We had been filming into the middle of the night, and come across a dark patch of shapes among a glowing sea, 500 metres (1,600 feet) beneath the boat. This figured with what Martin thought would give away the position of a giant squid, but those images would have disappointed any mega mollusc enthusiast, as they were hardly more than speckles of noise. Yet as is often the case it was not the final meeting with a monster that was important, only the thrill of its possibility, and the fear of the unknown. The film looked at how we went about looking for the giant squid, the details of our technique, and the glowing animals we saw on the way that hopefully built a picture of the ocean as you have never thought about it before – one where its gleaming waters are all important to life.

In Belize in particular I think we came across the most sophisticated example of light production by animals in the sea. We went to Dangriga, a town on the Caribbean coast in southern Belize, and to South Water Caye, a spot famous for its corals and diving across the whole of Central America. It takes about an hour in a fast boat out of Dangriga to the sandy bank that is the island of South Water Caye. The boat, filled to the brim with kit, bumped along low in the water under wheeling clouds of magnificent frigatebirds, their truly magnificent arch-winged silhouettes gliding smoothly in the wind. We passed their roosting sites on micro islands with tiny clumps of trees, the males surprisingly double-chinned, revealing red balloons on their throats, inflating them while making warbling calls with curious and noisy displays. Soon we were in site of the Blue Marlin resort, a collection of airy red-roofed huts perched on a narrow spit of sand at one end of the island. This was our filming studio, dive base and home for the next ten days.

Professor Emeritus Jim Morin, from Cornell University, was our scientific expert and had quickly become part of the team. Without his knowledge it would be impossible to find the tiny creatures we were looking to film. Jim is famous for making some breakthrough discoveries about bioluminescence in the sea and in 1969, with a co-worker, coined the term Green Fluorescent Protein (GFP), for a glowing pigment found in jellyfish. GFP has since been universally used to tag and understand the genetic code of many different organisms – it's a big deal, and its development received the Nobel prize for chemistry in 2008. Yet Jim obviously loves the sea, and has continued field research past an age when many would retire. He clearly loves Belize, too, especially Marie Sharp's Hot Habanero Sauce, a proud product of the country which we had with every meal. At mealtimes, over lashings of Marie's sauce and rice, we discussed everything from the details of his research to philosophy of life.

Jim is a very kindly and soft-spoken man, obviously patient with his students and meticulous in science, taking time over the routine work needed to crack nature's secrets. I would often see him working late into the night, a shadow on the insect mesh of his makeshift cabin laboratory, sorting the little glowing critters he collected and painstakingly writing down their details in scientific notebooks. You can tell when someone is good at something because they just get on with it, methodically making light of work that other people might shun.

Funny enough, for a place this far out of the way, I had been to South Water Caye before. It was in 1994, for the children's programme *The Really Wild Show*, when we dived with a local child from the nearby school in Dangriga, making a short inspirational film about the sea. What we were now coming to film in 2011 hadn't even been discovered then in Belize, and Jim had only just started to describe the animal in other parts of the Caribbean. And when I tell you the animal in question was the bioluminescent grassbed ostracod, *Photeros annecohenae*, I suspect you will be none the wiser. That's because the sea is full of creatures strange and mysterious to our terrestrial world, but not unusual in the ocean. There are about 13,000 species of ostracods alive today, and a further 60,000 have lived in the past, preserved as mini fossils. Not bad for an animal few have heard of, although to be fair most of them are microscopic or flea-sized at best. They are small crustaceans somewhat related to shrimp, but more round and encased in a thin shell. The largest of them is the deep-water giant ostracod, a bit like a small, orange, table-tennis ball, translucent, too, so you can see through. And inside this orange globe two strange eyes stare back like the raised headlamps of a vintage car, and two whip-like appendages poke out through a slit, to make it tumble through the water in a comical, haphazard way.

Not all ostracods glow, but the bioluminescent ones that Jim studies do, and in spectacular fashion. Moreover, it turned out that in the bays around the leeward side of Southwater Caye there were many other glowing creatures. A British expat dive guide I'd met sixteen years earlier when I'd first filmed here told us about starfish that glowed when they were touched in the dark. Martin knew they were here, of course, but it was such an outlandish idea I thought it might be a science fantasy when I first heard of it. He'd stayed here too long, I thought, this dive guide, as with unintended comedy he explained how his ex-girlfriend knew the starfish spot exactly. 'So "X" marks the spot, then?' I nearly blurted out.

We had ordered a lot of aquarium-grade silicon for aquariums from Belize City, and Martin planned to make at least three big tanks just outside the shacks of our 'hotel'. We sometimes use aquariums for filming big, close and magnified shots of small marine creatures, but whenever the press find out it's one of the techniques in wildlife filming they pounce and accuse the film-makers of cheating. It's done for several reasons, the main one being just physics. If you are using macro or microscopic lenses that have a large magnification, they will also have a really small depth of field, meaning the plane of focus is very small, and details either side of it will soon be out of focus. For example, if you were to film a fly at the magnification where you could see the facets of its eyes, then the top of its head and certainly the body behind would be out of focus. You can improve on this by 'stopping down', a confusing term because you actually *increase* the so called 'f-stop' values marked on the lens (often something like 2.8 to 22), in order to *reduce* the aperture or hole in the centre of the iris, making light just go through the centre part of the glass, with the effect of increasing the depth of field and making the sharpness better across the whole picture from near to far. However, this also drastically reduces the amount of light going to the camera sensor: obviously not helpful for filming creatures in the dark or near-darkness. The bottom line is that all the values you see marked on cameras are trade-offs – improve one thing, make another worse – but you maximise what's most important for the conditions and the desired look.

At night you want the lens 'wide open', with the maximum amount of light going to the sensor, and so you want a lens with an iris that has a very wide aperture: a value of 'f 1.4' is good, and there are even lenses with values as low as 'f 0.9' or better, as photographers will know. This gives you great sensitivity at low light, but also a vanishingly small depth of field. For good focus, this means you have to keep the camera extremely still, and that's something you can't easily do well in the swell of the sea. With aquariums, however, you can film close-up through the glass with a heavy, solid tripod that 'locks' the camera. Aquariums also allow you to use specialist lenses that no one has thought worthwhile to put in an underwater housing, as well as better lighting, and generally they provide a much more controlled environment, but the downside of course is that you have to catch the animal and put them in potentially unnatural conditions.

Nowadays, in order to be completely up-front about our techniques, all the behind-the-scenes methods are themselves filmed and put up on a website as 'Additional Material', so that, when the press think we have cheated, it's easy to say, 'No, have a look at this link where it's all explained and honestly revealed.'

That's not to say trying to make a documentary as honest and real as possible isn't vital for an audience's trust, but sometimes we also want to see super-interesting small things that are sometimes difficult, if not impossible, to film directly in 'wild' conditions. The vast majority of the time we use waterproof housings for the cameras and do take them directly into the sea, and by using wide-angle lenses make slight movements less noticeable and, even at lower f-stop values, when the iris is wide open, still keep an image acceptably in focus from near the lens to infinity. There is now also a move towards inventing ingenious, specialist cameras for detailed, high magnification underwater. That would be my preferred way to work, but they are not always available or affordable.

We set off at about 7 p.m. after filming the sunset and some of our preparation work. Several of us had small digital cameras sensitive enough to film well at dusk. *Hunt for the Giant Squid* being an expedition documentary for National Geographic's Expedition Week, there were no limits on filming both the marine subjects and the crew, who are normally never seen on camera. It's a bit more work at the time, but it makes it easier to structure and edit the film later.

Our little *panga*, a small fibreglass boat, skimmed along between the shores of Southwater Caye and the reef. It was so shallow here that we could see the coral below and the eel grass beds, but the boatman knew where the channel was just deep enough to pass. Now in total darkness, we used a small bank of infra-red (IR) LED lights and an IR-sensitive video camera to film the scene. The image is the familiar green of night-vision cameras, where people's faces look like zombies, especially because in the dark the pupils of the eyes are wide open and unfocused. The small outboard whined in high revolutions and there was a faint smell of fuel and fumes. In only fifteen minutes we were at our destination, floating over some thick underwater grass. Kitted up in scuba, we slipped into the water.

Below us it's Christmas. Blue lights briefly flash in rows, as if strung out on lines like flashing bulbs on a festive tree. The lines are short, perhaps two feet (60 centimetres), but it's also shallow here, and the rows seem to stretch from surface to seabed and form columns stretching backwards until they become too faint to see. This is ostracod fairyland, bizarre and beautiful, and first encountered less than forty years ago. Tiny male ostracods, as small as a pinhead, are courting their females with light, minute pulses of glowing chemical squirted out from their bodies at regular intervals as they swim. The females must be watching from somewhere near, but because they are so small and don't glow they are invisible to us.

Hundreds of male ostracods are found together in one place, and so this is an underwater lek: a sexual marketplace, where the females gather to check out the males and can quickly choose the best. It's a phenomenon found with many animals: I've filmed leks of Ugandan kob antelope, beautiful blue fish in Lake Malawi, black grouse and even midges. As here, the lek is usually of males displaying to females, though some, like hammerhead sharks, are the other way round, with females displaying to males. But this is something else. Never have I seen a lek that glows!

As Jim later pointed out, what we were seeing was not just one species, but males from several different species, creating more of a show by displaying together. How can you tell? Because each species has its own 'Morse code': blips of light that have different flashes and patterns. Depending on the species, males display while swimming upwards, downwards, diagonally or horizontally. There are even ones that stay in the same place. Each species has its unique flash pattern, rather like the way lighthouses identify themselves with the distinctive frequency of their beam. For example, each bout of flashing might start with an individual male making three to four bright pulses, a strong beginning that is thought to alert females from all around, followed by a sequence of up to fifteen shorter, more regular pulses, thought to act like a homing beacon for the females to locate the males and mate. The light itself is made with two natural chemicals that illuminate on mixing. We know this from fairground glow sticks because you have to snap them to start them off – causing a thin glass tube inside to break and two special chemicals to mix and produce light. In nature these chemicals are often ones called luciferins and they're activated by mixing with a catalyst or enzyme, called luciferase. The smart thing about the not even pea-brained grassbed ostracod, Jim told me, is that different species mix these two chemicals in different proportions to give the different light pulse durations.

There are many other wonderful examples of ocean biolu-minescence, from the light lures of deep-sea angler fish to the sparkling light the starfish we also found at South Water Caye makes when tugged by a crab – a spotlight or 'burglar alarm' to attract the crab's predators. Yet these pinhead-sized ostracods take the prize for their sophistication and add yet more won-der to the ocean. 'The luminescent displays of Caribbean ostracods,' Jim writes in a paper with his colleague Trevor Rivers,[1] 'are the most complex found in the marine environ-ment.' They are the apogee of what marine creatures can do

---

1 Trevor J. Rivers and James G. Morin, 'Complex sexual courtship displays by luminescent male marine ostracods', *Journal of Experimental Biology* 211 (2008), pp. 2252–62; doi: 10.1242/jeb.011130.

with light, and for the first time we were able to capture this on Martin's special underwater Starlight cameras.

Perhaps we saw the giant squid, perhaps we didn't, but Martin's theory that large animals reveal themselves by disturbing glowing plankton was magnificently demonstrated one morning before dawn in the Sea of Cortez, Baja Mexico. The sea had been glowing especially well that night in March 2011, and we had covered many miles of strange blue firework displays and fuzzy brightness in the water. It was just before dawn and we were about to have breakfast; we'd been filming all night and I was tired, and I just wanted a few moments of silence to myself. I had gone forward to the bow and looked into the water. There, just below me, was a pod of dolphins riding the wake of our boat like glowing rockets, their black shapes outlined by flames of blue bioluminescence. I shouted out in delight for the others to come quickly. There were cries from our partly American team of 'Oh, that's awesome! Awesome!' – something Brits often ignore, thinking there are several other words for 'good' before the word 'awesome' needs to be deployed. I could hear Martin frantically fumbling with the ungainly Starlight camera, and Elliot the camera assistant trying to keep up with him because he was holding the controlling laptop attached to the camera via an umbilical cord. But, well drilled, they came forward to film this magical scene and were on it in just a few seconds.

For what seems like ages, but was perhaps only ten minutes, the dolphins gave us glorious fireworks, every movement of their body amplified in a halo of glowing light: the rapid oscillating thrusts of their tails becoming curvy contrails in the water and sometimes crossing each other's paths with an 'X' of blue marine smoke left hanging like the aftermath of an aerobatic display team. When he'd finished capturing some of the most magnificent shots I've ever seen, Martin turned to my camera with a smile and said, 'And *that's* the kind of event for which the word "awesome" should be reserved, because it was utterly mind-boggling!'

13

A Big Blue in the Big Blue

Filming the biggest animal that ever lived

In a recurring dream I look across the curved edge of La Paz Bay, Mexico. We are on the deck of a large sports-fishing boat, standing at the stern with the captain and the film crew, watching the dual-propeller wake railtrack to the distance, passing local fishermen with small blue *pangas*, battered grey navy ships and a sprinkle of luxury motorboats. Receding behind are the bleached blocks of La Paz, and the much darker mountain background of Baja Mexico, where faint, jagged silhouettes of cactus trees crack the sky like lightning. A gentle breeze makes herringbone patterns on the water and, though just after dawn, it's already hot with anticipation, like a family outing: food, fuel and freedom stashed in the car and heading for the open road. This dream never concludes: it just motors on and on across a quilt of ultramarine ocean and glinting sun. In sleep the scene is timeless, but in reality it's March 1999, and the millennium milestone looms to remind us that it's later than we think, and we should be doing something good with our lives. At thirty-seven I'm managing a team tasked to film blue whales. That's something good, I hope, but as yet I've never seen one in the flesh, and have only my clichés to rely on.

Given that it's probably the biggest animal that ever lived, it's surprising how few people are familiar with blue whales; less surprising, perhaps, that not many have ever tried to film them. In 1999 we were just at the start of getting good blue whale shots into the living room, and perhaps it had not fully hit home that we share our planet with these extraordinary giants. I wished that our images could be like that of Zarafa, the first widely known giraffe, walking down the Champs-Élysées in 1827, in front of awe-struck Parisians seeing a mythical animal in the flesh for the first time. Of course, people had taken film and photos of the blues before, but we wanted shots of the whales from all points of view – at the surface, underwater, and from the air.

Blue whales are so big you'd have thought it was going to be fairly easy to catch up with some. The history of whaling tells us otherwise. Large whales, like blues and fins, are so fast and powerful that only the newly mechanised steam whalers of the early 1900s stood much chance of catching them, and so the biggest whales were the last to be targeted. When they did, whalers made up for lost time, and during the twentieth century the global population practically became extinct. About 400,000 blue whales were killed, and even today their population is only a tiny fraction of the numbers before their 'human apocalypse'. Virtually no one argues that there are more than about 15,000 left, and it might be fewer than 10,000. This is despite the hunting of blue whales being banned in 1955 in the North Atlantic, 1965 in the Southern Ocean and 1966 in the North Pacific. Though it took a further twenty years for almost all whaling to stop, many of the older individuals are still wary of us and the scary sound of big boats, which makes our quest all the harder. Though we catch them now only on camera, it wasn't going to be easy.

Big whales, it seems, need big kit to film them, and I find myself waiting in the departure hall of LAX airport, Los Angeles, on my way to La Paz, with no fewer than thirty-two full-size and some oversize cases, *by myself.* 'Do not leave luggage unattended!' I'll try, but a comfort break would be nice. Stopping over in LA on the way from London, I'd picked up eight more cases in nearby Burbank, too, where Vince Pace of Pace Technology made underwater housings for our cameras. A treasure trove for a specialist camera nerd like me, his fascinating factory was spread out in two aircraft hangars and included thousands of underwater lights for Disney, massive underwater rigs for Hollywood film cameras, and the prototypes of a 3D system that was the forerunner of that used to make James Cameron's feature, *Avatar,* ten years later. Vince and his manager Patrick were very generous with their knowledge of underwater filming, and we had some chats about how to get the best out of the kit, but also discussed the shape of things to come in the rapidly changing multimedia world, that in 1999 seemed more than ever to be exploding into the new century and was clearly going to change everything. It was two years after the birth of Google, and five years before YouTube. I remember talking with Vince about how great it would be if we could stream our own films on the internet. So naturally, we would have invented YouTube too ... if only we'd had a bit more time to chat ... instead of which we did absolutely nothing about it, pleasantly diverted by trying to get cool shots of blue whales.

Looking at the kit laid out on the marble floor of the airport, lugged into position by the van driver and me, I knew I was going to need help. I should have seen this coming, but sometimes when you're dreaming of whales common sense flies out the porthole.

In those days big airports still had porters; these days many don't, and they charge us for their trollies, now furious guests of a new country trying to find coins in a currency we don't yet have. So I found a porter and told him in my best British accent I was going to make it worthwhile, *really* worthwhile, for him to stay with me as we went together with the thirty-two bags through the slowish customs who must stamp our export papers lest we get taxed for kit we don't return, or kit we do return without papers. If I didn't have help I figured losing just one $20,000 lens was easily possible, so a $200 tip was the least I could do. Though folks in the office back home might not see it that way when it came time to put in the receipts. Somehow I muddled through, although the excess baggage was about $6,000 one way for the whole trip even after haggling on behalf of Aunty Beeb.

Despite all the kit, a wildlife film team is typically small: often just a director and camera person, sometimes only a single 'camera director'. One of the aims of keeping it so is to reduce costs and extend the time you have to film, that being the principal ingredient for capturing interesting animal behaviours. With underwater work there are more people needed for safe dive operations, and these can come from core staff or more usually a variety of local support people. Even though *Blue Planet* was based at the BBC in Bristol, the camera person may or may not have lived in the UK, as they are chosen for their excellence and not where they live, though if the two coincide that's great. Having said that, most core *Blue Planet* crews were American and British, with occasionally some other Europeans, together with the more cosmopolitan scientific experts we often teamed with, and of course the boat crew. Consequently every shoot started out with the assembly of people from the UK, USA, anywhere else in the world, and a local contingent.

Whenever possible I liked to be on location a couple of days before the camera crew, to make sure everything was ready and see the situation on the ground so I could form a strategy of how best to do things. This is why I was on the way to La Paz by myself a couple of days before our American DOPs would arrive. I was to meet them at a beautiful town called Loreto, on the Baja California coast, known for its whale-watching tours, fine Mexican architecture and good hotels. But since our boat was berthed in La Paz, a bit further south than Loreto, we would have to motor north to meet the rest of the crew. All great in principle, but in practice not having a film crew from the start was going to be unexpectedly frustrating.

Coming from a British winter into the full sun of a Mexican March is asking for trouble. The British in winter are like plants grown in a dark, damp cupboard, moisture drizzling to the point of fungus. Despite latherings of sun cream on my Caerphilly-white skin, within two days the backs of my ears were bleeding. More information than you need, but I was naïve to the amount of UV as I wandered along the planks of La Paz Marina with my modest trolley of thirty-two cases, listening to the familiar *tick-tick* of halyards and downhauls tapping against the masts of yachts in the wind. There, at the end of the quay, was the boat I was looking for: *Marylee,* sweetly named for the captain's mother, and spelt out in blocky italic letters on her stern in a cheerful blue. She's a big sports-fishing boat with apparently more space inside than out, but you could not mess up even such a Tardis better than to find a dive-film crew to fill it with all their kit.

John and Joanne Barnes, the owners, seemed happy to see me, but my bags not so much. John had a kind face, but his look of thinly disguised panic said, 'We're going to need a bigger boat!' I reassured him that this was the bulk of the kit, although there would be about ten more cases coming with Rick and David, our two underwater cameramen. Stoically he found spaces to stow the stuff, but later when it came out again it would be impossible to keep tidy, as in the heat of filming batteries are swapped, lenses changed, and boxes of film and video cracked open, not to mention the endless thirst for spare parts that underwater kit and cameras seem to have, especially when you mix them together. Today there's yet another layer of technological complexity, because we're not recording on videotape anymore but on digital camera cards, and you need a computer centre with tons of data storage to cope. Where possible it needs another hand to sort it, rudely called a 'data pig': someone whose main job is to manage digital rushes, although on a small boat there's usually no space for them and the photographer has to do it all, potentially adding hours of work to a hard day. So it's not surprising that the living space of a filming boat looks like a lost property office, and with wires flowing over the shelves like seaweed, boxes piled on the sofas or left in the perfect place for denting shins, it's a constant struggle to find order. Around all that weave the people, and it feels like constantly being pushed into a crowded railway carriage, elbows squeezed inwards, struggling to get your bag to the door.

Diane Gendron, our whale scientist, also joined us in La Paz, where she works. She was going to be our guide for the next three weeks, and also the guardian of the whales. Usually it's not possible to film whales without a scientist who has the correct permits. I'd heard about Diane's expertise through my friend and colleague, the whale writer, Mark Carwardine, and been in touch several months earlier for research. She had originally researched krill, the small, shrimp-like crustaceans that swarm in their billions and are among the main foods of blue whales, but had now moved from the small to the giants themselves.

Diane came to Mexico in the late Eighties from Canada, intending to stay a few years, but she never returned home. A French-Canadian, she did a master's funded by a joint Canadian and Mexican grant at the now famous marine research centre, CICIMAR (Centro Interdisciplinario de Ciencias Marinas), in La Paz. At the start of her research the scientific consensus was that blue whales 'fasted' in Baja during the winter months and fed mainly in the summer, when they migrated to the open waters of the Pacific. That seems unlikely, doesn't it, for the biggest animal ever to have existed, with presumably one of the biggest appetites?

Indeed it was, and Diane made a breakthrough when she showed they were feeding on huge swarms of krill (and sometimes similar pelagic crabs) in the winter waters of this semi-enclosed sea. Her work was so important that the Mexican authorities offered her a full-time position, which she seems modest about but is obviously a huge achievement and responsibility, not least to the whales of Baja itself, to which she has now devoted more than thirty years of study.

So now we get to the bit that replays in my dream: coming

out of La Paz harbour, light glinting on the bay, and heading north along the enchanting coast of Baja California, or the Sea of Cortez, depending on where you are from. We sail on and on, past a series of small, coast-hugging islands, to Loreto. I've been up and down this stretch a few times, and up on deck at all times of day and night, so I can tell you it's a magical place where you might see unicorns, and no wonder I sometimes see it in my sleep.

I had started to film behind the scenes to document what we were doing. I'd tried to sell this idea of a 'making-of-*Blue Planet*' show without success at first, and was even told by a TV exec from a topical magazine show I offered it to that 'underwater films are boring and only old people watch them'. At the time, to be fair, we had no idea that *Blue Planet* would become as significant as it did, but I knew we were doing something unusual and that it was worth recording what went on, the crew as well as the natural history. I had bought my own video camera, quite an expensive one and almost professional quality, so I could use it without anyone asking why. The days of directors 'not touching cameras' had gone, but some people were still uncomfortable with it, and others thought it a distraction to the primary job of organising and planning that a producer-director does in the field. Besides, as yet I had no film crew with me. That's when everything happens, of course, as you might have guessed.

Diane is on look-out right at the very front of the bow, on a narrow bit of deck, jammed into the protective stainless railings that outline its shape, and scanning the sea as we go. We're 50 miles from La Paz and just coming out of the gap between the coast and Isla San José, one of the bigger islands on the way. Now the calm sea fans out clear to the horizon in shades of white and light blue, with gentle silver herringbones of current reflecting the high sun. We are distracted by the beauty, but Diane keeps her concentration and keeps scanning all around: it's a good day to see whale blows.

Suddenly she calls out, practically screaming with excitement, *'There! there!'* – and then we see them all ourselves: orcas everywhere, following us through the channel between island and coast, becoming bigger every minute. Although I could see six distinct groups swimming within a mile, this was likely to be one large family, or maybe two that had met up. In every group (or sub-pod) there are between four and seven individuals, so perhaps forty animals, and they're moving fast, swimming in our slipstream and catching up with the boat. Soon we're line abreast, orcas on both sides and one group right behind the boat, enjoying a free ride. A small calf throws itself into the air and practically lands on the skiff we are towing.

By now Diane is jumping up and down in glee and brimming over with excitement, 'I have been studying here over fourteen years and I have *never* seen this!' I didn't really take that in at the time, but this was my first ever encounter with orcas, and pretty much one of the first times I'd been looking for any kind of whale or dolphin at all – beginner's luck. I was stunned into silence, taking it all in, watching the black-and-white shapes porpoising beside us, some jumping right out to get a look at us, huge dorsal fins splitting the water, doing about 8 knots as we sped north, sea mammals every one of us, in convoy to Loreto. The powerful black shapes rocked the sea, water draining quickly from their white saddlebacks and varnishing their ebony sides. A short blow of spray, a breath, and quickly ducking into the ocean again, 4 tons of sea mammal swallowed whole. I could see the hazy shapes of a mother and calf right beneath me, bow riding the boat, with an exhilarating sense of speed and whooshing sea spray.

'What's wrong with you?' Diane called over to me. 'Don't you realise what you're seeing? I have *never* seen this,' she repeated. 'Why aren't you showing any emotions?'

It's true. I wasn't – partly because I was so astonished, and also cursing not having a film crew, but partly too because I wasn't aware that it was compulsory to show your joy, though I'm pretty sure I was feeling something like it inside. I've often reflected on that moment since, so it must have left a big impression.

It set me worrying, subsequently, that I didn't show emotion: that my male mind, and English reserve needed to be overcome (especially at Christmas). Yet if I did display the required quantum of joy, wouldn't it just be contrived? Isn't massive outward excitement impossible if you are just reconstructing what you think others want to see, like a kind of gigantic false smile? It's been a point of discussion in close relationships over the years, all illustrated, believe it or not, by this orca encounter. My wife suggests that it's important to show your emotions so that others know what you're thinking, and I can see the sense in that. Doesn't mean I can do it easily, though, and I would prefer to be sincerely quiet! So for all the magnificence of the orcas and this exciting scene in Baja, what I remember most is being called out for not showing emotion. It's strange how we reflect the world inside ourselves and mix it up a bit. I wonder if orcas do that?

We stayed with this sea mammal family for at least another hour, until they sped off ahead of us and disappeared into the horizon. I do apologise, because that was one amazing event I didn't catch for you, and they never became 'whales in your living room', even if killer whales are actually dolphins.

Behind a sea wall of boulders and a line of tall palms appeared the Spanish looking town of Loreto. Although only blue and white, the boats in Loreto harbour could be called colourful. They are mainly *pangas,* the universal Mexican fishing boat. Mac Shroyer, the one-time Californian teacher who conceived the design in La Paz back in the Sixties, has now made over 3,000 of them. For some reason the interior is always painted sky blue, and the hull white.

Loreto is where our film crew came on board: Rick Rosenthal and David Reichert. Some people you work with you just have to be polite and professional to, and these you call 'colleagues'. Rick and David soon became my friends, and although they live in the States and I don't see them for years, we could pretty much pick up where we left off. But this was the first time we'd met. Rick was known to me as a well-respected underwater cameraman and marine biologist, and made his own films too. I'd seen a poetic film he shot called *Hunters of the Sea Wind,* about the 'tigers of the sea' – marlin, sailfish dolphin and tuna, and how they came together on the current known as the Sea Wind off Costa Rica. David at that time was just starting out. I didn't know much about him, but soon realised his endlessly cheerful, upbeat manner was going to be an asset to any team. An outdoor man, ski-racing and white-water kayaking, he lived in Jackson Hole, Wyoming and trained there as a camera assistant, somehow making the leap to underwater work. He's even filmed moose drinking from underwater!

That night we had a conference on board the *Marylee.* Aboard now were the boat team: John, Joanne, and Raúl, a very experienced Mexican sailor acting as first mate, as well as Rick, David and myself, Diane, and her colleague Sandy Lanham, our spotter pilot. Sandy is one of a kind: once a dancer and a print salesperson, then a flight instructor, she founded her own company after being asked to aerial survey pronghorn antelope in Mexico for the Nature Conservancy, a charitable environmental organisation in the USA. Soon she was also counting blue whales in partnership with Diane. I'd heard of them both through my whale expert friend Mark, who had recommended them as the best people to look for blue whales in Baja. Sandy owned and flew a 1956 Cessna, in faded matt-yellow and brown. 'Bad paint, good heart' she said of the plane, and it still flies today, one of the oldest models in the sky.

In the main cabin of *Marylee*, under low-watt lights, we plotted with the combined knowledge of whale scientist, environmental pilot, captain and camera crew as to where we might best find the blues. We laid out the map of Baja on the cabin table and everyone's fingers traced the coastline up and down, with likely theories about where the treasure was buried. You have some idea where the blue whales might be at a certain time of year in the Gulf, but it's a big place – about half the size of Belgium, if my maths is correct, and with apologies to Belgium, often used as a yardstick to measure other places in the world – although somewhere like Maryland might make more sense if you are in the USA.

In truth, the best way to find whales is from the air. We'd give Sandy a two-day head start to go look for them while the *Marylee* refuelled and restocked. Whenever I've tried to find large marine animals, be they whales or basking sharks, and more recently false killer whales, we've had most success with air support. As you can imagine, it isn't cheap, but it pays off, and the very next day Sandy soon picked up the blues, about 30 miles south of Loreto, not too far from where we'd seen the magnificent killer whale groups, but a bit further out into the open waters of the Gulf. After several years of doing annual surveys of blue whale numbers with Diane and her team from La Paz her experience was obviously second to none.

We'd heard the exciting news when Sandy radioed from the plane to the bridge of the *Marylee*, and it was decided to return to Loreto so Rick could take some shots from the air. Today this would be done with a full gyro-stabilised mount costing $2 million and attached to a helicopter, but back then we were bold or stupid enough to think it could be done just by pointing an old film camera out the window of a vibrating fifty-year-old Cessna. Rick would run the camera at double speed so that, played back at normal speed, some of the vibrations and bumps would be slowed down.

I came along, sitting in the cramped back seat of the Cessna, looking through the yellowing acrylic windows, and soon we were bumping along the runway at Loreto. Below I could see the wheelbarrow tyre of the non-retractable undercarriage, the square layout of Loreto, its ancient Spanish church and courtyards – and then nothing but blue, as the runway's end is only a couple of miles from the sea. As the plane climbs, the shape of the bay around Loreto and the nearby islands, with their slate-blue, split-rock mountains, became clear. The engine was loud enough that you had to use the army-style headsets to talk, but after a while it just became background noise. Past Sandy on the left and Rick on the right I could see the dashboard cluttered with mementos from previous flights: a plastic model of a pronghorn antelope, Sandy's other love, and a small statue of Jesus the more fainthearted would have said was a requirement in a plane of this age. In fact, Sandy swapped out the engine every couple of years and, I venture, planes that are used regularly and serviced often are safer than those taken out of mothballs only once in a while.

We are flying at only about 2,000 feet, and it's a calm day so there are no white wave crests below, and anything that flecks the water could be a whale. 'OK, I spot something over there,' Sandy calls over the headsets, and before we have a chance to see where she means the plane starts a steep turn, as if its wings and fuselage are just an extension of her body. Sandy radios the ship, now maybe twenty miles away: '*Marylee, Marylee*, we've just gotten a big blow. Probably is a blue whale, if you are ready to copy I'm going to pass the co-ordinates over to you.'

Then we saw our first blues.

From the waterline it's hard to say why they are called blue, being anything from mottled grey to almost black, but from the air they shine like sapphires and almost glow from beneath the waves. If you look closely, what's going on is that their bodies are very reflective, with some shiny paler patches on them, and that they're not really blue at all. Only the parts that are under the water near the surface are bright blue, and that's because their reflection lights up the sea like white sand under a blue lagoon, or more accurately like grey moon dust reflects sunlight from the moon. So as they break the water they show their mottled grey back, and just their tail and pectoral fins, still underwater, are blue, with a blue halo outlining the submerged body. To call them 'blue' the first whalers must have seen them from the crow's nest of the topgallant mast. They called them 'sulphur bottom', too, because they sometimes have a yellow haze from the underside that comes from tiny algae growing on the skin.

For the first three or four days Rick and Sandy flew over the blues, spotting them for us on the water and getting unique footage. Their only problem was that there were so many fin whales as well as blue that it was sometimes hard to see whether you were filming the right species. Fins and blues are so similar that they have been known to interbreed, and a calf that showed characteristics of both was found in a mother when the animal was butchered on a whaling ship back in the 1950s. In general, fin whales are darker and sleeker than blues, and have a small but distinct fin on their back shaped like a backward-pointing cheese knife, but that's not something you would notice from the air. The blue is lighter-coloured and more chunky, and when it feeds, gulping a huge patch of krill, it turns on its side and you can see its mouth expand like a balloon about to pop, with ribbed struts inside that are the rakes of its filtering baleen plates.

Very luckily, one day Sandy's yellow Cessna flew directly over a huge light-orange patch of krill that had come to the surface, with several blues quickly scooping their way through this food. Around each whale there was a clear patch of water, a patch they probably had just cleared of krill. These shots were unique at the time, and some of them still stand today as a rare document of blues from the air. Rick was worried that other film companies would copy us, and we had heard there was a National Geographic crew in the area. He was soon speaking in code like a special agent as he and Sandy flew up and down the San José Channel south of Loreto feasting on the sight of whales feasting. When Rick came over the radio saying, 'Send a taxi to Puerto Escondido,' you could be sure you'd meet some blues there!

For more or less the next twenty days we were on the trail of the whale. The big blue whales of Baja. A typical day started at about 6 a.m. with me bumping my head on the starboard console of the wheelhouse control panel, under which I had luxurious sleeping quarters decked out with a sleeping bag and a pillow. David Reichert shared similar accommodation on the other side of a central pillar – thank goodness I didn't snore in those days. The captain, John Barnes, was always up before us, looking across the water, working out what the day held. We drank black coffee, soft with the tastelessness of water makers, salt and trace elements removed from seawater through reverse osmosis. Even smelly dive crews take showers and hog more than the daily water ration from the tanks, so having the maker allows you to stay at sea for ages, using every waking hour to find whales.

It is a smooth day on the water. Another perfect day to find whales. Just after sunrise the surface is silver, with flecks of light blue, shadows of dark blue, and the white glare of bleached paper in the sun. Gentle currents swirl in small spirals all around, mixing the blues, whites and silvers like paint. If it were paint and you had a huge piece of paper to slide over it you'd get one of those swirling abstract creations you did in school, but of course since it changes by the second no two would ever be the same. These currents are there all the time; it's just that on calm days, when the waves are absent, they can be seen.

As we look to the horizon, John and I see the calm water being torn in a huge extended V coming towards us, with multiple tiny wakes. It's a pod of over 300 dolphins that seem to be leaping for joy, and are soon upon us and all around, slowing down to match our idle speed. As they come close, we can see the oval white patches on the side of otherwise glinting grey bodies. These are the long-beaked common dolphins found here in Baja and all down the West coast from California.

The adult dolphins are as long as adult humans, but of course far more athletic than us, and gliding three to five abreast in close synchrony. Within the distant amphitheatre of Baja's mountains and islands, this is an unforgettable performance, sleek bodies bending through the surface in perfect arcs, mothers and calves, brothers and sisters flying briefly into our world and then piercing the boundary again to return to the blue. Their joy is infectious, and clearly they do enjoy the ride with us, and when they break the water they look at the boat and the little 'stick dolphins' standing on its deck, and perhaps they're thinking, in their dolphin way, 'Oh, how strange – one of them has a box it keeps pointing at us!'

David has been pointing the camera from the bow, and playing the frustrating game of trying to get the moment when a group leaps out of the sea – you leave the camera running for ages and get lots of nothing, then you switch off at the exact moment they leap. Actually, technology has solved that one, as you now have a 'buffer' on a pro digital camera and can hit a button to record and capture up to ten seconds *before*. Seems to be a violation of time and a bit of a cheat, but there you are: dolphin leaps for dummies. Since the camera person will have already focused and framed up the image, the image will be good, and when the record button is pressed the camera saves the previous ten seconds as well. I said this technology was available on professional cameras, but I now notice that I have it on my humble phone. What will they think of next?

So how come, when motorboats like ours have only been around for just over a century, dolphins have learnt to have fun with them in this way? Well, I know exactly because I've seen the answer, and we shouldn't flatter ourselves: they've been doing it with great whales for millions of years. Once I saw maybe fifty riding in the wake of a blue whale in exactly the same way they do with a boat. Like cyclists in the Tour de France there's a lot to be gained by tucking into the slipstream of the bike, boat or baleen whale in front. The dolphin calves do it with their mothers, tucking in close just behind the fattest part of her flank and saving, it has been estimated, up to 60 per cent of their swimming effort.

Shots of dolphins bow-riding are as common as shore crabs, and usually only part of a bigger sequence in an ocean wildlife film such as dolphins corralling huge shoals of fish in well-co-ordinated feeding frenzies. Yet although commonplace it is always worth keeping your eye out for special moments that sometimes just seem to unfold in front of you, leaving you dumbfounded for a few seconds before you can say, 'Have you got that shot?'

Such a thing happened that evening when we again met a pod of dolphins, though not quite as many. The *Marylee* was motoring slightly faster than usual, and accelerating, and at a certain speed large waves were generated by some kind of resonance as our hull skimmed over smooth water. The waves spread out behind us in a train like those a surfer might catch. Indeed, surfers did catch them – dolphin surfers – and there was something about these 'standing' waves that seemed to trap the dolphins inside so that for a few seconds you could see their faces, head-on, clearly through the water. After watching this for a while, and marvelling at the beauty of it, it dawned on me that it would make some very graceful shots of dolphins, and that the angle was just right to make you believe you were in the water with them as they swam. Rick already had his film camera set up, so we turned around to do another run at the same speed. Rick shot it from a very stable deck on a smooth sea and ran the camera at high speed. The results were astonishing, and those shots became the dolphin faces you see inside the glass globe of the title pictures in the first series of *Blue Planet*.

Often you can be at sea ages and see nothing. Even the biggest creature that ever lived can be hidden in the expanse. This time it was different, and over the next three weeks we were to see blue whales on all except two days. Once we counted seventeen around us, the spray of their blows backlit in the sun like crystal fountains. That's not to say you can capture that easily on the film. You need to be close and, not wanting or allowed to chase them, we have to wait for them to come near. Even close up you can only see their enormous pebble-shaped back, often dark against dark blue water and not distinctive in a TV frame. If not close, then the lens has to zoom in, which amplifies any motion on the deck. So though you might think seeing lots of whales translates into great shots, it's only one or two very close encounters, of a complete behaviour like a blow or tail fluke plunging, that will make it to the final cut.

A blue whale can dive below for thirty minutes or more, although it was often shorter in Baja – maybe because it was shallower than elsewhere? Even so, travelling at, say, an average of 8 knots, it's possible they will be 2 miles away from their previous surfacing position when they next come up, and that's if they're feeding. If they want to, they can swim at three times that speed, which would explain why we were able to stay with a group only a couple of hours before they gave us the slip. All day long we would play this guessing game of where they would come up next. If it were more than half a seaside pier's length away when they first surfaced, you could forget any good shots. On average I counted a surfacing blue as making thirteen blows or breaths over about two to four minutes on the surface, and then they went down again. I even made a little diagram of our days' filming with some blues: the directions they went and how long between dives, in case there was any pattern, but I could never find one. I guess they were just following krill swarms, which in turn describe a random pattern in the current. Even if they were socialising, or just swimming, there was no pattern there either. We imagined a *Sea Mammal vs Human* scoreboard of the number of times whales teased us with their sightings but were not close enough to film, and the final score for the whole shoot was *Blue Whales* 158, *Humans* 2.

These days were Groundhog Days, each one a relentless focus on getting good shots of blues, but essentially the same kind of day. The sea, the whales, the islands and the mountains of Baja, the drone of the boat's engines, the smell of aircraft fuel: all seemed to become one, outside the boundaries of time. I can tell you, though, that on 18 March 1999 an entry in my dive log says, 'Setting dangle cam on garden eels'. That was one of the rarer days when we weren't seeing the blues and had anchored in 'an uncharted lagoon of the San José channel'. It might have been that the weather away from the coast wasn't great, but in any case we didn't like to be doing nothing, and so we went on a dive under the boat to see what was there. This is the seascape that Ed Ricketts, the famous marine biologist, already introduced, wrote about in the 1930s in his famous book *Between Pacific Tides*. Except that Ricketts never had any scuba gear, and what we were seeing was 'below Pacific tides'. Visibility wasn't great compared to the open Pacific: about 15 feet (5 metres), with a lot of silt and small plankton. Some of it contained tiny jellyfish whose sting on your face was exquisitely painful, although your swelling lips gave you a little of the Botox glamour of a Hollywood film star.

On the seabed was something comical and extraordinary. A forest of thousands of very long eels. But these were the vertical kind, each planted in a hole of their own in the sand. They are called 'garden eels' as it looks as though they are growing right out of the seabed. Curiously, they are very shy, and you only had to breathe out from your scuba gear for them all to retract into their holes. Since what you could see was about 4 feet (just over a metre) of eel when they were fully extended, their holes must be deep or perhaps spiral-shaped for them to be able to tuck themselves away until only their head and eyes peer out flush with the seabed. Since they didn't want to be filmed directly I had the idea of using one of our remote cameras, and just leaving it running outside the eel homes. 'Dangle cam' consisted of a small camera in a dome on the end of about 250 feet (80 metres) of cable, and it just dangled under the boat linked into a monitor inside the cabin, it had also been used to film lobsters at night and inside heavy sea storms. 'Garden Eel TV' soon became the top hit station on the *Marylee* because, sure enough, very soon after we left, they popped right up again, and the whole forest of eels swaying in the background, with some close-up in the foreground, looked very impressive. They seemed to be writhing to the tune of 'Walk Like an Egyptian', and even bent their heads as you do your hands in that dance as they snatched plankton from the current. You could see great detail on their skin, and the tell-tale signs of what's called a 'lateral line', which is the channel a fish has down its side that picks up vibrations. In the garden eel it is very big, which explains why they flinched so quickly when they heard the bubbles of the scuba. Perhaps sea lions or other predators go wild for them? That day's filming never made it to the show, which is a pity, because I thought it was great. I've always thought it would make a brilliant screen saver for your computer, as the eels could pop up when you walk away and retract into their holes when you come near.

After twelve days at sea continuously filming whales we had to refuel. We had been steadily working our way south, retracing the route where we had seen the orcas. There was no sign of them as we returned into La Paz bay, but in the distance were some big leaping black shapes, which turned out to be false killer whales, too far to film. It would be fifteen years later, in New Zealand, before I finally caught up with that species and realised how magnificent they were close up, and yet again how little we know about even the larger animals in the sea.

Further on our southwards journey I counted many other species of whales and dolphins in just one day, from grey whales to humpbacks, fins and sei whales, bottlenose, spotted and Pacific white-sided dolphins. Once we thought we saw a vaquita, the world's smallest porpoise, mother and tiny calf swimming very close to shore quite a distance from our boat. It was more likely to be another species, however, because we were too far south for this rare mammal endemic to Baja. How rare? Well, in 1999 there could perhaps have been 200; by 2019 only 22 were counted in the whole of the Sea of Cortez. By the time you read this it may be extinct, killed off by the banned gill nets used to catch totoaba, a prized fish that sells in Asia for thousands of dollars a kilo. We have known that this rarest of cetaceans was endangered since 1976.

The mountains of Baja are stunning. Ripped from the North American Plate somewhat along the lines of the San Andreas

Fault, they have been stolen by the Pacific plate and the whole gulf is continuing to tear northwards, one day to amputate much of California itself and cut it adrift into the Pacific. The mountains are a mixture of faults and volcanoes, and from a distance seem naked, but with a little moisture from sea mists blown inland from the Pacific they support a variety of interesting vegetation. The eastern side we look onto as we travel back towards La Paz is drier than the west and more sparsely covered. In places cardón cactus, the world's tallest species, can be seen, sticking upwards as if a giant had parked his fork in the sand with the intention of coming back to finish his meal. The smoke tree, whose fire is lit by occasional rain, billows with fine bluish clouds of flowers, and the medicinal creosote shrubs grow with yellow flowers that remind me of the gorse bushes on Welsh mountains near where I grew up. Higher up little else grows, but the rocks reflect the sun with every shade of red and orange you can imagine and, in the evening, mysteriously turn blue.

Soon we're back in La Paz harbour, where it was only a couple of weeks ago that I'd met John and Joanne and the *Marylee*. Already they seem like family and I feel a different person. No longer the etiolated Englishman coming out of the cold British winter, but sun-tanned, wind-washed, sea-salted, and confident. Confident that we've got something in the can to take back home.

We are paid by the working week, and that means five days' pay for seven days' work when you're on location. Most times we are hardly aware whether it's a weekend or not, but we feel we can take one evening off. I ask John if there are any local sites we should see, and particularly any really traditional Mexican places in La Paz. Without hesitation he recommends an old bar called Lord Black which he says is very 'traditionally Mexican' indeed. I ask him if I can buy him a beer there, but he says he's got too many things to sort on the boat.

So David and I get a taxi to Lord Black; the driver seems friendly and smiles when we tell him our destination, confirming our wise choice. Inside it's heaving (it was a Friday night, I think) and, after a struggle to get to the bar, the beer is good. The room is unusually long and full of locals; all men, in fact, now I come to think of it, and smartly turned out in dark jackets and white shirts. Yes, this seems just the flavour of local culture I'd been looking for. And then the music starts up, the crowd in the centre of the room parts to reveal a runway, and shortly several ladies strut along this platform. Naked ladies, that is, and then everything falls into place: the men's bar, the locals, the popularity, the smiling taxi driver, Rick saying he was cleaning his camera, and the penny drops as to where John has sent us. Still, in the warm bar sitting near the runway I feel a glow, the music becomes fuzzy, and I fall into one of those deep, contented sleeps you can only have when you've been outside all day and, work finished, you can rest at last. After a while a slightly blushing David nudges me, and when we get back to the boat, much to John's amusement, it's still only 9 p.m. 'Was that traditional enough for you?' asks John, grinning.

That coy episode bears little resemblance to that heady journey here of John Steinbeck and Ed Ricketts in the late 1930s, as I read in a memoir by Sparky Enea, a crew member who travelled with them both on the *Western Flyer*, a ship they chartered from Monterey. *With Steinbeck in the Sea of Cortez* is a savvy and humorous account by Sparky of that famous scientific expedition, and tells of the drinking and the numerous brothels they visited, and the affair Steinbeck's wife Carol had with the *Western Flyer's* captain, Tony Berry. *Human* biology was only an aside to the marine biology, of course, but it must have added a certain frisson to their trip.

Steinbeck and Ricketts were way ahead of their time in their thoughts on marine conservation. Writing the account of their trip, published first as *Sea of Cortez: A Leisurely Journal of Travel and Research* (1941), they tell of seeing industrial fishing boats taking huge and wasteful catches, 'committing a true crime against nature, and against the immediate welfare of Mexico, and the eventual welfare of the whole human species'. Again, that's someone pointing out the obvious over eighty years ago, when even today people still ignore the truth that if you keep on taking there will be nothing left.

Tragically, as mentioned (Chapter 9), Ricketts was killed when the Del Monte Express to San Francisco hit his old Buick at a crossing in Monterey. After his friend's death Steinbeck re-edited the initially unsuccessful story of their expedition, dropping the species catalogue by Ricketts, into another book entitled *The Log from the Sea of Cortez*, including a eulogy to Ricketts. But with regard to the little creatures it's Ricketts' book, *Between Pacific Tides* (co-author Jack Calvin), that endures. On the humble ecology of marine invertebrates of the West Coast it has been in almost continuous publication since 1939, going into its fifth edition and selling over 100,000 copies. In the foreword that John Steinbeck wrote in 1948, he suggests the book is a 'peephole' into tidepools that will 'fish in some new beauty and some new pattern, and the world of the human mind must be enriched by such fishing'. Still, books about spineless marine animals are not obvious bestsellers.

Yet Steinbeck's emotionally charged writing perfectly contrasts the scientific texts of Ricketts, and his descriptions of the glowing mountains around the Baja sea capture the mood of this special place and how it draws you in: 'The sky sucks up the land and disgorges it. A dream hangs over the whole region, a brooding kind of hallucination.' Ricketts and Steinbeck seem to me to be a great partnership between fact and emotion, science and expression. Maybe that resonates with me because that's what I feel a wildlife documentary at its best might be.

I have the luxury to think of that only in retrospect because, refuelled and rested, we needed to get on the 'blue road' again for the next leg of this shoot. Our mission now focused on getting underwater shots of the blues. We returned northwards to the San José channel just before Loreto and, sure enough, there they were still, waiting for us, perhaps. Getting really good shots of blues from the deck of a ship is hard, but in the greenish waters of Baja, when visibility is sometimes less than 20 feet, you might think it impossible or even dangerous to attempt underwater shots. Rick and David now gave it their best.

Rick, our main cameraman or DOP, is wise about the sea in a way I have seldom heard. When he tells you of the moods on the sea, what the birds are doing, where the bait lies, you would say he is being a mystic or superstitious, except that his knowledge was usually spot on and produced results. He knows when a 'moment' is about to happen; the moment that will make the cut. So it was that he put us in the path of blues several times. Most often the way to film or swim near big whales in the water on the surface is to use snorkels rather than dive tanks. Some use small pony cylinders, but Rick is a fan of free diving, and once, a few years later, I went in with him off the Azores, where he dived down to sperm whales and stayed holding his breath far longer than I could, and he twenty years older than me and by then in his early seventies.

On this blue whale shoot he took David, at the time a kind of apprentice cameraman, under his wing, and I often heard him say, 'Davey: no tankie, only snorkie'. The reason, apart from that it's not safe to dive deep and suddenly come up, as you might have to on a small tank, is that you are tremendously clumsy at the surface with your tank on your back, and pretty buoyant too, so it's difficult to position yourself quickly. Plus, the flare of bubbles that comes out is sometimes perceived as a threat by the whale, because if you can produce that many bubbles you must be very big. On many occasions Rick and David snorkelled out from the little *panga* and waited for the thundering train that is a swimming blue to come past. But every time a strange thing happened and it jumped the tracks.

The moment I remember most is when we were right in front of a blue whale mother and calf coming full tilt towards us from about a mile away. We stopped the *panga* and were just drifting. The mother boat, *Marylee*, was drifting too, about half a mile behind, with all echo-sounding gear, pumps and electrics switched off, in case anything deterred the whales. We held onto the small boat's hull and slid quietly into the water, 'sneaky like a snake', as David was fond of saying. I had the behind-the-scenes camera, hoping to get a shot of Rick getting the shot of the whales. He swam ahead, and, above the water, I could see the enormous shapes rapidly closing the distance. Underwater it had to be less than 30 feet before the visibility would allow Rick to capture anything. I'd seen mother and calf from the air, so I knew what awesome animals they were, but from the sky you don't really get a sense of their speed. Larger ships travel faster, and larger whales do too, the ratio of power to water resistance being more favourable for larger vessels. The blue whale has been clocked at 31 mph (50 kph) for short bursts, which is about the speed a water skier is towed, and more than twice the top speed of a fishing boat. So now 150, 120, 100, 80 feet away this mother and calf were surely going to almost run us over. This was going to be a great under-water shot.

But then they turned in a gentle curve, very blatantly, away from Rick. From the surface you'd think, looking at Rick's tiny figure silhouetted against the flanks of the whales, they were close enough to film. But underwater it was all green and dark, and you'd be lucky to make out anything at the distance they came by. 'They seem to have a sense they're not supposed to have,' said Rick, 'but something is going on.' It wasn't vision, because they certainly couldn't see us in that water either. It must have been something to do with their hearing.

Generally it is only toothed whales, orcas, sperm whales and common dolphins that are known to use echolocation at short range. Researchers at Cornell University have discovered that blue whales can bounce very loud, deep sounds off the seabed to help them navigate over long distances, but even twenty years later from our encounters in Baja I don't think anyone has yet shown that they can detect small things like puny human bodies at short range. They do, though.

The technique with trying to film from the *panga* never worked, but we had noticed that the blues sometimes took an interest in our mother boat *Marylee*. Even when it was just drifting, they would sometimes seem to come close to inspect, and then dive under its hull at tremendous speed. It was on one such pass that we got our only underwater shot. David and Rick had noticed that a blue was going to dive under our hull and quickly co-ordinated with John, the captain, to stop. Then they both went into the water, sliding swiftly off the stern with

David on the digital camera, just in time for the blue to pass right by him under his legs: a unique shot that lasted just twelve seconds.

They didn't tell me about it at first, but later, after David was sure it had been framed and recorded properly, they both made me close my eyes until they had lined up those twelve seconds on the TV in the central cabin, and then revealed it with glee. It made me realise how much they knew it meant to me and the whole team. David went on to be a world-class underwater cameraman, and for a series called *The Hunt* got amazing shots of the blues feeding from underwater, things beyond our wildest dreams in Baja in 1999. He recently told me he thinks it's to do with the visibility: he'd filmed the blues for *The Hunt* in clear waters off the Pacific coast of California. It may have been, he thought, that they didn't turn away or speed off because they could see him, and understand that he wasn't a threat.

Although the *panga* towed behind the *Marylee* hadn't proved much good for placing a diver, it was low to the water, and gave the chance for other more impressive shots of the blues. Again, the same issue applied of needing to be close, yet not chasing the whale. Even so David and Rick described their dream shot as to be so near that they were 'getting shade' under the tail or fluke of the whale as it tilted its body down to raise the tail before a dive. It was a shot that had optimistically been put on my storyboard from the start, but you'd have to be lucky to get that near, and blues don't always 'fluke', as it's called, either, sometimes going down without lifting their tail. All in all, it seemed unlikely they'd get the chance for shade, but the one big thing we had going for us was the time to find the right moment.

For the next few days David and Rick ventured out again on the *panga* whenever we got feasibly near to a blue. It had to surface almost next to us, and our scientist Diane, in her role of permit minder, was anxious we didn't push it. It was a delicate balance, knowing you must do the right thing by the whale, but also knowing how powerful a close shot of the fluke going down might be to millions of viewers. But how do you get behind a whale without slowly moving forwards? Sometimes the whales will dive shallow, and just come up again almost immediately: that was our chance – inching forward when we noticed such a short dive and then waiting. It would take all our skill and nerves. What are the chances, I thought?

You try and try for days, and such a shot seems impossible, and then all at once the impossible unfolds before you, as though you've learnt the choreography of a complex dance and suddenly one day you can perform it. In my mind I can play back such a scene: I'm on the deck of the *Marylee*, I'm filming Rick and David on the *panga* about half a mile in front of us, when it all just seems to slot in place. I can see them slowly come up behind the blue about to dive: David on the tiller, Rick standing at the bow as firmly as he can, legs out and crouching low to reduce his centre of gravity. Then, right in front of him, almost splashing water on his camera, if not *giving him shade*, the blue whale lifts its tail and dives.

When Rick retells the story he says,

> I'm running at double speed on the film camera, and I just see its tail come up in front of me. Dave is doing his best to steer, but I know that outboard

motor always makes a little clunk when it goes into gear, and I'm just waiting for the moment when he has to do that to keep us moving slowly forward. Sure enough, halfway through my shot, the engine clunks, and the boat makes a sudden start. But I've been expecting it: I'm spread-eagled, trying to lock my knees, keeping the camera as steady as I can and pointing right down the back of the blue, and I just keep running. When I look back at the shot you can hardly see that sudden jerk, but I know where it is.

I look down the arching back of that blue and I can see all its vertebrae – in fact, that individual looks a bit thin, perhaps – but then I see its tail lift up, with silver trails of water running off the wings of its fluke, so near you can see barnacles that have attached like brown strings. In my whole body I experience a moment of utter joy and relief, knowing we've got something special.

It's not impossible that by now a billion people have seen that shot, with Sir David Attenborough pointing out that a blue whale has a tailfin as wide as the wings of a small aircraft. On Netflix it's used to trail the whole first series, and so perhaps *that* was the moment when the whale revealed its magnificence, let us breathe in its size, and came into the living room and closed the door.

It's human nature that, as soon as you've got what you want, it doesn't seem so desirable any more, and you're on to the next thing. From the films you've seen since the first series of *Blue Planet* you'll know that the standard is raised every time, until nowadays you can stare right into the eye of a whale filling the frame of your TV as though it's looking right inside your house. One of the shots I desperately wanted was to see the whales open their nostrils, or blowholes, as they surfaced and blew a spume of water right up to the lens of a camera hovering high above. We couldn't do that in 1999 because drones hadn't been invented, but shortly before this adventure I had been reading a book called *Kite Aerial Photography*, and I knew of a shop in Covent Garden in London that made large kites to order. I worked out the size needed to lift a 26-lb (12-kg) camera in an average wind and ordered it, but a little too late, unfortunately, for it to arrive at the Natural History Unit in Bristol before we went out to Mexico. No matter I thought; we'd have it sent on. Three weeks later in La Paz it arrived in the scientific field station I'd addressed it to. Or at least its control lines did. The canopy, made from light-blue ripstop nylon, was nowhere to be seen, which was a bit disappointing to say the least. My career as a kite cameraman would never get off the ground, but, hey, we had a lot of other stuff to do. About four months later, back in the UK, the mystery was solved. I got a big parcel, untidily wrapped, with bits of light-blue cloth sticking out. Inside was a note from customs in Mexico City that stated this material, clearly meant for a wedding dress, is subject to Wedding Tax duty, and that the owner must come to Mexico City, where the parcel is being held, to pay the duty in person, otherwise it would be sent back to the UK. I never got the message, or the wedding proposal.

So March 1999 turned out to be the most amazing feast of blue whale sightings: some captured, some missed, like the evening a blue turned over right in front of us to reveal its filtering baleen plates, but it was too dark to film. But film-making is about what you capture, not what you miss.

* * *

Twelve years later I'm in La Paz again for another documentary, standing under the hull of that same ship, the *Marylee*. She's been hauled out of the harbour and sits forlorn and rusting in a cradle, in what might be a steel graveyard if her overhaul is left unfinished. Her bright-blue, blocked name is still cheerful on the stern, but panels are missing and the engine covers are open. I stand still for almost an hour looking at the rivets, the copper-green prop blades, the broken deck rails and the orange rust streaks that leak like tears from her portholes. Wind gently whistles through her frame to stir the ghosts of passengers past, and the twenty-five days we spent on those decks at the end of the century. It does seem like a dream now.

14

Blue Whales II

Filming blue whales with Sir David Attenborough

David Attenborough caused me to lose my sunglasses. I don't blame him, of course, because it was my fault – I left them in the hire car going to the airport to pick him up. I remember it because I had never bought expensive sunglasses before but, mindful of the huge amounts of UV you get off the water in the open ocean, I thought I'd better be serious about some eye protection. I was distracted because I was thinking of what Sir David meant to me and to millions of other people. I don't like celebrity much, but not because it is shallow, as most people have done something to deserve it, if only to put up with the pestilence of the press. It's more because it seems to make the individual concerned live in an artificial little bubble of fame. Sometimes I wonder about the mega-famous people of history, and whether Albert Einstein, Florence Nightingale or even, say, Amy Whitehouse as we know them were actually real people. Their fame transcended the fact that they were just humans, and the real person inside was manipulated by the press and by public opinion until all we are left with is an assumed personality that might bear little resemblance to the actual person and how they lived.

What I have noticed about David, on the few occasions I have met and worked with him, is that people seem to want a piece of him: something that will give them reflected glory and raise their status, although of course no one would admit that, even to themselves. My experience is that he'd just like to be treated normally, without too much fuss. Yet it's true he has profoundly affected many, many people in good ways he will never know. I've met countless examples of people whose careers he has changed, or simply their belief in themselves, merely with a little encouragement and inspiration. A lot of that inspiration, of course, comes indirectly from watching the films he narrates.

Normally I would only see someone as famous as Sir David for a couple of hours when he comes into a studio to read a narration on almost-complete films. He gets those scripts at least a week in advance and spends several days amending, making them better and putting some parts into his own words, to make for more fluent reading. At other times, when he is nearer the subject matter – for example, in *The Life of Mammals* – he writes the script mostly himself. He is of course fully knowledgeable about the subject matter and always enthusiastic about the biology, but it would simply not be practical, with all the demands on his time, to be present and involved all the way through a production. Even in his nineties he can finish reading a fifty-minute script to pictures in about fifty-two minutes with just a couple of retakes. So he comes into the recording studio, and he's off again before you know it. Usually my conversations are just grabbed ones with him at the start and end of such sessions. Although he's always friendly, these tend to be a bit stilted, as you can't but help to be in awe of the man.

'How are you, John?' he asks. How he can remember me from any other John is always impressive. He was Controller of BBC2, for example, responsible for the start of colour TV. I wish I could remember names so well.

'I'm OK, David, but I've been travelling too much lately,' I find myself blurting out, and then realise I'm talking to probably one of the most travelled people alive.

He sees the funny side too as his eyes have a cheeky sparkle. 'Oh, you love it really, don't you!'

'Yes, but I have a young family and I'd like to see them more.' Again, words randomly escaping from my head, but curiously truthful.

He becomes more serious. 'Oh yes, I know what you mean. I felt that too when I was away so much and the children were young.'

For a moment I am silent, contemplating something I'd never thought before: that a man who has travelled the world to tell us about life on Earth might also have some personal regrets about doing that. That's what I mean about famous people: we forget they're only human.

So it was a treat to spend three days at sea finding blue whales with David and the team over one weekend in early October 2000, only a year before the whole first series of *Blue Planet* would air, and one of the last field shoots before editing. For *Blue Planet*, David was to do a piece to camera, ideally with a blue whale in the background. That's what's called a 'two-shot' – the presenter and the animal all in the same shot, which gives it a more immediate, authentic feel. Alastair Fothergill, series producer, suggested I should direct the *Blue Planet* bit, but had also done a money-share deal on this shoot with *The Life of Mammals*, already planned as the next series out the door after

Blue Planet, so there was going to be another producer for that, Neil Lucas, joining us for the key days. The plan was to get David on a boat and do two different scripts, one after the other.

We all checked in to a convenient motel in Half Moon Bay, near the marina where the filming and science boat was tied up. A young person at reception asked David to spell his name, and he quipped that they probably didn't watch Public Broadcasting Service (PBS).

We got down to the dock early, and I remember a nose-singeing sulphurous smell, and that all around there was rotting seaweed, some still intact and recognisable as Californian kelp, and some that looked melted, as though someone had poured a giant vat of green custard into the sea. There were flies everywhere, black clotted masses on the rocks and over the kelp. These, I learnt, were the well-named 'kelp flies' that feed on kelp, and 'bloom' when there has been a storm, as there had been only a couple of weeks ago. The increased frequency of those storms, by the way, is thought by some to be a further indicator of climate change, but just twenty years ago I don't think we even discussed that.

We met up with the science team on the research boat, but it too was thick with flies, as someone had obviously left the doors open overnight. Hundreds of small black dots flitted about the cabin and flew to the light of the windows buzzing to get out. Out of the corner of my eye I saw David roll up a supplement which probably belonged to the famous Californian newspaper the *Mercury News,* which had been lying on the table. Then he started to swat the flies on the window with it. I could only watch this for so long before I had to comment, 'That David Attenborough, he wouldn't hurt a fly!' He grinned back a little sheepishly.

Remembering that story has caused me to look up the scientific name of the kelp fly in question: *Coelopa frigida*. It's named after the cold winds that herald its arrival with the storms and, being one of the most widespread of all seaweed flies, appears to be one of the winners of climate change, as more kelp is washed up on the beach. It seems its larvae, at least, don't eat kelp itself, but the bacteria that grow on rotting seaweed. It just goes to show that all wildlife has its story, although for obvious reasons we tend to concentrate on bigger, more charismatic and awesome animals like the blue whales.

Given that it had taken us over three weeks to get good shots of blue whales in Mexico, how were we going to do that in just the three days we had of David's time? The answer was to go with a scientist who had a satellite transmitter on some blue whales. Bruce Mate at the University of Oregon is a prolific author of research papers on large whales – the blue and its close relative the fin whale, for example. At the time we met him his focus was on tracking the blue whales off the Californian and Mexican Pacific coast, some of which were also going into the Sea of Cortez, where we had been doing that detailed film shoot a few months earlier. We know very little about the lives of blue whales – where they go, where they breed, and how and where they raise their calves – and by using the satellite tags Bruce's team aimed to find out a little more. They had already got several tags out in the previous season, but wanted to attach a few more to some blue whales off the Californian coast in the fall of 2000.

One of the reasons we go with scientists to film, apart from the fact that we can share some of the costs, is that they have the valid permits to get close to creatures like blue whales. That was the case with Diane, as I mentioned, when we were filming in Mexico, but the USA has even tougher laws. The Marine Mammal Protection Act, 1972, gives all marine mammals within United States waters strong protection, and rightly there are heavy fines for 'any act of pursuit, torment or annoyance'. You can forget filming marine mammals off California if you don't have at least some permitted access. One of the valid reasons to get close to whales is to do marine research that will benefit the animals, and Bruce's work, trying to understand the migration and breeding patterns of the whales off the West Coast of the US, was a good example. While Bruce was doing his tagging work, we would be allowed to come close to film him and the blues too. Some of this 'behind-the-scenes' science would go into the ten-minute 'making-ofs' I was producing at the end of each episode, which also fulfilled the remit for 'outreach' and publicising the research on blue whales at the University of Oregon where Bruce's lab was based. In real terms this kind of collaboration means paying your way as a film crew and contributing to the cost of the satellite tags, which in 2000 for a blue were about $13,000 each. This would be an unusually large cost, and only a show with a *Blue Planet*-type budget could even contemplate it.

It was amazing to sit in that cabin with David as we chugged out to sea, heading north towards San Francisco into the Gulf of the Farallones, where Bruce Mate's satellite tags had told us the blues would be waiting for us. We couldn't resist discussing David's time developing TV in the 1960s, when he was brought in to mould the new BBC2 channel and commissioned such epics as the thirteen-part *Civilisation*, in part to show off the new innovation of colour television. He'd been involved with series like *Play For Today* and knew, indeed helped the careers of, famous playwrights like Dennis Potter, and he also knew all the senior management of the BBC in those formative days and beyond: people I'd seen walking down the corridors from a distance but never spoken to directly, like the chairman of the BBC in the 1980s, Marmaduke Hussey, a Second World War veteran; people who have just vanished like the dinosaurs while David's TV career has carried on and evolved like the life of mammals themselves. I would have liked to hear so much more about his time shaping British television, and his memories of some of the major figures of the twentieth century.

The satellite feed Bruce was able to download on his computer, with only a few hours' delay, would give us a rough fix on his study whales' location. But that's not quite enough if you only have three days and need to be right near a whale. Besides only a few of the whales had satellite tags, although it was likely those that did would be swimming in a loose pod with those that didn't. So we needed some air support, and had hired a helicopter to locate the whales precisely, and guide the surface team on the boat right to the blues. In the sea there is a hell of a lot of difference in knowing roughly where something is and knowing exactly where it is – try finding a hat twenty seconds after it has blown into the water. I had assumed the helicopter radio and the marine radio on the boat could talk to each other, and there was an embarrassing moment when I discovered that, Sod's law, the marine and aerial radios were on incompatible frequencies. As fast as we could we arranged a way of relaying the chat via cell 'phones, which worked, but it was a sweaty moment for me and wasted half an hour of helicopter time.

Despite the small setbacks I could see something we'd planned for months now unfolding as intended. With the helicopter and the researcher's expertise there was more control over how we could film a blue whale than the previous time in Mexico. Close now, we deployed the RIB from the mother ship, and directed by the helicopter we soon heard whale blows in front of us. Blue whales are perhaps the fastest of all, which is why they were among the last to be hunted, but when calmly swimming along they can be caught up by your average RIB. You have to be within about 3–10 metres (13–32 feet) though to place the satellite tag, which is very close indeed to such a massive creature.

Bruce loaded the tag into a small crossbow, standing ready on a raised metal gantry on the boat's bow, looking intently in the direction of where the whales had last surfaced. The tag itself was relatively big, because it needed a lot of battery power to track whale movements over months and communicate to a satellite every time it surfaced. It had a short barb at one end, and that's how it stayed on the whale, with a blob of antiseptic on it too in case it caused infection. Bruce assured us that to a whale this was a pinprick, and there was very little noticeable reaction when it was inserted. Indeed, there are natural things like giant whale barnacles that penetrate the skin even more deeply. However, I can't help thinking of 'Cranston's law'.

Bob Cranston was the cameraman I had worked with a lot on *Blue Planet*, and it would not be an exaggeration to say we had had many life changing adventures together – so I always listened closely. 'When a scientist tells you the tag is harmless that's fine, and probably true,' he used to say, 'but just to check, I think they should put one in themselves to make sure it doesn't hurt!' It's true, though, that we hardly saw the whale flinch when one of the tags was put into its skin. Satellite data from Bruce's tags also show the whales don't change their speed after being tagged either, suggesting they are indeed benign.

The helicopter had to leave to refuel, and I felt a little of the certainty of what we were going to get leave with it. But after perhaps forty minutes of drifting under cold and unusually grey Californian skies, almost in sight of San Francisco, we heard the deep rumble of expelled air as four blues surfaced close to us. None of them had a tag. The scientist, now fully animated, called out curt directions to the driver, and DOP Mike DeGruy, focussed on the action, began shouting to Bruce to help him keep in the frame of the closely held camera. The sound guy, Mike Kasic, had an extra-long boom pole stretched across the deck towards the action, and so from a distance the small boat looked like some kind of weird artisanal fishing craft, moving with frantic intent. The rest of us, hiding from the sea spray, were crouched over the camera monitor in the stern, linked to Mike's camera by a thin cable, and trying not to get the electronics or ourselves wet as we bumped over the waves. Soon we were right alongside a blue, close enough to see the mottled texture of its skin, the clouds of spray that shoot upwards with its breath and the 'bow' wake they make as they drive through the water.

'Left, left, left – straighten up,' Bruce was calling to the boat driver. 'Keep steady. Steady . . . ' and in a swift manoeuvre, almost too fast to see, there was the muffled thud of the dart and Bruce had the tag in the whale. There was an almost imperceptible twitch from the whale, but it continued swimming as if nothing had happened. We saw several attempts, successful and otherwise, to place the tags, which even up to a year later would give invaluable data about the blue whales, data that in future might be used to argue for plans to safeguard their feeding grounds and migration routes. Then, the work of science satisfied, we got ready to do the piece David was going to do to camera, while also trying to co-ordinate the shots of whales in the background.

When you are in the field you live for these hopefully planned moments, sometimes finding it hard to imagine they could ever happen . . . and then, there they are, just unfolding in front of you. It's a thrill to see a blue whale close up, and for a documentary director an even bigger one to see your presenter in front of it as the proof of the animal's existence.

'I can see its tail just under my boat here,' says David, looking into the water at the huge blue triangle. 'It's coming up, coming up, the blue whale!' He's shouting and looking straight into the camera, excited laughter on his face like a small boy with the best birthday present. 'The biggest creature that exists or has ever existed on the planet.' Then there follows the only passing *underwater* shot we ever got of a blue whale, which is particularly gratifying for me because it was the fruits of our effort in Baja several months earlier.

When the whole shoot was finished it fell on me to take out the whole team, scientists, film crew, boat crew and David for a good meal. Sitting next to Bruce and Sir David I overheard the professor ask him how he got his knighthood.

'For slaying dragons!'

15

The Red and Orange Sea

Coral wonders

Phil is standing on the shoreline with what seems like a fast-flowing river behind him, but in fact it is the main entrance to the lagoon of Fakarava. We are in the centre of the Tuamotu Islands, in French Polynesia about 200 miles from Tahiti and stretching eastwards in the largest chain of atolls in the world: a place I had hoped to see when I was a boy, though did not know its name, as I trailed a stubby finger over the blue area of a revolving classroom globe. It's about four o'clock and the light is starting to get low, although there are fantastic towering clouds moving explosively upwards, tingling with electric energy from the day's heat. Fortunately, it's going to be quick to do this short piece to camera with Phil. He knows what he's talking about and, as an ex-US Navy captain, able to express it clearly and in a way that commands you to listen:

We've been at science a long time, but now let's go into *coral* science. We've been naming diseases by names like black band disease, dark spot disease; it reminds me of medieval days when we used to bleed people for ailments, and you think of the advances we've made in medicine and that's the kind of advances we need to make in coral-reef science.

There: in the bag in one take. It's only a sentence, or two, but it will get the scenes about coral off to a good start.

To our left I can clearly see the glow of a full moon rising above the waves. The Moon: the timepiece, meshing with the Sun and Earth in precise orbits that can be predicted thousands of years into the future. The last entry in the *Five Millennium Canon of Solar Eclipses*, the current guide to the subject, is for the Moon to block the Sun in a total eclipse on 26 April 3000, when it will even be visible in the UK, though of course it'll be cloudy, I suppose.

The canon's predictions presumably only stop where they do because any further would take you into a second volume; theoretically, those tables could be calculated with reasonable accuracy for at least another 600 million years. But nature just knows this stuff, and the creatures of the sea in particular rely on that big white pocket watch in the sky to tell them when to party. It helped us too, because we knew that the first rising tide after the full moon would signal an ocean spectacular.

Captain Phil Renaud was executive director of the Khaled bin Sultan Living Oceans Foundation. Phil's a man with a great empathy for and obvious love of the sea, and I liked him a lot. He's something of a mixture between gentle officer, marine scientist and diplomat. Retired from the US Navy, he'd been in charge of a research vessel, but was now navigating the cultures of Arabia and the USA to manage an ambitious project to map all the corals of the world: the Global Reef Expedition, which I began to tell you about in Chapter 2.

Working for the BBC has its moments, but since I left its staff I found a freedom that goes with the precarious freelance life I now lead. Working with the Living Oceans Foundation allowed me more latitude, and longitude too, come to think of it, in filming at sea. The foundation had an excellent research platform in the shape of the Motor Yacht, *Golden Shadow*, the unusually large 67 metre, (220 foot) yacht in Prince Khaled's fleet which, best of all, had a sea lift in the stern, a moveable platform that lowers smaller boats into the sea. With it you could work in swells that would shut down more unwieldy ships.

As large support ships go the *Golden Shadow* was great, but they can also be a pain for film crews trying to do detailed filming work at sea. The sixty people a ship that big can accommodate will all have different schedules and agendas, and no one has told the sharks. A scientific survey like the Living Oceans Foundation's needs to sample a lot of locations over hundreds of miles. Yet when nature's action is happening, it just doesn't work to break off from diving in one area because the support ship needs to move on. Film-makers are fiddlers and need time to fiddle, especially when filming wildlife, to get their eye in at a location and stay there while something good is happening.

The Living Oceans Foundation team understood all this, as they'd done many filming trips and we'd worked that way together before in the Galapagos, where I'd met Phil, and their communications director, Alison Barrat, very experienced as a respected TV exec in science and wildlife documentary. That's why for some of the filming we'd chartered the *Heiva*, the

56-foot (17-metre) catamaran that could double up as a diving platform and work independently from the larger mother ship. The name comes from the Polynesian, meaning 'to assemble', which seemed appropriate, although we were now a more compact team, with a total of just eight people, and with the helpful French captain, Yvan Neault, we could set our own agenda. It was an ideal situation: the facilities of the larger ship close to hand, but freed from its schedules to concentrate on the detail of the coral reef. From the *Heiva* we'd do the natural history parts of the film, and on the bigger ship we'd cover the scientists' work. Scientists can, on the whole, be told what to do; fish can't, which is why you can film a whole scene with a scientist in an afternoon but a specific bit of fish behaviour might take many days, and on the catamaran at Fakarava we would have the time.

Coral atolls are mostly found across the central belt of the Pacific and those of the Tuamotu Islands are the most spectacular. It was Charles Darwin, no less, who first suggested how they might form, when the evolution penny hadn't yet dropped and he was studying coral, something the British Navy, whose wooden ships were often shredded on reefs, was keen to understand. He observed that living coral needed shallow, light-filled water, and noted that it grew just below the shoreline, roughly in a ring around volcanic islands. Over geological time spans many of these islands would eventually sink beneath the waves, but the living coral ring would continue to grow upwards on its own dead skeletons to the light, so it never sank. The hollow left by the fallen island became a shallow lagoon surrounded by a ring of reef – a proverbial 'blue lagoon' in fact, surrounded on all sides by the darker blue of the open sea.

From the air, atolls like Rangiroa and Fakarava, which no longer have their central island, take you by surprise. It seems they really shouldn't be there in miles and miles of deep sea, tenuously popping above the surface, causing waves to crash on them and reflecting beautiful shades of turquoise. They are not small rings either: Fakarava Atoll is over 1,000 square kilometres and 37 miles (60 kilometres) long and 13 miles (37 kilometres) wide, while Rangiroa, the largest of the Tuamotu archipelago, is half as big again. I have worked in both these spectacular hotspots, and both are amazing places to dive, though in my experience Fakarava offers shallower and more pristine reefs.

Though our official task was to highlight the importance of coral reefs, or just to get people interested in corals, we wondered if people were really interested in the mechanics of coral science, knowing there was of course no point in making a film no one sees. Sharks, on the other hand, *were* popular. Thirty-plus years of Discovery Shark Week told us that. What if we mixed a story of corals with sharks? It had to make sense and have a purpose, but as it happened there had been much discussion in marine science journals about whether the decline of sharks was hurting coral reefs. Fortunately, French Polynesia is known to still have pockets of healthy reef shark populations; how healthy we were about to discover.

There is still much to learn about how sharks shape ocean ecosystems, but for coral reefs in particular there is a theory that goes like this: sharks check the population of smaller predatory fish, ones that in turn eat beneficial herbivorous fish that clean up the algae. When sharks are overfished it follows that the smaller predatory fish will take over and decimate the algae-grazers. Then there will be nothing left to clean the coral, and it will be smothered by matted filaments of green algae and die. Many reefs, such as those in parts of the Caribbean, have already succumbed in this way. At any rate, intuitively, taking large predators out of the ecosystem seems a very bad idea, but in the multifaceted webs of ecology the exact way it breaks the strands is likely to be complex.

Science, though rigorous and tested, but done by humans, is not immune to 'wishful thinking', especially when it comes to neat theories. In this case although shark and coral dependency is commonly mentioned, it's odd that few have ever seen a wild shark eating predatory fish, or any kind of living fish at all. Most of the encounters filmed on TV use bait – buckets of meat or 'chum' thrown over the side of a boat to draw in the sharks. There's nothing natural about this, and it doesn't give great insight into the predatory habits of wild sharks. Even so, our research showed that Fakarava might yet give us a good chance of filming natural feeding and some new answers about the relationships between sharks and coral reefs. At any rate, now we had the guiding aim for the film, a skeleton on which to build our story and, with the richness of Polynesian seas, one that could include all the animals of a reef, from the humble coral polyps to the charismatic sharks themselves.

From the inception of the idea to wetting our toes was about five months. On the *Heiva* catamaran we assembled our experts: an excellent local dive guide, Rudolphe Holler, whose normal gig was to show world famous billionaires the reefs, our two main diving DOPs, each with a camera, the boat crew and a scientist. We asked Australian shark biologist Will Robbins to advise us and to be part of the film. He was very articulate in expressing his detailed knowledge of shark behaviour, his PhD was on grey reef sharks, the predominant species in

Fakarava, and it was clear from the start that he fitted in well with the team. We left the comfort of the *Golden Shadow* behind and, for the next seventeen days, the eight of us were to call the *Heiva* home. Albeit the usual kit-cluttered home of a diving camera crew. For most of that time we were just moored in the main channel of the South Pass at Fakarava, and I was happy with this because it meant we would have time free from travel to really concentrate on this one amazing spot.

The South Pass of Fakarava is so beautiful I'd want my ashes spread there one day if it wouldn't place such a financial burden on my relatives, or the ashes wash away on the tide and pollute the sea. In the whole ring of Fakarava, about a hundred miles (160 kilometres) in circumference, there are only two 'cuts' or passes between the shallow central lagoon and the deep open sea. To the north a wide cut is interesting but not as spectacular or concentrated in life as the south pass. Here, the fluctuating tides force water through the pass to equalise the level between the lagoon and the open sea. At times of maximum difference this flow bottlenecks in the narrow channel producing lethally fast currents. That's why it's vital to dive on what's called the 'slack' part of the tide, when the waters in and around the lagoon are almost level. It's wise too to dive only on an incoming tide so you are never washed out into the open ocean. But this dangerous current also brings life, stirring up the lagoon to make plankton-rich waters. And it attracts sharks, hundreds of them, for which the currents of the pass seem almost like a playground, and for which Fakarava is famous.

Weeks of planning, somewhat stressful discussions over money and the strain of second-guessing the right time to film all disappeared in an instant as we back-flipped over the side of a rubber dive boat, once again breaking the line between air and water. We would do well to be humble asking nature to give up her secrets, I thought, and to *us* rather than anyone else; secrets that she's held close for millions of years.

The moment we tumble into the water is often filmed in slow motion, as if to make clumsily kitted water creatures look good. Flipping backwards you tumble upside-down and fall through a plume of stolen air from the surface, so that it does indeed give you a feeling of slow motion as a curtain of bubbles slowly opens to reveal the world below.

Shallow corals are fussy creatures. They feed on plankton in the water, while also obtaining nutrition from symbiont algae inside their cells, called zooxanthellae. As such they need the right light and temperature, and enough current to bring them their plankton dinner, but not too much to sweep them off their polyps, or too little so they silt over and choke. The South Pass, a great canyon in the seabed, is a biblical scene in which the waters have parted the corals, being too fast for them to settle in its central area. Yet all along the sides of the pass are terraces of coral where the current is slower. Many of these corals look like giant cauliflowers, with a few more branched and pointed like enormous forks, and others spread out like dinner plates laid on the seabed, but strewn randomly over one another like a badly loaded dishwasher. There are massive boulder types of coral too: dense iron-brown clusters bigger than a table, looking like contemporary sculpture but in fact hundreds of years old. Never usually encountered in the everyday, their names are unfamiliar to us, but a bluffer's guide might suggest you talk of *Acroporids*, those branching cauliflowers which are part of the staghorn family, *Porites*, the stone corals, or *Faviids*, the brain corals, that do indeed have the wrinkles of a human brain, and you might also throw in a mention of *Montipora*, those plating corals, for good measure.

Around the terraces of coral that line the pass from lagoon to blue ocean flutter millions of brightly-coloured and often curiously-shaped fish: yellow snappers in their hundreds, each the size of a hand and all ploughing the water in the same direction, interlocking like a giant, moving, yellow wall. Here they are stunning, because they are the 'blue striped' variety – their ultra-yellow struck through with four blue streaks, like a glorious new flavour of Bertie Bott's Every Flavour Beans. There are many more varieties of fish too from the same confectionery, like the red big-eye scad, raccoon butterfly fish (yellow with black-and-white faces), damselfish of all kinds, giant trigger fish, and magnificent Napoleon wrasse, the largest of its kind, hunted almost to extinction in many parts of the world for its beauty as a prized aquarium fish, and for the restaurant live-food trade.

Normally water steals red light first to cast everything in a haze of greens and blues, but here in bright shallow waters, where warm water corals grow, there is still an abundance of red. That's why in our colour chart of the Saltwater Country I like to think of coral reefs as the 'orange sea', because elsewhere in the ocean reds and oranges are relatively rare under natural light. I can't call it the 'red sea' because that would be confusing, so 'orange' it is.

As per usual, the advertised attraction is nowhere to be seen. The minute we drop into the water the main animals we've come to film have just gone. I mean, I know the shark's senses are pretty amazing – but really, how did they know we were coming? This state of affairs – *The animals we have come to film have left the building* – is pretty normal. The only question is, how long will it take to find them?

Sometimes it can be excruciatingly long, as day after day you see nothing and feel sick at all the money you know is being spent with no brilliant pictures to show for it. That's one of the differences of being here for work and here as a sports diver for an afternoon of recreation: the worry that you come back with nothing. I guess, too, it has become a mark of pride among wildlife film-makers to make sure you 'always deliver', although I do feel responsible when I am spending the price of a house in about three weeks.

As we descend the terraces of the canyon, like a forgotten vineyard made of coral, the warm waters soothing me, I think I see sharks over every boulder. We go deeper, and Will Robbins, the shark scientist, is in front of me now. He's a big man in his dive kit and I can't see easily over his torso but, as we reach a white patch of sand that at 35 metres will be the canyon floor, four grey reef sharks appear above his head. Then four more in the distance, and some more grey outlines behind. We follow them and, as the range improves, what I see is just astonishing. Will is staring up at a wall of sharks.

There are not just four or eight or eighty, but, stacked up like planes in a holding pattern, 400 or so sharks are hovering in the water. They have more or less an equal distance between them, and so I do that thing we were taught at school: count how many squares there are along the top and then multiply by the number of squares along the edges – only for 'squares' read 'sharks'. Four hundred is probably an underestimate as the wall of sharks disappears out of view, and it confirms that this is the place on Earth with the highest density of sharks.

This is our planet as it was in the depths of time when no man had interfered with the cycle of life and the abundance of the sea. This is one of the hope spots that the famous marine conservationist, Sylvia Earle, talks about when she tells us there are few places in the ocean left untouched, but the few that are give us hope of what the sea can be, and what those places now so degraded could become if we only gave them half a chance. Out of this saltwater, like a miracle, comes all this abundance of life, the tiny molluscs and the urchins, the millions of brightly-coloured fish, the trillions of hungry coral polyps pulsating in the current and these, the cheetahs of the sea, classic looking grey reef sharks in their hundreds, the silver grey of their immaculate, streamlined bodies formed up like links of chain mail, blocking this passage to the open ocean, looking with an all-knowing kind of stare and waiting patiently for food.

To one side I see Peter Kragh, one of our two main cameramen, stealthily getting nearer to the sharks. In black, tightly-fitting Neoprene that clings to his strong physique he looks like a member of a SWAT team. He is also using a rebreather, which in theory allows Peter to get closer to the sharks, although, contrary to what you may think, they are not after us at all, and in fact have a 'stand-off' distance of perhaps 15 feet (3 metres). If you move forward, they move back. If you continue to move forward and persist in bothering them that's when they will arch their backs and drop their forward pectoral fins, which is a warning posture. It takes a lot to provoke them, but woe betide you if you ignore it.

In his youth, the famous underwater DOP, Mike DeGruy, decided it would be a good idea to get a picture of this interesting behaviour. He got very close: a grey reef shark arched its back, and he took a still picture of it with an underwater flash. It was the straw that broke the shark's back, actually, because what followed was a swift warning bite that went right through the joint of Mike's elbow and required multiple operations to put right. He probably knew about the signal, but had he known that that particular arching shark really meant to follow through with its threat I guess he'd have reconsidered. Even a grey reef, a smallish shark, 4 to 5 foot max, not even 2 metres, can do a lot of damage when it wants. Mike told the story often, so maybe got something out of it and we fellow diving film-makers got a good warning.

Jacques Cousteau, as I've mentioned, warned us never to be complacent around sharks, but he also knew that 99 per cent of the time most sharks are placid, and doing pretty much nothing apart from swimming. That now became our problem. Apart from cruising up this underwater pass, hovering like seagulls in the wind, these sharks were doing nothing, and 'nothing' doesn't make an interesting film, or at least for very long.

You can tell what sort of prey a shark eats from the shape of its teeth. Great whites eat seals, and so have large and savage serrated triangular teeth that rip through mammal flesh like a chain saw. Tiger sharks also have large teeth, thinner than great whites, but they have a 'shoulder' on them like the head of a can opener, and that is exactly what they are: can openers to open up the shells of turtles, their key prey. Fish-eating sharks, like the greys, have thin, pointy teeth, on the lower jaw, to spear their prey. Their upper jaw teeth are wider and serrated, allowing them to slice into their prey with a characteristic shark head shake. Yet although we spent hours diving with the grey reef sharks in Fakarava, with thousands of fishes around and almost bumping into them, we never saw a shark eat a living fish under normal circumstances in daylight.

In bright light grey reef sharks have eyes with vertical pupils like cats, and the shark eye is at least twice the size of a cat's;

something that is probably near the maximum sensitivity it could be as, after a certain point, size isn't the issue. Also, sharks have further spectacular senses we don't – like the ampullae of Lorenzini, grandly named for the scientist who discovered them in 1678. These are electromagnetic sensing organs, arranged in small, jelly-filled pits all over the snout and down the side of the shark. If you look at sharks closely it seems someone has left pinpricks all over their faces, and these are the ampullae. They are sensitive to tiny electrical currents, and said to be able to pick up the heartbeat of a fish (presumably the very fast heartbeat) as the shark comes close. It is also believed that larger migratory sharks use this sense to navigate long distances using the earth's magnetic field.

Although we weren't seeing it, we knew fish-eating sharks must eat fish, because how else would they grow big? But the question is when? Of course, there is always the exception to the rule and some scientists diving and taking samples here for only a couple of hours saw a fish eaten, but that was the only time we heard of it during the day, and it's typical that people who visit for merely an afternoon often see the stuff it takes us weeks to film. During the day, the nonchalance of sharks confronted with food but not eating seems common to many species. In this part of French Polynesia you'd be more likely to see a blacktip reef shark before a grey, as they seem to play in the shallows with the exuberance of young puppies. They are small, hardly more than a metre (3 feet), but beautiful, with distinctive black-flecked dorsal fins that shear the surface like miniature windsurfers. But all this activity seems to come to very little, because we'd not seen them catch living fish either.

Obviously we were going to have to move to a 'plan B', changing our timings or location.

There are not many buildings on this side of Fakarava Atoll, and not much land either. A French settlement called Tetamanu was once here, and for a while was the capital, but this was moved north to Rotoava, where you fly in today, and where the atoll is appreciably wider. Tetamanu is mostly dark, volcanic-stone ruins amid tall grass and palm trees and white coral rubble. There is a small but impressive and beautiful church with a red corrugated roof, and a few 'pensions': scattered, palm-covered huts that are the accommodation for divers, and closer to a Robinson Crusoe camping experience than hotels.

At the lagoon end of the South Pass in Fakarava there's a tourist café – surprising, as you might not expect enough tourists here, and of course almost all will be sports divers. It's the only spot to eat if you want a night off from the ship's galley, a delightful place sitting on long stilts above the water, where you can see into the kitchen and all the way to the palm trees on the island beyond.

One day I saw the chef preparing fish and tossing their heads with glee through the cookhouse window, where they landed in a foaming sea of hungry blacktips, now accustomed to visiting the café themselves. He paused from his recipe to wonder at how quickly and efficiently this natural garbage-disposal machinery worked in his kitchen, and I saw him staring into the water with the kind of morbid fascination that seems to overcome us all watching sharks feeding. It made me realise sharks don't miss a trick and remember likely food sources very quickly.

This happy fish-gutting scene was only trumped for blacktip shark sightings by an unplanned event a couple of weeks later.

I was waiting to film a fishing trap of an ancient local design that we could weave into our story of the lagoon and tides. Used since Prehistoric times, today these traps are made from stones and wire netting and catch fish in their funnelled bottom end as the incoming tide sweeps through. We had been dropped at a jetty, cameraman Ernie Kovaks, scientist Will Robbins, and I, while the rest of the team where diving elsewhere, to meet some local fishermen to pick us up and show us the tidal trap. The fishermen had had a good day, and when they arrived their boat was full of brightly coloured parrot fish, which they started to gut right in front of us on the jetty. I was in a kind of trance looking at this scene of handsome fish, metallic greens, sky blues and tomato reds all mixed together in a heap, in awe of their beauty and its destruction in the quest for food. I hadn't noticed the little dogs, the fisherman's friends, until they started barking loudly. Then the dogs were jumping in the water, and what they were barking at were the black-tipped sharks – tens of them, ploughing the shallows like little torpedoes homing in on the fish heads.

'Are you seeing what I'm seeing?' I whispered to Ernie. We needed to film this scene in front of us – for one thing, how often do you see dogs swimming with sharks and chasing them as if they were cats?

'Yeah, of course,' he replied in his calm Californian voice. Ernie was already reaching for the camera. With no time to put on the underwater housing he was only going to get the surface shots – the beautiful fish, the fishermen working, their crazy dogs and the blacktip sharks they were barking at. In my hand I had a smaller camera with an underwater housing. I waded into the shallows with the dogs and the sharks, wanting to prove to the world that these sea dogs were fearless, albeit

298

the blacktips were only a little bigger than themselves. If anything, the dogs were more scared of my black camera housing, which made it difficult to get the shot I wanted: little dog legs treading water as seen from underwater in front of hungry sharks, like a scene from a parody of *Jaws*. Anyway it had all become a bit of a blur now, and both Ernie and I were grabbing any shots we could, and sure enough the whole thing was over in about five minutes as the fishermen finished gutting and the sharks ate all they had been given and left, the little dogs looking menacingly after them. Lucky for the dogs the sharks hadn't learnt how *they* tasted, or TV directors for that matter.

Plot and research as we do, that 'grabbed' scene made it to the top of the show, as a colourful way to illustrate how sharks come to the camera for 'bait'. Of course, the dogs helped to engage viewers, as they wondered whether we also meant 'canine' bait. But since we'd challenged ourselves to film their natural feeding behaviour it would of course be good if we could deliver.

Back in the south pass of Fakarava, we'd obviously been thinking that if we couldn't see sharks feeding naturally during the day, and if they had very big eyes, which like the famous wolf were, 'all the better to see you with', and fish eating teeth, 'all the better to eat you with' and ampullae of Lorenzini (Little Red Riding hood never mentioned that), then the chances were that what we wanted to see was happening at night. But it probably wasn't going to be the safest thing to dive in the pass at night. And if we timed the dive wrong and got caught in the outgoing tide we'd be swept out to sea. There were no lifeboats here, and an aerial search would be too late to help. In the light of all this I felt I had to give the team the chance to assess the risk themselves. At a meeting that evening in the *Heiva* I looked along the row of expectant faces in the dull yellow light of the cabin: Peter tinkering with his camera; Ernie loading batteries into a charger; Phil, the boss, looking serious but excited; Paula the cook wondering if there would be fewer for dinner; Yvan wondering what the fuss was about; Will pondering new research papers; and Rodolphe, our guide, used to dealing with unreasonable billionaires, startled we were even having a discussion at all. 'So,' I concluded: 'hundreds of sharks at night and strong current,' and I asked if they really were happy diving here in the dark. There was a short silence. They all nodded seriously, making me wait for suspense as on a quiz show, and then they shouted, 'Hell yes!'

The café would be a good spot for an evening meal, we thought. The evening meal *of a shark*. Looking down at the wooden pylons beneath the decking we could see this would be a relatively safe place to try out a night dive. The pylons would shelter you a little against the current, and this part of the pass was in any case shallow, starting out at only 6 metres (20 feet) and shelving off gently.

Rodolphe worked out that the slack incoming tide that night was at about 9 p.m. A 'slack' tide, as I've touched on, is the period between an incoming and outgoing tide when the water reverses and for a little while the current becomes weak or 'slack'. Since at peak flow the current at Fakarava can run at a frightening 8 knots, more than enough to rip off a diver's mask, it was vital the tide calculations were right, and our life was literally in Rodolphe's and Yvan, the captain's, hands. They in turn were taking their tide times from the most trusted of local tables. You can find some suggested tide times for Fakarava South Pass on the Internet, but these can be up to a couple of hours out because of local conditions, or because they are accurate only to the nearest port where measurements have been checked. There are further complications with small passes and big atolls, as the water inside and outside the lagoon must be at equal levels for the current to stop, but since it can't get out or in fast enough through a small gap this equalisation lags behind the exact point of slack tide. Additionally, ocean swells can cause the lagoon to fill up more than usual, and these are variable and not tide-dependent. The wisest course, then, is to note the tide times from the best sources and still observe the current just before you dive. Rodolphe knew this area well, so it was mainly his advice we took, and just after the advertised slack tide the current seemed to slow and it was deemed safe to go in at about 9.30 that evening and stay for an hour.

In our little rubber boat we set out across the pass towards the café. The little RIB was hardly big enough to hold us all, and sank a little into the water with our weight. We passed by tourist diners having their candle-lit dinners, and the bar looked very inviting. For a moment it seemed a much better option to go and have a beer than plunge into the dark water for unknown encounters with sharks. The coloured lights of the café shone down the wooden legs in shades of acid green and yellow, illuminating curious crowds of fish and making the whole scene even more moody than we expected. One by one we slipped off the side, and the rubber boat bobbed higher again as if catching its breath in relief.

Ernie, one of the two cameramen, had brought the most impressive lighting rig with him, consisting of a bank of six large LED dive lights set into a frame – something like a portable version of the floodlight towers used in football stadiums and, it seemed, almost as bright. He had two banks of these, giving one each to the captain, Yvan, and one to Rodolphe to hold either side of him as lighting assistants. On full power these banks would last for about forty minutes.

The LED – a Light Emitting Diode – has its origins in the work of a British engineer, Captain Henry Joseph Round, who in 1907 found that faint yellow light was produced when applying electricity to certain 'cat's whisker' crystal detectors used in radios. It only takes a principle to be understood for it to be refined into something useful, even if it takes time. In 1994 Shuji Nakamura invented the ultra-bright blue LEDs, based on the same principle but using gallium nitride diodes. Soon afterwards it was discovered how to change this to ultra-bright white LEDs, and now we have lights that use 80 per cent less energy, are brighter than ever, and last twenty-five times longer.

Such LED lights have changed underwater photography. In the first series of *Blue Planet* sixteen years earlier, for example, we would have had to have a generator, a very bulky lamp head and a thick electric cable to get even half as much light as from Ernie's floodlight set. The generator would be sitting on a boat above, and the cable would inevitably get snagged on everything from rocks to seaweed and usually be too short to get it in the right position, and would tug wildly as the generator boat bobbed up and down in the waves. Not to mention that all this extra hardware added a huge bill to an already expensive shoot, or that generators are a pain to source as the fuel in their tank means they can't be air-shipped easily.

We began our descent under the café and, as the light beams swept across the pass, filtered through water they were more akin to car headlights in fog than the piercing beacon of a lighthouse. It made it very atmospheric, and I thought I heard the dark but uplifting soundtrack that would play over these images in the final film.

The lights lit the bubbles of exhaled air from our scuba tanks too. I noticed the air wasn't going upwards as usual but sideways, and that the current was still very strong. We had to brace ourselves, holding on to some rocks on the seabed. No sharks – maybe it was a bit too shallow? Then suddenly we saw them, in ones and twos, flying past like jets on a reconnaissance mission to see what we were, arching in to the light from either side and coming very close, but being careful, thank goodness, not to hit us. Flashes of grey silver in front of the lights, and dark silhouettes as they shot behind.

For a while we hovered above the seabed ourselves, transfixed by the light beams and the shark silhouettes and waiting for the current to slow down a little. Life that had not dared come out during the day was crawling all across the coral rubble on the ocean floor. I watched an octopus squeeze itself out of a crack between two boulders and crab its way sideways to another rock, almost disappearing but keeping one eye peeping out from a crevice to see what we were doing. I had a smaller camera, and I now started to film these 'secondary' characters, useful for so-called 'cutaways' when editing the main action of the sharks. An amazing moving slipper made from several dotted-yellow and blue-edged panels, with two pockets for the toes, walked by. 'Wow! a slipper that comes to *you*!' I thought, before realising that this was actually a real creature called a blunt slipper lobster, something I wouldn't even have known was here unless we had dived at night. A moray eel, never the most cheerful-looking of creatures, but twice as grim at night, wound its way across the coral.

The sharks seemed to be becoming braver by the moment, and the number of fly-bys became intense. Perhaps we'd flattered ourselves that we were causing all the fuss, but then we realised that for the sharks we were not the centre of attention. A huge cloud of silver fish, scad of some sort, began to mill above our heads as if in panic, trying to flee towards the mouth of the lagoon behind us from what was now a pack of sharks in hot pursuit. The sharks seemed to be trying to co-ordinate their efforts, blocking and herding the fish into a ball as if to help each other catch them. Being in the midst of this melée was undeniably thrilling, the dangers of shark impact only adding a little spice to the current and the night crawlers on the seabed. More satisfyingly for a wildlife documentary-maker, this was the first time such behaviour had ever been filmed in grey reef sharks. Will Robbins and Phil Renaud would eventually write a scientific paper about many of these observations in the October 2015 edition of *Coral Reefs*, the journal of the Coral Reef Society. Now we were getting somewhere in our story.

By about 10 o'clock we had returned to the *Heiva* full of adrenaline and excited that we had got something unique. We also had that soggy feeling that comes from being underwater for the best part of an hour, a tight Neoprene wetsuit clutching your skin and trapping tepid seawater: it feels like you've peed yourself. As we gratefully unburdened ourselves of our kit all over the deck, washing it down and generally trying to keep parts together like masks, fins and regulators, I noticed that Yvan had cut his hand and was bleeding quite a lot from between his fingers.

'Oh, it's nothing,' Yvan said in his quiet way. 'Just a scratch.' But it was a scratch *from a shark*. He had been holding the lights, and the shark had just bumped them, grazing his clenched hand with a half-open mouth. There was no intent to bite, but even a bump with super-sharp teeth is enough to make a nasty cut. I remembered our evacuation plan had this been worse and he had been losing lethal amounts of blood. It would be touch-and-go if you could get to Rotoava in time, at least two hours north by boat, where there was an air ambulance. As it happened Yvan only had two very small nicks in the skin between two fingers, though when he cleaned them you could clearly see they were slashes from shark teeth. Nothing more than a big Band-Aid and antiseptic were required, but the next night we put the lights on poles so they could be held away from the body.

For the next two nights we repeated the same operations, hoping we would see the sharks corralling scad again, but although there was plenty of shark activity the large shoals of fish had disappeared. The consequence was that we only just had enough footage, and no close-ups of the scad, for example, which is why we couldn't identify them exactly and called them 'silver fish' in the final script. The reason you go for it over several days is to make a polished film, with all the exciting different angles you could wish for, but in this case the behaviour warranted putting the scene together as best we could, with the help of a good editor and some carefully chosen cutaways such as moody silhouettes of the sharks against the water surface, and that self-presenting walking slipper.

Now that we were gaining our confidence in the shallows at night, we dared broach the idea of going right out into the centre of the pass, where the current would be stronger and the waters deeper and more full of sharks. A large white patch that we'd seen in the centre of the pass during the day gave us a point to orientate on. It was decided that a smaller team should go in, as more sharks meant more trouble.

Again we checked the right tides, and this time it was even later when Rudolphe, Yvan, Peter and Ernie went in together at around 11 p.m. Will Robbins, who couldn't dive due to a gear issue, and I stayed on the *Heiva*. We saw the little rubber dinghy crawl into the centre of the pass lit only by a small beacon and Cyalumes, those chemical lights with a different colour defining each diver. Then we saw them go in, and the large batteries of lights switch on to make an eerie turquoise halo in the night sea. We waited anxiously, timing their dive: twenty minutes gone, and yet the halo was roughly in the same place as when they went in; forty minutes, and the rubber boat was circling expectantly, waiting for the divers to show their heads. At about forty-five minutes the first of them returned to the surface, and all were safely recovered.

Back at the haven of the *Heiva* there was a lot of noise as they climbed aboard. All the divers had big grins, but if I wasn't mistaken it was a slightly nervous laugh as they offloaded this nocturnal shark encounter in excited voices:

'It was wild!'

'Yeah.'

'Yeah!'

'Sixty sharks!'

'More.'

'They were hunting everything, anything that moved on the reef; it was intense,' Peter reflected coolly in his precise Danish-American accent.

'It was an exciting great experience, but I think you'd be pushing to do that every night,' said Ernie, confirming my suspicions that we were crossing boundaries. In fact, two years later a BBC team would be back here trying the same thing, only this time with the latest type of shark-protective dive suits.

In the cabin we played back the footage and Will, even with his research experience of these grey reef sharks, watched in awe. At the beginning of the dive there were one or two sharks, but gradually they increased in numbers and activity. Then they really got stuck in.

'I've never seen anything like this,' said Will. 'Normally sharks don't want to spook the fish, because they know that the fish are probably faster than them, at least in the short term.' He paused, looking back at the night footage again. 'So here they quietly glide up next to the fish and get as close as they can to its head from the side – and then just flick and grab the fish. The fish also play this slow dance, as the faster the fish swims, or the more excited its motions are, the more nearby sharks become interested in it.'

Excitingly, this was the first scientific record of natural grey reef shark predatory behaviour captured without artificial attractants or baits.

It's always a question as to whether taking artificial light into the dark at night changes the behaviour of the very animals you are trying to study. It's one we had back in Costa Rica filming the whitetip sharks at night too. Certainly, shining a light on sleeping fish makes some stir, and that is when the sharks will notice them, tuning in to the electrical activity in the muscles, although no doubt using their smell to a great degree too, and their vision when they get close. But this hunting behaviour was so premeditated it was likely to be happening in the dark regardless of our lights. As Will explains,

'It may be possible that our lights might be giving the shark some advantages in pinpointing the fish, but they've clearly developed this strategy long before we got here. Indeed, we see the sharks continue on with the same strategy of gliding up next to the fish as they disappear into the darkness.'

I've watched the feeding behaviour we recorded in the pass a hundred times on playback and in slow motion. I sit transfixed in slightly horrified fascination as the prey fish and shark swim side by side in their deadly joust, each uncertain what will happen next. Then suddenly the shark makes a fluid sideways movement of the head, as if it has some kind of hinge in its body and could bend its head at right angles, and it scoops the fish right into its mouth like sucking on melon segments, to frame an eerie smile.

Many times the shark wasn't successful. Actually, I can tell you *exactly* how many times because Will analysed the footage and, in a paper he wrote with Phil Renaud (the Living Oceans Foundation director with us on the *Heiva*, and now at Woods Hole Oceanographic Institution), he found that the sharks were only successful at catching the fish in 16 per cent of their attempted bites.[1]

The footage also clearly showed that the sharks were eating *all* kinds of fish, not just big predators. While we saw the greys eat predatory fish like snappers and cod as expected, we also saw them eat a unicorn fish, named for the short horn on its head and the soulful eyes of a unicorn; an algae eater. And fusilier fish were being taken too, a beautifully sleek and

---

1 W. D. Robbins and P. Renaud, 'Foraging mode of the grey reef shark, *Carcharhinus amblyrhynchos*, under two different scenarios', *Coral Reefs* 35 (2015), pp. 253–260.

blue-striped plankton eater. All this seemed to go against the idea that sharks keep reefs healthy by taking just the top predators among the reef fish, the ones that eat the algae-eating fish. In fact, it's the sharks themselves that are directly taking algae-eating fish when they get a chance. It's curious that the literature reinforces the theory of how sharks regulate fish life on the reefs when few people have seen natural feeding behaviour. It seems that some scientists can propagate myths as well as anyone.

In fact, in documentary TV, the truth is it doesn't matter whether a theory is wrong or right, because either way it gives you a story to spin out. You just need it as an excuse to talk about the images and a direction for the film. It's something akin to Alfred Hitchcock's 'MacGuffin' (actually a term attributed to Hitchcock's screenplay writer, Angus MacPhail): an event or plot line necessary to the motivation of the film and its characters, but irrelevant in itself. Even so, this MacGuffin had come up trumps, and in the space of a few nights we had uncovered new behaviours that had never been seen.

Peter and Ernie told me that towards the end of the dive the sharks were getting very feisty, learning perhaps that divers were responsible for an increase in fish activity and there could be good pickings around these funny stick-like animals with bright lights. On several occasions Peter was bumped, and we all agreed we didn't need to repeat the risk at night, especially now we had the images. That didn't mean we couldn't repeat it during the day.

While all this was going on, we'd being looking at the waxing moon every night, frankly a bit squiffy and upside-down compared to the UK, because the orientation to the sun's reflecting light alters with latitude. I was surprised how such a small change to the long familiar unsettled me, but that's not why I was looking at the Moon. It was because I knew it was about to trigger an extraordinary ocean event, and why we'd come at the time we had.

Every year at a certain time, thousands of groupers come to spawn in the pass at Fakarava. It's something that's been going on for millions of years, and the locals may have known about it for several thousand, but it's only recently the wider world has become aware. There's some discussion as to whether it's a good idea to publicise it at all, but in this age where everything can be seen online it may also be an idea to tell people about it in order to protect it. Recently this area has become part of a giant marine national park, and in theory should have the protection of the President of French Polynesia and the French government against any illegal fishing of sharks and reef fish.

The brown marbled groupers that congregate in Fakarava and other islands of the Tuamotu Archipelago are magnificent fish. Found right across the Indo-Pacific, they remind me in shape of large and expensive ornamental koi carp, but are in fact of the sea bass family and stouter than carp, with aggressively-spined dorsal fins that stretch along their back. Like all their family they have big mouths and thick lips; so big that just opening their mouths causes enough suction to pull in crabs and small fish prey which they bite down on with impressive canine teeth. They've got big, alert-looking eyes, and the marbled variety has a military-brown and dirty-white camouflage. Guidebooks oddly describe them as 'solitary', because they're *groupers*, but when they navigate to lagoons like Fakarava to breed in their thousands they sure know how to party, coming from who knows where out of the blue. How can a fish do that? It's another ocean mystery.

This mass arrival of groupers is triggered by the full moon in June or July. We couldn't afford to stay over two months, so it was a one-moon shot, and critical that we got our best calculated guess for the right full moon. If there's a full moon in early July that's probably when it's going to happen, but in 2013 the new moons fell somewhat indecisively, with one at the end of June and another in late July. So would the spawning be early on the late-June full moon, or late on the late-July moon? Or maybe split across both? After much consultation, particularly with people like Rudolphe, who had dived French Polynesia most of his life, we decided to opt for the earlier full moon in June, and prayed to the sea gods that the spawning might happen.

Near the start of the shoot there were some nervous emails back to base when we didn't see many groupers. At the time it felt like putting all your chips on the red, but now I wonder why we even worried because, once committed, there was little we could do but hope. Sharing such anxieties while at sea thousands of miles from the office is a new occupation, by the way, as only a few years earlier in such a place you would have had no contact for weeks. As it was, there was a better cell signal from the French Telecoms tower at Tuamotu, South Pass, than I get back home.

An email I wrote to the office at 23.25 on 21 June 2013 sounds more optimistic:

Hi,

We have got a little primitive email connection on the ship! Not sure how reliable it is but working for the moment.

The groupers are here in good numbers - although some of the locals say much fewer than in some years - they are however carpeting the entire pass from end to end and looks promising.

The groupers had started to appear in ones and twos, and then in tens and twenties, and then in hundreds, and thousands – 'carpeting the entire pass' the day before the full moon is right. If anything they seemed to be more active at dusk, with some feeding, rooting around the base of rocks and persecuting crustaceans. Many seemed to have lost their appetite, and were just patiently hovering above the seabed. There were two obvious kinds: the slender males and the very fat and egg-full females, with stretched bellies waxing like the moon. Their big eyes stared back at you expectantly, and you got the impression they knew something was up.

The full moon of 23 June 2013 was a perigee full moon, a supermoon: in other words, a big one. This happens when the Moon flies slightly closer to the Earth, looks a little bigger, and pulls harder on the sea for higher tides. That was probably a bonus to the groupers but not a necessity, but it reminds me how perfect this planet is for life. The full moon provides a natural call alert, so groupers know when to group and spawn, and the high inward tide from the open ocean washes the fertilised eggs into the plankton-rich lagoon, helping little fish grow up. Without such a celestial clock life might not have been possible at all.

Just before sunset we did the piece to camera with Phil that opens this chapter. We were tying up some loose ends in our shopping list of shots (the 'shotlist'), but also trying to distract ourselves from the possible success or failure of the following day. Rudolphe assured us that the spawning event would happen just at the end of the inward tide, at 8.24 in the morning, to be exact.

At 7.45 a.m. on 23 June, we trundled to the centre of the pass in our little rubber boat and our now familiar diving formations, loaded with filming kit of all kinds. At 8.05 we entered the water. By 8.15 we were all mustered on the seabed in the slightly dark morning water in two groups close to each other, and all surrounded by swirling clouds of groupers. At *exactly* 8.24, as Rudolphe had predicted to the minute, it all kicked off.

The first thing I noticed were what looked like smoke bombs going off above our heads, detonating every thirty seconds or so, causing pandemonium among the sharks. I could hardly believe that this thing we'd planned to witness for months was really happening in front of us at last.

Blanched white and keeping just a black dot on the stem of the tail, male groupers had become conspicuous among the females. Tens of thousands of fish floated together, a sea of hands pointing in the same direction, motionless themselves but swaying with the ocean swell. The females looked so fat they might explode with eggs at any moment, held only on a short fuse with seconds to run, and they would. Males nearest the female when they spawn have the best chance of fertilising the eggs, a simple but compelling rule that drives their behaviour completely. Breaking ranks, they fought to win the gravid females, sparring with their fat mouths and rotating around each other, kicking up a seabed sandstorm.

Fight club won, the female is courted with a quivering display, but one not always well received, and she can turn back into the crowd. Successful males nudge her belly and trigger the final act, as the breeding pair rush upwards like a rocket propelled on a cloud of eggs and sperm – the white detonation. This is instantly followed by all males in the vicinity also rushing in to spawn, typically resulting in groups of about five groupers in each spawning event. But it's not so much the visuals that alert the sharks, rather the deep drumming of the groupers' tails as they break the cover of the reef and propel themselves towards the surface to mate. It sounds a dinner bell for the grey reef sharks, moving faster than I had ever see them move in lethal but beautiful arcs of fluid motion, catching the courting fish unawares and trying to shred them apart as quickly as they can.

Too big to swallow in one gulp, the comatose grouper flops out of the shark's mouth, but the grey's thin teeth act like fish hooks securing the prey. The second stage of the rocket now ignites, as many other sharks follow, trying to grab the fish right out of the mouth of the feeding shark that got there first. The whole formation shoots into a higher orbit near the surface, but if the successful shark manages to swallow its prize, its fearsome colleagues immediately stop the chase, level out and dive again into the melée below, looking for their own fish.

On all this action we have two main cameras, three secondary cameras, and several smaller 'action cameras' mounted on the divers themselves. Rudolphe's camera is mounted on the air pipe of his rebreather, and the sound carries through the small underwater housing. As a 'rocket scene' explodes in front of him I can hear his squeals of joy and amazement, without the slightest tinge of fear, a 'Ho-ho', not an 'Uh-oh'. His excited laughter and exclamations last for a while, and as the guide of this shoot he must feel that his intuitions and calculations were right, letting go of the great burden of expectation from the team.

With my small camera I try to get a good shot of one of these 'shark rockets' too, and although I do, I also get into the edge of the frame that Peter is shooting on the main camera below. To be fair, there's so much going on now I don't know who is pointing their camera where, as all across the pass the groupers are spawning. Both shots make the final cut and, although I feel embarrassed at being in the shot, part of me also wants to shout out, 'Look, mum! That's me!' I'm only in silhouette, but still . . .

The scene in the pass is starting to look like the battle of Waterloo, as over the corals charge a brigade of blue fusiliers. These are taking full advantage of rich pickings as they form thick walls around the groupers and the sharks, the water now milky with spawn. Fish like these are one of the reasons the groupers group to breed in the first place: to overwhelm their enemies with the sheer abundance of their eggs so that some will survive. The blue wall of fusiliers parts, and there for a moment I see Phil Renaud, perfectly still, hovering in all the chaos with his camera, cool as a sea cucumber, looking as if he'd seen it all before. But I know under his mask he was grinning.

Like a firework display it all seemed to end too quickly, and although there was still a lot of activity the rockets had all gone off. If we'd been in the water for ten minutes before it started, and it was a fifty-minute dive, the whole event from the first detonation to the last was less than half an hour. The groupers, some now carrying big serrated scars from unlucky escapes, headed back towards the lagoon in the slack tide. Through my mask I could smell the oil of their ripped flesh.

I have rarely felt such a sense of elation. I surface still filming, lifting my small camera above the sea to capture the joy of my colleagues, who are laughing with glee and punching the air. Peter the cameraman just smiles and says, 'A good day'. Phil, the head of our organisation, makes an impassioned plea to the camera, 'It's really exciting to see the sharks here and the numbers that should be on most reefs of the world. You know we take approximately 100 million sharks out of the ocean every single year – I can't even wrap my head around 100 million sharks.'

I haven't told of how we filmed little scenes in the corals when the sharks were away or the tide in the pass too strong to be with them. We filmed solitary brown damselfish tending their algae garden on a coral head – a patch of seaweed it ferociously guards and farms for its own use. We briefly filmed the corals with special UV lights that make them glow in beautiful colours and show the exquisite deal of their polyps. We gathered footage of all the different coral fish species, filming a giant Napoleon wrasse as big as a diver, as it came near the surface in a rainstorm that from underwater looked like drops of glass falling from a chandelier. We filmed communities of more brightly coloured blue damselfish that take residence in their hundreds in the staghorn coral heads. We filmed Titan trigger fish, the largest species of trigger fish at nearly a metre (3 feet), with yellow and orange patterns warning that they have a somewhat venomous bite should you invade the giant nests, huge craters 2 metres (6 feet) across, which they dig for their eggs in the sand.

Elsewhere we filmed massive nurse sharks in the lagoon, enjoying this different environment siltier than the pass, chomping molluscs and crabs with their somewhat stubby teeth. Muddy green, they have a blunt head and somewhat sleepy eyes and rise in a plume of silt when you come near. They seem docile, but don't take much nonsense from human divers, or at least those that are dumb enough to underestimate them, and that might explain why they are at number 4 in the top 10 species for shark bites on humans.

We also filmed the crown-of-thorns starfish (COTS), looking like the crown of Jesus on the cross, I presume, and about the same in circumference. They eat coral and can destroy unhealthy reefs, but healthier reefs are more resilient. We used a small camera and the giant echinoderm crawled over it, giving us a menacing view of hundreds of tube feet, the locomotion of choice for starfish, urchins and sea cucumbers.

On the outer side of the lagoon near the open sea we dived on the edge of the reef, the infamous 'drop-off', over impressive and unending walls of plate corals spiralling down into the depths and reminding us of how the abyss stares back to tingle your sense of fear and fire your imagination about what may lurk in the dark blue deeps. We also dived the wider North Pass at Fakarava, where we filmed schools of colourful parrot fish and long silver trumpet fish skulking among the coral in thin horizontal lines, or manta rays attracted into the shallows by the plankton-rich current of the turning tide. One banked right in front of me, revealing its wings, and swam over my head, giving a beautiful shot.

I can't tell you if the reefs at Fakarava are exactly like they were before humans ever went to sea, but in the present day they are among the finest that exist on our planet. The film we made there, *Mysteries of the Coral Canyon*, documenting the wildlife and work of the Living Oceans Foundation, was released on PBS in the USA in 2016 and won an Emmy for the best environmental film that year, and can be seen on the PBS website. The scientific report on the health of the reefs in French Polynesia can be found on the Khaled bin Sultan Living Oceans Foundation website. It is part of the largest coral reef survey in history, the French Polynesian section alone involving 73 scientists, sampling 1,600 reef surveys and 2,200 fish surveys at over 264 dive sites. Sadly it shows that reefs are less healthy the closer they get to large human populations, so those at Fakarava, far from the biggest settlements and pollution sources, show what's called good 'resilience'. That means they are somewhat better at bouncing back from coral bleaching, disease and attacks from crown-of-thorns starfish because, like us, being healthy in the first place puts you in a good position to survive illness.

Yet all reefs hang on a knife-edge, and as I write there is again another major bleaching event in Tahiti and the southern part of French Polynesia. This is happening without it being a special El Niño year, when it is normal for the weather patterns to fluctuate, and it is devastating coral cover, warm water killing the symbiotic micro algae inside the coral that it needs to live. Some of this is normal, and French Polynesia is exposed to many currents, with slight changes bringing dramatic temperature fluctuations. But these bleaching events are happening faster now than the reefs can recover, and threaten to destroy them entirely.

Spots like Fakarava, though tiny compared to the vast ocean, are vital breeding grounds for marine life that's borne away on the currents to seed areas all around. As it says in the Living Oceans Foundation report, 'The reefs of the world are already declining; saving this precious ecosystem is not only critical for the people of French Polynesia, but the downstream reefs of nearby countries in the whole South Pacific.' In 2012 French Polynesia also declared one of the largest shark sanctuaries in the world. Today there are seventeen ocean locations where shark fishing and finning is banned, covering an area twice the size of Europe. It's a good start, but it remains to be seen how effectively they will be policed, and whether these magnificent predators, and the beautiful ecosystems in which they live, can be saved.

Since the *Heiva* was returning to Tahiti with Yvan its captain, we realised that we didn't have to use the plane at all, and could sail back with him, spending the time to pack and clean our kit properly. It was about 355 kilometres (or 200 miles) to Papeete, the capital, and it took us 36 hours, with each taking turns on the tiller through the night, in sometimes stormy seas.

Shattered and craving a hot bath, we landed on the dockside in the early morning. I walked up through town to take a look and went into the Notre Dame cathedral in the centre of the city. It just looked like a giant version of the smaller churches seen at Fakarava: a colourful yellow with a red roof and a sharp, thin steeple. Inside a choir was rehearsing, male and female voices chanting in waves of song that echoed around its high wooden arches; it was a melodic and dramatic Tahitian song but with a recognisable European influence. I am not religious but the sights that nature had given to me would make me so for this little while.

16

Coming Clean

Talking rubbish

Plastic has a beauty. It's what got us into it in the first place. Our love affair has lasted more than a century, but like all lovers we've been blind. Plastic is spreading like a disease in our oceans, multiplying and damaging our world irreparably. Suspended in fluid and stirred like the particles in a planet-sized snow globe, it's travelled everywhere. Producing *Blue Planet II*, we knew we couldn't ignore it any longer. As much as we wanted to show the magical lives of creatures in crystal blue, it wasn't the whole story.

I'd worked on the first *Blue Planet* series twenty years earlier, when plastic was surreptitiously infiltrating our marine life, but few people noticed. Fewer really cared. This time the mood was different and the problem more serious. But while we had strategies to capture stunning sequences of sperm whales and spinner dolphins, we were struggling to come clean about the dirty seas.

My passion is the sea. I love every last salty seawater drop of it. I love the horizon and the way it pulls you forward to explore beyond its edge. I love diving beneath its dappled skin, looking for mysterious wild treasures, taking a lucky dip, with a new surprise every time. So I was delighted to be asked to make the 'Big Blue' episode on the wide expanses of the open ocean far from shore. It was a challenge to take your breath away: go and film the 90 per cent of the ocean we don't know about. A brief taking in more than half the surface of the world. But the journey it took me on was more surprising than I ever dreamed, and made me re-think all my years of ocean film-making. A journey of emotion as much as geography.

'Do you want to see the most beautiful thing I have ever filmed . . . and this bag was just dancing with me, like a little kid begging me to play with it . . .'

That's from what's been called the perfect scene from the perfect film, *American Beauty* – you know, the one where there's an amazing sad piano track over a plastic bag dancing with leaves. Wanting to find new ways to make us think about plastic made me think of it: how the bag seems to have a life of its own, and the poignant music underneath introduces a level of emotional engagement. I know in *Blue Planet II* it wasn't done for the same motivation, for the joy of the aesthetic beauty in itself, but still, it proved, in a left-field way, that it's possible to get emotional over plastic. In *American Beauty*, the plastic bag is the hero; in *Blue Planet II* it would be the villain. Yet even now it's difficult to make this wonder material the criminal, though its beauty soon fades and, discarded, it becomes useless and ugly in so many ways.

In the past I might have left it there, but in the past YouTube wasn't available to a TV producer. So, I stuck 'plastic bag' into the search engine, and up comes the scene from *American Beauty* again (of course), great and unusual re-uses of plastic from the lifehack channels, and some worthiness from CNN: 'Plastic bags and the environment'. Does what it said on the tin, I guess, and hey, 19,000 views in six years. My eyes flick sideways and catch on: '*UNBELIEVABLE* Items Found After Tsunamis!' It's got a stranded fish, six times the size of the person walking on the beach nearby. I'm pretty sure rock pool gobies don't grow that big but, still, I'm hooked, though how they contained themselves to only one exclamation mark I'll never know. Nine months, 11,570,983 views, well done, Talltanic Channel!!!!

I mention it to the editor, Mark Fox, who's sitting next to me. After three years of filming we've just started cutting. He pretends he hasn't been watching. 'I was wondering if you had completely lost it,' he teases gently. 'It's always hard to tell,' and he looks up from the double screens that shine a blue light on his face.

'Yes, but you know that scene in *American Beauty*?'

He does. He might pounce at any minute, but luckily I've just found another YouTube gem. 'Well, look at this: two and a half million views in seven years – they can't all be wrong.'

A husky-voiced wildlife narrator* strikes up in time-honoured tradition: 'The open plains of the asphalt jungle, home to many creatures great and small, and the pupping ground for one of the most clever and illustrious creatures, the *plastic bag*.' *The Majestic Plastic Bag – A Mockumentary*.

Now we've seen the light, and we're both hooked. Within the bounds of what's called blue-chip natural history (because it's posh), what we could do is to film a plastic bag *as if it were a beautiful animal*. Sure, that's only a very small part of the mix, but the novel take has already proved to be worth approximately two and a half million hits more than the worthy style of 'Plastic bags and the environment.' 'Today,' the narrator continues, 'we explore the cycle of life for this curious creature, the plastic bag, on its migration to its home, the Pacific Ocean . . .'

We like to think of ourselves as more sophisticated than our ancestors, but many thousands of years ago hunter-gatherers likely used better shopping baskets than we do, woven from biodegradable materials. In its native supermarket habitat the plastic bag is OK: it's a very useful, cheap and convenient way to take your food home – but when it escapes into the wild it's a nightmare. How much of a nightmare we're not really sure, because the work on what happens in its afterlife is far from complete. Yet even a superficial glance tells us that it's not a good idea to release it, looking like a jellyfish meal for sea turtles, and potentially suffocating and trapping all kinds of creatures. That's just the start of it, of course, as the painful fragmentation of the bag leaves particles still harmful to living things in ways we are only just beginning to understand. Some countries, it's true, have been trying to do something about it, but with the plastic bag as with many other forms of plastic in the sea we have been very slow to understand its toxic potential.

In fact, it's shocking to realise *just* how long we have known about the harmful effects of plastic in the sea and done nothing. Based on the current uproar and what you read in the press, you'd think the following was written last week.

Plastic particles, in concentrations averaging 3,500 pieces and 290 grams per square kilometre, are widespread in the western Sargasso Sea. Pieces are brittle, apparently due to the weathering of the plasticisers, and many are in a pellet shape about 0.25 to 0.5 centimetres in diameter. The particles are surfaces for the attachment of diatoms and hydroids. Increasing production of plastics, combined with present waste-disposal practices, will undoubtedly lead to increases in the concentrations of these particles. Plastics could be a source of some of the polychlorinated biphenyls recently observed in oceanic organisms.

When was it written? The answer is 1972, when marine biologists Edward Carpenter and Kenneth Smith were surveying thousands of miles of the Atlantic with a 1-metre 'Neuston' net, that catches minute plankton swimming in the surface film at the very top layer of the water. Ken, now in his early seventies, was a postdoc working alongside Ed Carpenter aboard the *Atlantis II*, a research ship belonging to the esteemed Woods Hole Marine Biological Laboratory in Falmouth, Massachusetts. I caught up with him recently, still doing marine research and now at the Monterey Bay Aquarium Research Institute (MBARI). 'We were sampling for plankton near the great clusters of seaweed, called *Sargassum*, which is right on the surface,' says Ken. 'We were doing about 1,300-mile transects from Woods Hole, where the ship was based, down to Bermuda, and what we were seeing were chunks of plastic broken off from bigger bottles or beakers or whatever.' The samples that should have only contained plankton had hard, white, cylindrical pellets. A few were green, blue or red, and there were also tiny sheets. I asked him if he was surprised.

'Right, right. Now, we were very surprised by it, and that's why, you know, we published in *Science*; it's a high-profile journal for sure. Tar balls from the oil industry were a big thing, and we had some chemists with us, so that's why Ed Carpenter and the chemists wrote about the polluting chemicals from plastics in a follow-up paper a few months later.'

I'm talking to Ken on the phone, but I can see a picture of him on the web. Behind his neatly trimmed white beard and a wind-worn face from a lifetime in the open sea, I imagine his glimmer of surprise at the discovery, almost fifty years ago, and nearly a thousand miles from anywhere. This alien material, back then, only in mass production for about twenty years, had got everywhere. Every one of their samples had it, and it was already very widespread.

'I notice the *New York Times* picked up the story,' I said. 'So it caused a stir even back then. Though people didn't do much about it – or did they?'

Ken chuckles knowingly. 'Not that I'm aware of, no. But I mean, I drifted away from that and did other things. It was just a flash in the pan. It was a different era and never carried any further. For me it's buried history, and we weren't really anticipating all this interest now, so it's pretty amazing.' Back then, it seems, it was nothing but a curiosity, easily ignored.

Science is more about tolerance to tedium than romantic breakthroughs. This was both, not that the world noticed. The particles were manually sorted from the plankton, then sorted into size ranges and weighed. You do the maths: at this speed a 1-metre-wide net filters about 244,000 gallons or 4,000 bathtubs of water an hour. So when you've counted your haul, with a little brain ache you can work out how many particles there are over a given area, which is how they got to between

290 and 3,500 pieces, or about a quarter of a kilogram (about half a pound) of plastic, per square kilometre (just under half a square mile). This is a somewhat rough figure, of course, because it assumes not even a millimetre of depth below the surface. Yet if the sampling is always done in the same way it gives a baseline for comparison: today the sea's plastic particles average between 63,000 and two *million* per square kilometre, depending on where you are in the world's oceans, and well over 1,000 times more in most places than in 1972, and Ken's trawl might produce not a quarter of a kilogram but two tons of material or more in the most polluted areas.

Carpenter and Smith's short paper is the first known published scientific account of plastic particles in the sea. It is not, of course, the first clue about the durability of plastics in the ocean and the effects they have on marine animals.

Leach's petrel is a beautiful satin-black seabird, slightly bigger than your hand, with a white V mark on its back pointing backwards. It's hardly ever seen from land, as it spends most of its non-breeding days far out over the colder northern areas of the Atlantic and Pacific. Even when it breeds on the coast it's nocturnal, and so mostly avoids us. It can travel 1,000 miles just for one meal for its chicks, and migrates many more thousands every year up and down the coasts of North America. Not for nothing is its Greek name *Oceanodroma* or 'ocean runner' and, foraging far and wide, it is a natural sampler for ocean plastic.

As early as 1963 the biologist Stephen Rothstein found plastic in the bodies of dead Leach's petrels he collected from Gull Island in Witless Bay, Newfoundland. Some of this plastic was very similar to that found by the Neuston-net trawls of Carpenter and Smith ten years later. Stephen pointed out that, since the petrels spend most of their time at sea, the plastic probably came from the open ocean rather than the coast. In his short communication to *Condor*, the peer-reviewed journal of the American Ornithological Society, he notes: 'Leach's petrel evidently consumes any ingestible object occurring within a few centimetres of the ocean's surface. Before the occurrence of plastic particles, it is probable that nearly all such objects were edible. Thus natural selection could not have favoured petrels which avoided non-edible material.' In a tone reminiscent of Conan Doyle's Professor Challenger in *The Lost World*, he continues, 'The sudden, widespread appearance of non-edible floating objects such as plastic particles represents an evolutionary novel event to which birds do not respond in an adaptive manner.' In English this means they can't change their habits fast enough.

Stephen points out that the fine-meshed Neuston nets have only been in use since 1963, and the only way to determine when plastic particles first appeared in the sea is to examine seabird stomachs from preserved specimens. This doesn't seem to have been done with any precision, but still there's the blindingly obvious that scientists sometimes miss: it can't have been there *before* plastic was invented and used in massive quantities. And it wasn't until the 1940s that that happened, after the plastics used in the Second World War were widely released for domestic use, so we can guess that the first significant plastic particles probably showed up in the open ocean, and in marine creatures, sometime in, say, the early 1950s.

Our edit suite has a very rare technical innovation in modern digitally equipped video-edit suites. It's called a *window*. Through it, it's pretty much spring, and there's a beautiful magnolia just coming into blossom in a garden on the other side of the road. We know from the number of times our cuts have already been chewed over and returned by those higher in the editorial food chain that we're in for the long haul. 'That magnolia tree will be losing its leaves before we get out of here,' we jest, more than partly believing our own joke. Mark and I have been around the block more than a few times now, and we smell the scent of nervous managers a mile off, and wafting even further away from the tribal hierarchy in London.

In many ways that's fair enough. *Blue Planet* has a reputation to keep and, as with the first series, there's a lot of money been put up without a certain return. In BBC terms that means paying back value to the licence-payer, but projects like this are minority-funded by the licence fee, and the largest stakes are from international broadcasters who buy in with a whole raft of different agendas. A simpler view, however, is that it boils down to well-paid people in power making sure they keep their jobs or, better still, gaining kudos and more power through spectacular success, like football managers.

This time, though, there's another factor in play: the series is to have an environmental slant. We're well into the twenty-first century, and it is high time we dropped the idea that wildlife films can be representations of a perfect world untouched by humanity. As in the first series of *Blue Planet* there will be a final show on conservation and the ocean. But this time *every* programme in the series will have an environmental story. We'll build it into the scripts. Why didn't we think of that before?

I'm surprised when I hear there's no money for that final environmental show, and that it'll have to be made from the budget and scraps of all the other shows. It's difficult to get to the bottom of why. Preachy conservation shows don't do well for the co-funders, or the BBC for that matter. Generally, people don't want to be depressed by global Armageddon when they come home from work. The primary role of television is entertainment, so making people feel guilty just for living, as worthy messages often do, isn't a crowd-pleasing strategy.

Then there's also the issue of confusing broadcasters with green NGOs. Sensible broadcasters strive for political impartiality and cannot be seen as campaigning organisations. Environmental shows therefore dice with two of the primary laws of documentary:

1) don't be boring
2) be credible.

There are of course ways to work with this and make engaging environmental stories, but it is inconvenient. So it was welcome that the overall thought for *Blue Planet II* was to have better eco information in every show.

Producers, as a species of broadcast journalists, are cynics. Older producers are professional cynics. It comes from years of checking flaky facts and questioning everything. But now I have to come clean: for years I believed that environmentalism was futile in wildlife film-making. How could anything we say make the slightest difference to the industrial juggernaut of annual growth and the relentless cash register of consumerism? It's very probable that we are causing our planet to change fast, but the environment is so interlinked and complex, how is it possible to say anything with absolute certainty? Where are the incontrovertible truths? And if the dire predictions are right it's probably hopeless anyway. Film-makers, therefore, could only fall back on their role as entertainers, showing the beauty and fascination of the natural world through rose-tinted camera lenses.

When it comes to making environmental films the hypocrisy of our job is also inhibiting. At the back of my mind I know we should be trying to limit how much we travel, even though we need to get to exotic locations to show the wonder and diversity of the world. Like many of my colleagues, my green sins are among the worst. Film crews fly to Australia to do a piece on how climate change is killing the Barrier Reef when, ironically, aircraft emissions are cited as causing nearly 10 per cent of the world's global warming. Flying across the world for nearly thirty years I'm so deep in carbon debt that even if I never had another hot bath or shower I could never pay it back. We are all keen on creature comforts, but the environmentally damaging things we will *voluntarily* give up are few.

Earlier in my career I was somewhat selfish, wanting more and better places to go, and wondrous animal behaviours to film and show to people. There was very little thought about making conservation-type films, and the nearest it got was the vain belief that if we show the beauty of wildlife people will want to protect it. But slowly I was taking on board the turning tide, and listening to the expertise of the ocean researchers and the vast experience of the camera dive crews I worked with.

Rangiroa, French Polynesia, 10 October 1999

We're on one of the world's largest coral atolls, a beautiful ring of coral rubble, about half a mile wide, and about 180 miles in circumference. Cameramen Bob Cranston and David Reichert and I are here to film the legendary wall of sharks for *The Blue Planet*.

I don't remember Rangiroa being covered in plastic twenty years ago. I've got some detailed photographs I took then of the beaches, made from chunks of dead corals, but there's not a speck of plastic to be seen, even at high magnification. There must have been some, of course, though the amount in the sea was many times less even twenty years ago. It's more likely I didn't see it because I wasn't looking for it and, as for so many other people back then, even those working in the sea, it just wasn't a big echo on my radar.

After one spectacular dive, when Bob got great footage, I asked him to do an interview for the behind-the-scenes show, though it was never used. I realise now he was telling me something important.

> We are living at a time where we have the technology to go down and see these sharks, which nobody's seen before, and it's, ah, perhaps the last great herds, the last great herds of buffalo kinda thing, I mean, we are, like, going out across these plains and seeing these sharks just like the frontiersmen used to go and see buffalo.

We've been lucky enough to have these glimpses of the ocean as it was before industrialisation. Places like Rangiroa, Fakarava, Cocos and Malpelo, and other places where we've dived and been pushed back by silver clouds of fish barring our path like glinting armour. 'Hope spots' that show us what the sea and our planet can be if we took more care.

Back in the edit suite Mark has had enough of me staring out of the window. 'Where's that shot of the Portuguese man-o'-war, the one that shows how well it can sail over the waves – you know the windy one?'

I do know, or at least approximately. 'Bin 615, I think. About halfway through the clips.'

We're only two weeks into the edit but we've already cut three sequences. Mind you, I know of hour-long documentaries we've made in just a month, although that's usually with a presenter in vision. Presenters make it easier to cut pictures together. You can usually get them to say something relevant, and if nothing happens, or if you haven't got the shot, you can get them to say why. That's not possible in the pure blue-chip style, with a world of landscapes and animal behaviours that must string together in seamless unpeopled stories.

Chagos, British Indian Ocean Territory, 16 April 2015

Another human may not have walked the beach we have landed on in forty years. We're on one of the small islands of the Great Chagos Bank, officially the largest acknowledged atoll structure in the world. After controversial displacements of the local people by the British government in the 1960s, the whole northern part of this Archipelago is deserted.

I'm with the reef expert Professor Sam Purkis and wildlife cameraman Doug Allan, and we're trying to find a spot where the coral rocks are exposed to do a piece on how the islands are formed. Only it's a bit of a job to find the right spot: I'm wading knee-high in places in plastic bottles, flip-flops, fishing floats, plastic bags and Crocs, and that's just the plastic stuff I recognise. It might take you three whole days to sail here from the nearest civilisation in the Maldives. It's one of the most isolated places on Earth, and yet?: hello, plastic bottles, fancy seeing you here . . .

This may be the moment when everything changed for me, when the penny dropped. I look back at the fifty or so films I made about the sea and find memories that are like asking for your first dance. The embarrassment that comes with the realisation of your innocence before adult life, the things you didn't notice, and their awkwardness in the light of the obvious truth that now confronts you.

Like us all, I've been very slow to catch on, but even if I had read that paper on plastic particles in 1972, when I was eleven, I would not have understood its significance, or that plastic would harm the sea. Neither would the great inventors of plastic, the Victorian chemists who started to mix the new petroleum chemicals together, producing foul-smelling, lumpy substances that were the forerunners of modern plastics.

Leo Baekeland, inventor of Velox photographic paper and Bakelite, the first mass-produced, synthetic plastic, left behind forty-nine boxes of papers, sixty-two diaries, several thousand photographs, laboratory reports and notebooks of his work. They describe in detail how he came to make a wonderful new durable and mouldable material, and all the useful things that could be done with it. But never once did he mention what might happen when it was no longer useful. It's no use asking, 'What were you thinking?' because he wasn't thinking about recycling at all, and it didn't occur to him that his invention of a deliberately indestructible material that was cheap enough to throw away would wreak havoc on the natural world.

I'm looking now at a photo of a happy Leo on holiday with his wife, Céline. He's obviously a man of achievements, and the twinkle in his eyes lifts an otherwise serious face. He's staring out to sea from the deck of his 120-foot yacht, *Ion*. Leo Baekeland, father of plastic, loved the natural world. He fished, collected seashells on the beach, loved aquariums and sea turtles. In his later years he spent many happy moments sailing in Biscayne Bay, Miami, near his home in Coconut Grove. He made many adventurous missions on *Ion* deep into the Florida Keys. His diary entries in 1936 comment frequently on the clarity of the seas:

> *March 30th:* We proceeded to sea over the shoals in clear blue water (Virginia Key).
> *April 23rd:* Marvellous calm landscape and calm clear water. A large number of sponging vessels and these boats are out fishing for sponges, during these calm days when the water is so clear (Biscayne Bay, Miami).
> *May 4th:* Water of Biscayne Bay remarkably clear and transparent. Arrive at our dock at 3.20 p.m.

Being on the doorstep of Miami, Biscayne Bay is today, not surprisingly, saturated with plastic. Styrofoam fragments, plastic bottles and their caps, straws, plastic bags, fishing gear and all sorts of plastic trash are found by the ton along the shoreline, in fish nets and floating on the rip lines out at sea, and on the seabed. Many of the beaches of the Biscayne National Park Islands loved by Leo are so covered in plastic you can't see the sand. Turtle-nesting beaches so clogged that the egg-laying females cannot find their way up the shore. Like so many of us, neither he nor the politicians that should have added a clean-up tax to plastic manufacture ever foresaw the nightmare of this ocean apocalypse.

Baekeland died in 1944, but if he were alive it would surely be only a very short conversation, perhaps over a few pictures of these modern shorelines, that would have changed the way plastic was manufactured forever. More usually, views don't change overnight, and obviously educated people can choose to ignore what they don't want to see, are too busy for, can't be bothered about, or for whatever reason just don't get.

Outside the edit suit the magnolia tree's leaves were falling. In the time they grew and died I counted nearly thirty-five reversions of the script, and no fewer than twenty-six weeks in the edit – for *one* hour. It had been a big team effort, too – teams within teams, even. It's been estimated that over a thousand people around the world had a part in the making of *Blue Planet II*.

Surprisingly, the outline I had written almost three years earlier was still recognisable – but almost at the last minute we had swapped out the final sequence for another. The cameraman Rafa Herrero and his colleague Andrea Cassini had offered us beautiful shots of pilot whales from the seas around the Canary Islands, where they lived. The opportunity to be with your filming subject for months on end – years in Rafa's case – trumps anything we could have got by sending someone from the BBC there for just three weeks. It meant he was able to capture moments with the pilot whales few had ever seen. But Mark Brownlow, the series producer, and I felt that these pilot whale sequences were too similar to the sperm whale footage we already had at the top of the show: both told the story of how a big family of mammals can survive in the wide-open ocean, and both couldn't be in the film.

Then, at the eleventh hour, Rafa showed us new some shots of a dead pilot whale calf in the mouth of its mother. It was likely that it had been killed by toxic plastic residues in its milk.

We knew we had to use it. We wanted to end the show with the issue of plastic pollution: this fitted, and had huge emotional impact.

Mark Fox and I spent a week writing the script around Rafa's shots of pilot whales and cutting it together to see if it worked. Rafa had got intimate and beautiful shots of a whole family of pilot whales in the clear blue water of the mid-Atlantic, sunlight flickering over their shiny round heads, and soulful-looking eyes looking straight back to camera. Watching them appear to be mourning the dead calf was heartbreaking, and when Mark had finished cutting, and adding sad music underneath, I found tears welling up. Though often bittersweet I love those moments in film-making when pictures, music and words ignite on contact, becoming more powerful than you ever thought, and allowing emotions to flow unrestrained across the screen.

One last mystery of film-making – perhaps the biggest – is that, despite the best intentions of a lot of committed people, you never really know how it will turn out. How it will be received in the living room. You may have an intuition, but you never truly know if it will connect with the audience, or indeed 'succeed', until the curtains open on the night of its broadcast. But at that moment – I had to gulp before I could speak – we suspected that something important had happened.

We double-checked the science on whether whales can indeed show such emotions. Yoland Bosiger and Joe Treddenick, researchers on the team, told me that one piece of evidence comes from the so-called 'spindle cells' in a whale's brain. Named after their long, spindle-like bodies, as seen under the microscope, spindle cells in humans are credited with allowing us to feel love and to suffer emotionally. In whales, it appears, these cells are much longer, and, even accounting for the size of their heavier brains, they have about three times as many as we do.[1] We also checked back with Rafa, who confirmed he had seen the family he filmed with the dead whale calf keeping it for at least two days, most often in the mouth of the mother, but also passing the dead body around the whole pod. Because the scene was so emotionally charged it was also run by several knowledgeable experts and what we were saying was carefully analysed by the series exec, James Honeybourne. Sir David Attenborough made further changes, simplifying all our writing, and making it more powerful and fluid, and in the final lines he nailed it:

> The creatures that live in the 'Big Blue' are perhaps more remote from the influence of humanity than any animals on the planet. But not remote enough, it seems, to escape the effects of what we are doing to their world.

Broadcast first on 19 November 2017, that episode did indeed make an impact. As now we have instant responses from digital services like Twitter we could see immediately the effect on the audience too. This is typical of many thousands of tweets:

HEARTBROKEN

for the mumma whale carrying her dead baby around with her as she can't bear to let go. ALL BECAUSE OF US!!!! #BluePlanet

---

1 Andy Coghlan, 'Whales boast the brain cells that "make us human",' *New Scientist*, 27 November 2006.

The *Daily Telegraph* headline the next day – 'Shocked *Blue Planet* viewers vow never to use disposable plastic again after heartbreaking whale scene' – also captured the reaction of many. The majority of the scientific community backed it, too, although there were some cries of 'fake news' from a few that wanted the certainty of an autopsy to prove definitively the calf died from plastic toxicity. That is why we had been so careful in our scrutiny and wording of the piece and had made sure it was based on good and verified research. It was not possible to autopsy the individual calf filmed – how could you take it from the mother or follow them for over two days and then be lucky to find it in perhaps hundreds of miles of deep open ocean? Yet a research study by WWF, for example, published in 2017, autopsied 100 marine mammals in the Mediterranean, and shows a very high concentration of a plastic derivative called phthalates in all the animals tested, including pilot whales. The average was over three times the threshold for what is considered a high level in fact, and phthalates are known to have harmful effects on foetus development and fertility, disrupting reproduction hormones. There are countless other studies like this, too, all that I know of pointing to the lethal stresses caused to marine mammals by plastic particles or their derivatives. Additionally marine mammal milk is among the richest of all mammals, being about 60 per cent fat, and sadly the fat carries the toxins and transfers the burden to the calf, so that, in severe cases, even if it is not stillborn it may subsequently get a lethal dose from its mother's milk. There is absolutely no doubt in my mind that the pilot whale family filmed will all have had plastic toxins in their tissue and that what we were suggesting was true.

So the emotion we had felt in the cutting room was shared by the audience in the living room: in the UK alone no fewer than 14 million people were watching, with the *Blue Planet II* series being the most ever watched wildlife series in the UK. Broadcasts worldwide, especially in China, showed a similar trend and with the repeats since on subscription services like Netfilx, the total audience may now exceed a billion.

The week after the programme on the open seas, 'Big Blue', with the grieving mother and its dead calf was shown, the shame of plastic pollution in the sea was acknowledged by the Secretary of State for the Environment, Michael Gove, and even by the Prime Minister herself, Theresa May, both of whom had watched *Blue Planet*. Gove said he was 'haunted' by the images of the damage done to the oceans in *Blue Planet II*. On 22 November Chancellor of the Exchequer Philip Hammond referenced *Blue Planet II* in his announcement to investigate the viability of a new plastic tax in his autumn budget speech of 2017. In March 2020 one of his successors, Chancellor Rishi Sunak, announced a tax of £200 a tonne on packaging containing less than 30 per cent recycled content. The last programme of the series, produced by Orla Doherty and Will Ridgeon, called 'Our Blue Planet' was devoted to the environmental issues affecting the oceans and featured a large section on microplastics and pollution, and their harmful effects in the ocean – something for which marine conservation organisations had been campaigning for a very long time. So the *Blue Planet* series became the catalyst for a movement, albeit late in the day, to have a plastic tax and to abolish single-use plastics in the UK. In January 2018, Prime Minister Theresa May gifted the *Blue Planet II* series boxed set to President Xi on a visit to China in recognition of its popularity in China and as a symbol for global ocean protection. The clip of the 'grieving mother and calf' won the Virgin BAFTA award for the 'Must-See Moment' of the year, as voted by the public, and was shown at the National Television Awards where the series won the Impact Award for the most impact of any TV series that year. In accepting the award, in front of the *Blue Planet II* team, David Attenborough summed up how what we were trying to do was to bring vital environmental issues that will affect the whole future of our ocean and the whole planet, to the forefront of public attention: 'If our television programmes have helped stir the consciences of people around the world and that we are going to do something to protect our beautiful world then all of us will be very pleased.'

What creates moments like this? What makes people sit up and take notice, when all along the NGOs and scientists have been telling us the same thing, and the signs have been obvious? 'Sir David Attenborough' seems to be one good answer, but timing is everything, too, and when that's right even small triggers can ignite big changes in society's behaviour that were already ripe for taking place.

Even so, at this point it seems almost traditional to remind you again of the troubles of the world, the attack on nature, the threats to all aspects of the ocean in particular. A series of reports such as the 'World Ocean Assessment', approved by the United Nations General Assembly, highlight the importance of the oceans to all life on Earth while at the same time giving evidence of serious degradation of most ocean habitats, especially near the coast. If we were realists, we might give up now. At best we're in a race between the ocean's, and therefore the Earth's, salvation and its impending collapse. It's going to be a close-run thing. Maybe the tipping points have already passed, and we're in such deep trouble that the problem is insoluble. But what sort of attitude is that? How could we go on if we didn't have hope; didn't believe there was a way to make our planet whole again? Despair is no use: we must be inspired to act by the beauty and ingenuity of nature just as much as we are motivated by fear for our future.

Honestly, though, I am a creature of convenience as much as you, surviving day to day, burning fuel, not paying as much attention as I should to the bigger picture. At times the environmental problems seem overwhelming too, and I feel small and helpless as to what I can do. Despite what I often hear about the need for more messaging on the environment, I think most people are aware that the world is in trouble, that every living species of animal or plant is 'endangered'. The important bit, however, is our engagement with those facts: that we care enough to do something about it, and that they are not ignored. On an individual level I can resolve to try harder consuming less of everything, I can actively partake in my local community's initiatives to lower carbon use and to re-use and recycle, and I can resolve to support the political parties that have genuine environmental policies. But since we are prone to take the easiest route to get what we want, it will in large part be technological fixes that will change our behaviours as much as anything. Some will be forced on us, like the switch to electric cars and more efficient light bulbs, and here too we can choose not to grumble and to give our support to what are most often win-win solutions that save money and the planet.

What, then, of the visual messages that came into our living room from the sea? How have they changed our view of the world? In 1914 the journalist J. E. Williamson invented the 'photosphere', an iron tube large enough for a person to get inside, with a window to take photographs through underwater. In a recently rediscovered film he captures a shark baited with the body of a dead horse and, for added drama, kills it with a knife in front of the camera-tube. We have thankfully slowly moved on, via Hans Hass and his 16-minute film *Pirsch unter Wasser* (Stalking Under Water), first seen in 1942, and the first feature-length full-colour underwater documentary, Jacques Cousteau's *Le Monde du Silence* (The Silent World), shown in 1954, which still depicts a shark massacre and even a census of life on coral reefs using dynamite to kill everything and let it float to the surface – although later Cousteau did become a champion of the environment bar none. The *Blue Planet* documentaries too are now part of the history of the sea in your living room, and even between the two series there has been a progression to a greater discussion of environmental issues – hopefully one that mirrors the majority outlook on the conservation and beauty of nature.

I am driving through some beautiful English countryside with my then eight-year-old daughter, India, in the back. The light is flickering through the trees on each side of the road. It's the height of summer, and the sense of nature's power is all around. Suddenly she offers up a thought of the kind that often only children have.

'Daddy, I don't know if I am here or just in God's dream?'

I'm tempted to say, 'Ask your mum!' But it's a beautiful question, capturing the mystery of life itself and how we could possibly be lucky enough to be here on this unique living planet.

The green flicker from the trees as we drive along merges with memories of some filming I've just finished – sea grass flickering in the sunlight around the Chagos Islands in the Indian Ocean. It's a place that holds some answers to that question of how the complexities of life have evolved on Earth and why the sea is so important. It's just a tiny patch on the seabed, hundreds of miles from anywhere, isolated in a universe of sand, with only the occasional sea turtle passing by, but home to a diverse and unique residential community. At least eleven different kinds of vivid green, brown and yellow fish; sage-coloured sea breams like the 'Slender Emperor', various olive goatfishes and green parrot fishes, and some no doubt unnamed, but all perfectly adapted and camouflaged in their minute underwater meadow. So it only needs a little patch for life to evolve like this, a little three-dimensional patch held in saltwater. Maybe that's why this whole world, with its massive water store, has nurtured life in the first place; a life unlikely to be alone in the universe, but rare and certainly precious.

My wetsuit is a salt-bleached grey and slightly hardened now, but I can feel that tingling in my feet, the kick of the fins and the swimming movements in my arms as I dream of diving back into our beautiful and surprising blue planet. There's much more to show you, and now I think of it I didn't even mention when a whale shark flew over my head, when a remora suckerfish wanted to be close friends, when we got the first shots of mother and calf sperm whale diving into the abyss, when I came upon what was probably the biggest bony fish alive, or evidence of two kinds of dolphins hunting together and co-operating across species, and much more . . . Those stories will have to wait, but your visits to beaches and rock pools, swimming and snorkelling, diving and exploring, or just walking by the sea, do not.

Of course, always hoping that we give the sea the chance to thrive, an ocean more of secrets still awaits to be discovered, and I never stop feeling thrilled by the wealth and variety of creatures that live there, or by those that might live there that we've not seen yet, or by those we may never find. Not long ago we could only look through a dappled surface to see what lay beneath the waves. We had no idea how it really looked below, and how important the life there was to us all. And now the sea, as much as we know it, has been revealed – indeed, seen glass-clear as though we too were fish. It has flowed across cinema screens and through the TV into the living room, championed by the whale, which, despite being among the largest creatures that ever lived, has itself been largely unknown and unappreciated until the present day. Yet the sea keeps many of its secrets close, as it should, defined in large part through its vast open blues, its dark depth and its endless mystery.

Acknowledgements

From the first teachers and the lollipop lady (crossing guard) to our work colleagues, or even people who just take the time to ask how you are doing, people around us play a bigger role than we know – their friendship giving us the confidence to be ourselves.

Of course, it starts with our closest relationships. My mother is the only person I know to have successfully bred captive axolotls using unfluorinated Welsh stream water. She encouraged all my interests in wildlife, turning a blind eye to a dead axolotl I had frozen and put in the deep freeze for safekeeping when I was ten, and eventually far surpassing my animal husbandry skills with that species herself. It is clear now looking back that I owe her a lot for this encouragement.

I thank my wife Lucy and our children, India and Will, too, with all my heart for their patience, encouragement and cheerful teasing while I was in the writing shed. Lucy's common sense kept me on the straight and narrow, and I would often ask her how to write what I was trying to say. Lucy's mum and dad, John and Liz Bowden, are exceptional too in their support. John Bowden gave the most thorough criticism of my early drafts, which was very helpful and encouraging, and I take it always as a great compliment when someone bothers to read your work (watch your film) and comment in detail. Liz's great love for our family and her endless support and down-to-earth 'Not that bloody book again!' were invaluable too, reminding me to prioritise my family over all else.

It was Mark Carwardine, the whale and dolphin expert and writer, who got me into this mess in the first place. He would often say, 'If I write another book, shoot me!' and then went on to tell me I should write one. Co-conspirator and wildlife film-maker Peter Bassett and I spent many hours discussing all aspects of writing, film-making and photography with Mark, and taking it in turns to tease each other, discovering as we age that we are morphing into Compo, Cleggy and Foggy from *Last of the Summer Wine*, although I am not sure who identifies as who. Having himself written nearly a hundred books, Mark was very generous in putting me in touch with his fantastic agent, Caroline Montgomery, whose tireless efforts found me a great publisher and another new set of friends at Robinson.

I quickly realised that, although we come from different media worlds, Duncan Proudfoot, Publishing Director of Robinson, understood me and took the fear out of print publishing, which can be daunting to a newbie. To cement our friendship I popped a small recycled plastic model of a deep-sea anglerfish into the envelope with the completed manuscript. It fell on the floor unnoticed for a while but, after some puzzlement, is now on his desk, I understand, in full line of sight. I meant it as a talisman of good luck, but also as a metaphor, as the anglerfish illuminates the ocean, which is what I hope I have done in some part in this book. It is Duncan who suggested the title, *The Whale in the Living Room*, which I was surprised by at first, then grew to love, because of the way it connects us to the whale and *its* living room, and subtly suggests the development of marine imagery flowing into our living room through the TV for over sixty years. It also has shades of 'the elephant in the room': of things left unsaid that shouldn't be.

Of all the thankless tasks, and so I especially need to thank them, is the work of script editors, picture editors and the legal team. Graham Coster cut through my excesses in what I thought were obviously witty diversions, but were obviously not, and made things better, as only an experienced editor can do. Similarly, managing editor Amanda Keats has had much patience with me, taking on the second pass of changes when the 'mark-ups' on the Word document started to look like the Battle of Waterloo in the blues and reds of dead and wounded sentences that had been annotated by various people. Amanda calmly unravelled those bloodied pages and made it something that could be read again. Felicity Price, legal adviser, was very helpful, and was generous to mention that she had enjoyed the manuscript. She spurred me on to recontact Barrie Osborne, producer of *The Lord of the Rings*, whose ideas I discuss in Chapter 2, and who kindly gave me permission to talk about developing them for an ocean series.

There are lots of scientific facts in this text. Impartial as it pretends to be, science is actually done by humans, and so is fallible, and of course the exact details about most things can be interpreted in different ways. Add to that that there are a lot of unknowns anyway about our oceans, and you can have great difficulty finding scientific consensus. Therefore it was a great relief to me that marine experts Julian Partridge, Ron Douglas and Jim Morin all kindly looked over the scientific aspects of my ramblings. Julian and Ron, experts in deep-sea vision and the creatures of the deep, once took me with them on a fascinating voyage to see the abyssal wonders of the San Clemente trench off California; Jim is one of the leading lights (pun intended) in his pioneering research on marine bioluminescence. Jonathan Watts, cameraman and filming engineer, filming gizmo inventor, also checked the script to give me feedback on the details of optical physics, and much more. Over the years we have filmed everything from flying seeds in wind tunnels to making deep-sea camera tags for sperm whales on his kitchen table, and his encouragement has never faltered.

Another partner in crime was Fergus Keeling, a long-time friend, colleague and presenter from the days when we made *The Natural History Programme* together for BBC Radio 4. Trekking together across the salt pans of remote northern Canada (another story) cemented an honest relationship which allows us to be brutally blunt about each other's work, and Fergus was helpfully so about this book. Irritatingly, he is now writing his own book, which is, I think, head and shoulders above mine in writing style and human insight.

Alison Barrat, a fantastic executive editor from the documentary filmmaking world, and now VP Production and Development at Love Nature, gave me some of the most amazing filming assignments when she was communications officer at the Khaled bin Sultan Living Oceans Foundation (KSLOF), the Washington-based NGO. I have greatly enjoyed working with her, and the confidence that comes from a supportive and positive working environment fed into this book and much else. Similarly, I would like to thank Doug

Allan, cameraman and polar explorer, who put me in touch with Alison in the first place, and has always been a good friend since we met way back at the BBC Natural History Unit. To this day we still enjoy making short films together.

Rick Rosenthal, David Reichert and Florian Graner, cameramen and camera directors, who became my friends from the first series of *Blue Planet*, also gave me supportive comments. Rick in particular, who was the cameraman filming the blue whales, reminded me of details I had forgotten, like the code he invented for discrete sightings of blue whales from the air: 'Send a taxi to Puerto Escondido!'

I am lucky to live in the lovely village of Hawkesbury Upton, South Gloucestershire. People here have all been very supportive too, in a way only the visible community of a village can be; here I would especially like to thank Mike Wareham, who read the manuscript in detail, with much knowledge of the sea as a high-ranking naval officer.

Then there are people who sit at the crossroads of your life with signposts that point to unknown places in the future: ones you drive past at the time, hardly noticing, but without which you would never reach those destinations. Simon Roberts, a great friend and fellow radio producer in the 1990s, who died of a brain tumour in 2010, was one such. We enjoyed many of the same interests and practical jokes: I once put a whole packet of sunflower seeds in his garden when he was away on assignment, and he was surprised to find them taking over when he got back. He returned the compliment by sending me an out-of-date copy of *Railway Modeller* magazine as a homage to my trainspotting tendencies, but knowingly underpaid the postage so that I would have to collect it from the depot and pay the excess at 6.30 a.m. one morning. One of the camera tags on the sperm whales we filmed for *Blue Planet II* in 2016 (yet another story, if you'll let me) I named 'Simon'. Now you know why.

A special mention must go to Alan James, an outstanding photographer, and one-time owner of an underwater-photography shop in Bristol. It was through Alan that I discovered the amazing world of underwater images and, on the workshop trips organised by Alan and his wife Heather, from Cornwall to Sulawesi, I was fully introduced for the first time to this beautiful other planet that is yet our planet. And because this hobby gave me a lot of experience, I was given the chance to work on *Blue Planet*, by the series producer at the time, Alastair Fothergill, who must have been somewhat persuaded to take me on by my excited burbling on the subject of marine photography.

Going back deeper in time still, I'd like to thank my biology teacher, Rex Dibley. In 1979 he introduced us as A-level students to a series called *Life on Earth*, which we watched in class with amazement, wondering how they got those pictures. At the time I would never have believed that I could work on such films too, so if you are reading this and thinking the same thing, there is a lesson on how we must not self-limit ourselves: there are quite enough other people who will try and do that for you. I am proud to say that my biology teacher founded a very successful specialist plant nursery. Filming the history of potted plants (yet another story) in Tanzania in 1993, I found what I thought was an unusual species of African violet, and scooped up its seeds and sent them to him in an envelope for propagation in his large greenhouses. Just outside this writing shed I have a pot that says 'Dibley's Nursery' on it, from an African violet plant I subsequently bought. That's him!

ACKNOWLEDGEMENTS

I must also mention my siblings, Ginette, Iona, and James, who all product-tested the book's manuscript. And especially thanks too to my cousin Andrew Findlay, who read many passages, and who is frequently an ally when it comes to taking my side. Andrew took me sailing several times around the Channel Islands in California, where he lives, and reminded me of my father's (Archie's) love of the sea, and what were obviously some of the happiest times of his life sailing off the coast of Essex in a little boat called *Indoona*.

My word count and time have run out and, like the proverbial contestant on a radio show getting their one chance in the limelight, and fearing that he has forgotten someone, I must say, '. . . and hello, too, to anyone else that knows me.'

Index